THE "PEOPLE'S WAR"
IN FRANCE

THE "PEOPLE'S WAR" IN FRANCE

1870—1871

BY

COLONEL LONSDALE HALE

The Naval & Military Press Ltd

> "There is for a Leader nothing more oppressive than a situation that is not clear, nothing more trying than bands of armed irregular troops, aided by the population and the nature of the country, and relying for support on a strong army in the neighbourhood."
> PRINCE FREDERICK CHARLES OF PRUSSIA.

Published by

The Naval & Military Press Ltd

Unit 5 Riverside, Brambleside
Bellbrook Industrial Estate
Uckfield, East Sussex
TN22 1QQ England

Tel: +44 (0)1825 749494

www.naval-military-press.com
www.nmarchive.com

In reprinting in facsimile from the original, any imperfections are inevitably reproduced and the quality may fall short of modern type and cartographic standards.

TO MY

MANY BROTHER-SOLDIERS OF ALL RANKS

FROM

FIELD-MARSHALS TO PRIVATES

TO WHOM I HAVE, IN VARIOUS CAPACITIES, TALKED ABOUT WAR FOR NEARLY FORTY-THREE YEARS, THIS LITTLE "SOMETHING TO READ" IS DEDICATED AS A MEMENTO OF THE ENCOURAGEMENT THAT I HAVE ALWAYS RECEIVED FROM THEM IN MY WORK, AND OF AN ENDURING CONNECTION WITH THEM, WHICH THEY HAVE ALWAYS MADE SO PLEASANT AND WHICH I VALUE DEEPLY

L. A. H.

CONTENTS

CHAP.	PAGE
I. Introductory	1
II. Conditions of the Second War : State of Affairs to the End of September	11
III. October	33
IV. Human Nature in War and the " Personlichkeit " of the German Leaders	56
V. The first fortnight of November	67
VI. The Grand Duke's Detachment from November 14th to 20th	95
VII. The Second Army from November 10th to 20th	114
VIII. The Grand Duke's Detachment from November 21st to 23rd	126
IX. The Second Army from November 21st to 23rd	139
X. November 24th	160
XI. November 25th	173
XII. November 26th	184
XIII. November 27th	195
XIV. November 28th—Battle of Beaune la Rolande	202
XV. November 29th	215

CONTENTS

CHAP.		PAGE
XVI.	November 30th	222
XVII.	December 1st	228
XVIII.	December 2nd—Battle of Loigny-Poupry	236
XIX.	December 3rd—First Day, Second Battle of Orleans	251
XX.	December 4th—Second Day, Second Battle of Orleans—Capture of the City	265
XXI.	Conclusion	282

MAPS

General Map of the Operations in France 1870–71
To face page 1

Large Scale Map of Country round Orleans *not reproduced in this edition*

PREFACE

In a long course of the study of War I have acquired quite enough knowledge of the subject to deter me from ever making the futile attempt to write "Military History." That work must be left to the gifted few. So in these pages I am simply a narrator of some incidents of War, though in my narrative I have from time to time endeavoured to lay before the reader some of the lessons which seem to me deducible from the incidents narrated.

Very many years' close connection with British officers of all arms and branches of the Service has led me to the conclusion that urging them to read and study Military History because Napoleon and Wellington did so, raises in them no responsive echo. The examples given are far above their ambitions; they aspire to become good soldiers, but not Napoleons or Wellingtons. But they will all admit that the more an officer, field-marshal, or subaltern, on taking the field, knows of what has happened, and what may happen, in War, the better practical soldier he will be; for to those who know nothing of the past, everything that comes is new and unexpected, and they are taken by surprise. One night about Christmastide during the South African War, a piquet guarding a very steep hillside was surprised by the Boers, who had clambered up, and the camp was rushed; but if whoever was in charge of the piquet had ever been at Bude, on the north coast of Cornwall, and, not necessarily with a volume of military history in his hand, but with a threepenny guide-book, had explored the neighbourhood, he would have learnt of the incident of war at Stamford Hill in 1643, when Sir Bevil Greenvil, with a band of Royalists, clambering up the steep sides of the hill, surprised and defeated the Parliamentarian forces on the top, with an eventual loss to these forces of 2000 men, their ordnance and baggage train; and he would have been doubly watchful.

So in these pages I have narrated for the British officer "something to read" about War.

This small book does not pretend to be an erudite work; so I hope if the aforesaid British officer takes up the book to read it, he will not think it necessary to sit at a table on which to rest his elbows with his head between his hands, and with a pair of compasses by him to measure distances. Let him repose in an arm-chair with, on his knees, the excellent map thoughtfully provided by the publishers, and I think he will be able to follow the narrative quite easily. He will find also that the first time a place is named I have appended to the name, in rectangular brackets, the distances at which the place is from important points; and further, in those brackets are illustrative or explanatory remarks of my own.

The English rendering of some of the many extracts from the German archives will doubtless appear stiff and unpolished;

PREFACE

but I have most carefully endeavoured to adhere as closely as possible to the originals. On active service, "elegant" composition gives way before the need for brevity and for saving time, so even the best staff officers are apt to write "inelegantly." So as v. Stiehle wrote to v. V. Rhetz that the latter was to send off at once his "intaktesten brigade," I have designated the brigade by the equally horrible English expression "the most intact brigade."

"Qui s'excuse s'accuse," but, nevertheless, I must say that probably grammatical slips in these pages may be easy to find, in spite of the efforts of a young friend who has read the proofs with me, and to whom I am deeply indebted for doing her best to persuade me to write English; but after years of relating the incidents of War colloquially from brief notes to listeners, the transition to communicating them in cold blood from a study chair by means of a pen I have found to be somewhat trying.

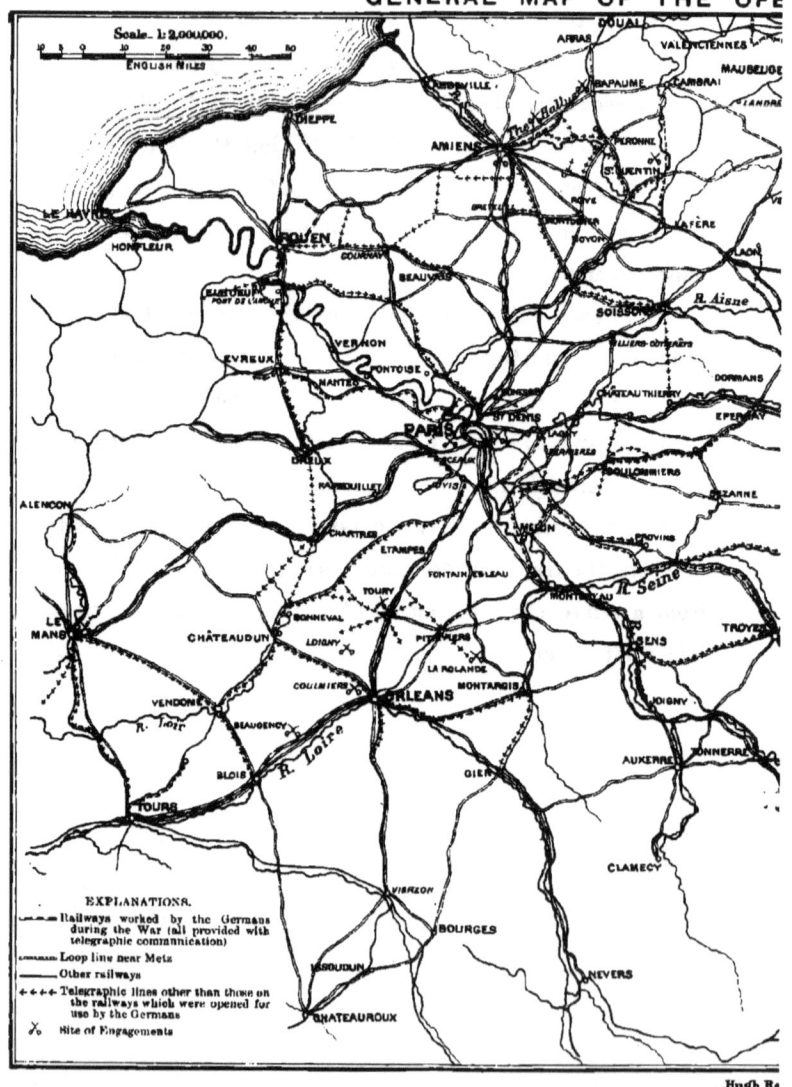

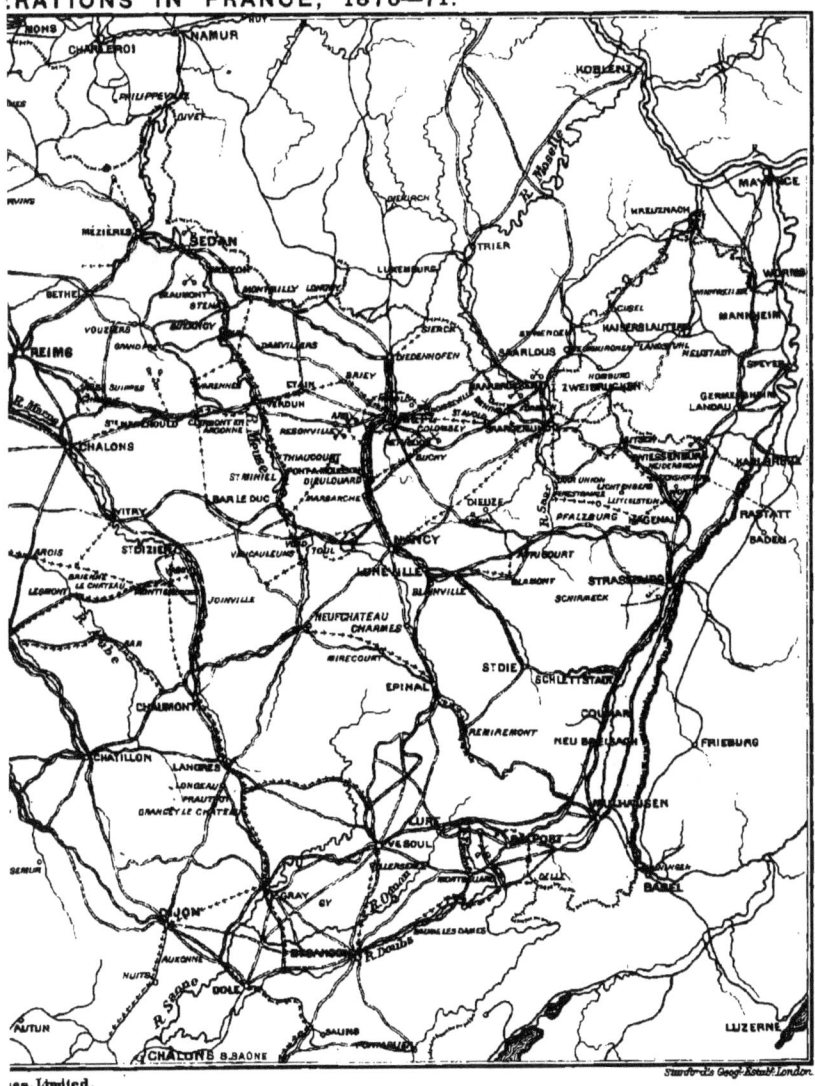
OPERATIONS IN FRANCE, 1870—71.

THE PEOPLE'S WAR IN FRANCE
1870-71

CHAPTER I

INTRODUCTORY

In every country, even in those where the law of universal liability to military service is most widely applied, there will always be of the adult male population a certain portion for whom no place can be found in the organised Field and Fortress army, or who, for some reason or other, are exempted from liability to serve. In Germany, the number of these men is very small, in Great Britain it is very large. At a Conference on the "Usages of War" held at Brussels in 1874, shortly after the close of the Franco-German War of 1870-71, one of the most important questions raised and most warmly discussed was the extent to which this portion of the population might actively participate and take a share in the defence of their country against an invader. The great land Powers, Russia and Germany, did their utmost to induce the Conference to restrict the defence entirely and absolutely to the organised army; the smaller Powers, Belgium, Holland, Switzerland, and others, insisted with equal energy on legalising the participation of the whole population, both civil and military, in the war. Great Britain, little to her credit, took a neutral position in the discussions. Eventually the disputants came to a compromise; the men not included in the ranks of the organised army were to be allowed to defend their country provided they carried some distinctive mark or badge, and had been accepted as part of the defending force by the Government of their country; but as regards the civilians, the decision was practically shelved, and, as one of the delegates, towards the close of the Conference, said: "The Conference will, then, break up without deciding whether a civilian who destroys a bridge in rear of the invaders may be shot for so doing." At first sight it appears almost absurd to question the right of any man to take part in the defence of his country; theoretically, active participation in that defence is not a mere right, it is a bounden duty; whether he shall do so or not is, however, a question of expediency. Humanitarians, whose sympathies are, of course, with the invaded people, assert that with the participation of the non-military population in the war, reprisals enter into the war, and it becomes embittered and barbaric; they assert that the sufferings resulting to the whole country in consequence are not in any way counterbalanced by the value of the assistance given to the general defence. There are also military men who would restrict participation in a war to the organised army only, and on the grounds that the population outside the army is unreliable as an instrument of war, and also, that the mere increase of numbers is rather a probable cause of confusion in the operations than an increase of defensive strength. But it was none of these reasons that influenced the greater land Powers at the Brussels Conference; it was the knowledge of the enormous increase in the difficulties to be encountered by an invader, if the resistance is not confined to the organised army alone. So long as the opponents are the respective organised armies only, the struggle is a species of military chess, in which victory must inevitably declare itself on the side where the players are the better, and the pieces are the stronger. There are certain data, mainly those of time and space, known to both opponents, and on these are based calculations for movements; sentiment does not enter into the proceedings or influence them, and the game is played by professional experts only. Moreover,

INTRODUCTORY

every Power has for reference in the pigeon-holes of its Intelligence Department the strength and composition of the organised armies of its opponents; so at the outset of a campaign it knows the probable strength of its adversary, and can make its plans accordingly. But if, in the course of the invasion, the population outside the organised army throws itself into the fray, there comes in a disturbing element, the composition of which is unknown to the invader, and of which the resisting value cannot be ascertained except by practical experience; patriotism may work wonders; and, moreover, patriotism very often declines to confine its action according to the rules of the game; so the situation sometimes becomes very perplexing and embarrassing to the invaders. This sort of war is a war of defence carried on by the whole people of the country, and is therefore denominated a "People's War." The recent war in South Africa was a "People's War," and although its long duration was mainly due to the vast size of the theatre of war, some of the greatest difficulties encountered by our invading army arose from the fact of it being a "People's War."

Most persons, if asked to name the latest "People's War" in Europe, would give the war in the Spanish Peninsula in the early years of the last century, for it is not generally known that of the seven months' war between France and Germany in 1870-71, whilst during the first seven or eight weeks it was a war between only the organised armies of the two countries, during the remaining five months it was a "People's War" for the defence of France. This great campaign is usually regarded as a single war which commenced with the Declaration of War by France on July 19th, 1870, and terminated with the surrender of Belfort to the Germans on February 16th, 1871. But in this campaign there were these two phases, so different from each other as forms of warfare that virtually they were two distinct wars, the second commencing immediately after the conclusion of the first. The first, carried on by the organised armies of the two countries, came to a close on September 1st, 1870, with the Battle of Sedan and the surrender of the Emperor Napoleon III. and of MacMahon's army of Châlons; the second, in which the German Army found itself opposed by the French people as well as the French organised Army, began on the 4th of the same month, when the Germans commenced their march on Paris, where, on that day, the Imperial Dynasty was dethroned, and there was established in its place a Republican Government, which at once assumed the title, "The Government of National Defence." So complete had been the overthrow of the original organised French Army which took the field at the commencement of the campaign, that when, on September 19th, Paris was invested by the Germans, the only remaining organised units of the regular army available for operations in France outside the capital were three three-battalion infantry regiments, a single battalion from each of three infantry regiments, nine regiments of cavalry, and, according to de Freycinet, there was only one battery of artillery complete in material and personnel. Of depôt troops there were a large number. With every battalion there was a depôt company, consisting of "the halt, the maimed and the blind," and untrained soldiers. Besides these there were a number of trained soldiers who had not joined the army in the first stages of the war, or who, having taken part in it, had managed to escape being captured. The depôt companies had, before the catastrophe of Sedan, been collected into three-battalion regiments denominated Marche Regiments or Regiments de Marche; but in all the new formations it was in the want of good officers that their deficiencies were most apparent. It was out of these indifferent and insufficient regular troops that the nucleus of the French armies which fought during the "People's War" were formed. The resources of material and men in the provinces were abundant, but the men were not professional soldiers, they were the People; and even when subsequently they wore some distinctive dress or badge, carried some sort of firearm in their hands, and were designated by military appellations, it

INTRODUCTORY

was as the People that they fought against the invader. And besides all these, a multitude of men, ordinary civilians, and of women as well, took their part in the defence. So the second war was a real "People's War."

The forces that the Government employed in the national defence were hastily improvised; the organisation of the defence was hastily arranged, and time was wanting for its completion. To these causes, and to the absence of unison of views between the chief civil and military authorities in the provinces, was due the eventual collapse of the national defence; but notwithstanding the disadvantageous conditions under which it was carried on, it brought the invaders to the verge of a catastrophe; and it is impossible to study the struggle without arriving at the conclusion that a country which relies for defence on its organised army alone, and does not avail itself of the defensive power outside the ranks of that army, deliberately deprives itself of auxiliary aid of the very greatest military value to itself. On this point there are two witnesses whose evidence must necessarily have great weight. Baron v. d. Goltz, who was an officer of the German General Staff of the Second Army during the war, says, in his "Gambetta und Seine Armeen": "The war revealed the existence of forces for war that, without that experience, we should still to-day undervalue"; and Prince Frederick Charles the commander of that army, when he was in a very difficult situation during the war, spoke as follows: "The Franc-tireurs, aided by the country, have done the French good service. Now I am reduced to a waiting attitude. . . . There is for a leader nothing more oppressive than a situation that is not clear, nothing more trying than bands of armed irregular troops aided by the population and the nature of the country, and relying for support on a strong army in the neighbourhood." At the Brussels Conference, the leading German representative was Colonel v. Voigts-Rhetz, who had been the Chief Staff Officer of the Third Army Corps, which took so conspicuous a part in the Franco-German War, both before and after Sedan; and he knew, by bitter

6   THE PEOPLE'S WAR IN FRANCE, 1870-71

experience, the difficulties to be overcome in a "People's War"; hence his energetic resistance to any legalisation of the participation of the people in a war. From the narrative recorded in the following pages will be clearly apparent the great potentialities in a "People's War" for defence against invasion, provided that the part the people are to take in the war has been as fully and carefully thought out and organised beforehand as has the work of the organised army.

The "People's War" in France was mainly confined, in its thoroughness and intensity, to a comparatively small area: the district bounded on the north by the Seine from its mouth up to Melun; on the east by the country between its tributaries, the Loing and the Yonne; on the south by the Loire from Gien to Tours; and on the west by the railway from Tours through Le Mans and Alençon to the mouth of the Seine. The war may be said to have reached its climax with the second occupation of Orleans by the Germans on the night of December 4-5.

For many years past there has been available all the information ever likely to be forthcoming from the French side as regards this war, but for twenty-three years the Germans were reticent with respect to their share in it. V. Moltke was always a believer in the maintenance of "prestige," so in the Official History of the War, drawn up under his supervision, there is little to lead the reader to imagine that either v. Moltke himself, or any of the other leaders and Generals of the German Army, ever made mistakes, or were other than marvellously perfect soldiers. And undoubtedly he was, for many years, right in maintaining this reticence, for at any time war might have broken out again between the old foes, and had the French known of the blunders and shortcomings of the German leaders they would have entered on a new war with but little fear of any innate superiority in their opponents, whilst the faith and confidence of the German soldiers in their own commanders, and even in v. Moltke himself, would have been most seriously shaken, and dis-

cipline might have suffered. So *suppressio veri*, very seldom,
however, carried to the length of *falsificatio veri*, was, when
expedient, one of the chief principles applied to the compilation of the German Official History of the War. We
may be quite sure also that strict censorship must have
been exercised over the numerous Regimental Histories
of the War, which were published from time to time, and
that officers, who had written home from the seat of war,
took care when their letters contained uncomplimentary
criticism on the operations, that they should be kept
strictly confidential. Similarly, the favourite form of record,
the "Tagebuch," or diary, must have been carefully stowed
away under lock and key, or saw the light only after such
an amount of expurgation as ensured that its publication
would in no way injure the professional prospects of the
diarist.

Yet it was not necessary to apply this principle with
equal rigidness indiscriminately to all the operations of the
campaign. Any one simply following the narrative, and
reading between the lines, can mark the mistakes made and
the terrible unnecessary waste of life caused by them in the
period from the battle of Weissenburg to that of Sedan.
But in this splendid continuous series of victories, and their
ultimate decisive result, the shortcomings fell into the background, and were condoned by the successes achieved. It
was in the subsequent war, the "People's War," that things
went so badly, that it was considered necessary to carry the
suppressio veri to its extreme. The reason why things went
wrong was that this new war was a "People's War," a form
of warfare of which the Germans had had no previous experience, and which was quite new to them; and in it the supreme
and the superior German authorities made mistakes similar
to those our own authorities made in the "People's War" in
South Africa, and which will be made in every "People's
War" that ever takes place. For in every such war, owing
to the density of the "Fog of War" that confronts and
surrounds the invader, his plans and combinations are

frequently based on guesses and hypotheses only, and his operations are then those of blindfolded strategy and blindfolded tactics.

For some twenty years this scrupulous care of prestige lasted, and then the German military authorities came to the conclusion that the *suppressio veri* was not only no longer necessary, but was now a danger to the efficiency of their army; for they argued, and rightly so, that the representation of the experiences of the "People's War" of 1870-71, as given in the history, was one-sided, erroneous, and incomplete, and yet it was this untrustworthy representation that, for a score of years, had been before the younger generations of the German officers as a guide and exemplar for the future. To Captain Fritz Hoenig, who had served in the 57th Infantry Regiment during the campaign, the compilation of a real history was entrusted, and he was given access to the official archives at Berlin. This history is in six volumes, of which the first was published in 1893, the last in 1897, carrying the history to December 6th, 1870, the account being confined to the operations against the First Army of the Loire. But there are certain indications in the work that Hoenig was not altogether free in the amount of information he was at liberty to give to the public. Hoenig's history always will be, and must be, the starting-point for any study of this "People's War," but excellent and admirable as it is, it can but serve as the introductory step to the study of the inner life of the German operations, for as years go by more and more information will come to light. Even since the publication of Hoenig's last volume, there have come before us the Journals of General v. Blumenthal, who was Chief of the Staff of the Third Army, and these throw a new light on the subject, much of which now assumes an aspect very different from that it presents in the pages of Hoenig. In this war, Prince Frederick Charles played, in the field operations, the leading part. It is believed that for many years the Prince's Diary has been ready for publication, but it is still withheld from all except the favoured few.

INTRODUCTORY 9

Without that diary, and similar materials from others of the leading soldiers, such as the Grand Duke of Mecklenburg-Schwerin, General v. Stiehle and others, judgments on the leading and on the leaders must be provisional only; and even the narrative is not altogether complete. In v. Moltke's own published correspondence during the war there is sometimes a remarkable hiatus. Still, from the materials available, much may be learnt, not only of this "People's War," but of war in the widest sense of the word, for in Hoenig's work we are presented with a striking picture of the German control and command during the period of which he treats; and we see that, admirable as is their staff system, and their system of devolution of responsibility, those systems sometimes failed in difficult circumstances, as every system worked by falliable human beings must fail. With the three great battles of this war, Beaune-la-Rolande, Loigny-Poupry and the second battle of Orleans, Hoenig deals in the fullest detail, and, notwithstanding the great changes in modern firearms, his accounts of them are full of valuable lessons.

In the following pages, Hoenig and his extracts from the archives, together with v. d. Goltz's semi-official "History of the Operations of the Second Army," have been taken as the chief sources of supply for the material of the narrative; and though many other works have been consulted and utilised, there is no pretence at composing a military history from even all the materials available at the present time. This small work is merely an introductory sketch of a war, of which the study and thorough knowledge appears to the writer to be of far greater value to the British officer than that of the part of the campaign of 1870–71 which alone is regarded by most military men as the "Franco-German War," and which began at Weissenburg and terminated at Sedan. From it soldiers will learn the "seamy side" of command and of staff work; the regular army will form a better appreciation than they at present possess of the capabilities of the rank and file of even the shortest service soldiers; the auxiliary forces will be impressed with the value of a highly trained army in the field, whether for offence or defence; and rifle clubs will realise that whilst they can be of great value in home defence, there are distinct limitations to the sphere of their operations and of their usefulness.

CHAPTER II

CONDITIONS OF THE SECOND WAR: STATE OF AFFAIRS TO THE END OF SEPTEMBER

IN order that the situation at the commencement of the second war may be better understood, a brief epitome of the original organisation of the hostile Armies, and of the events of the preceding war, will now be given.

The German forces were under the supreme command of King William I. of Prussia, with General Baron v. Moltke as the Chief of the Staff. The forces were grouped in three Armies. The First Army, under General v. Steinmetz, comprised the Ist, VIIth and VIIIth Army Corps and the 1st and 3rd Cavalry Divisions. The Second Army was under Prince Frederick Charles of Prussia (a nephew of the King), with General v. Stiehle as Chief Staff Officer, and included the Guard Corps, IInd, IIIrd, IVth, IXth, Xth, and XIIth A.C. (Saxon Corps), and the 5th and 6th Cavalry Divisions. In the Third Army, under the Crown Prince of Prussia (whose Chief Staff Officer was General v. Blumenthal), were the Vth, VIth and XIth A.C., the Ist and IInd Bavarian A.C., the Wurtemberg and Baden Field Divisions, and the 2nd and 4th Cavalry Divisions.

At the head of the French Army was the Emperor Napoleon III. The Army was composed at first of the Guard, 1st, 2nd, 3rd, 4th, 5th, 6th, and 7th A.C. Later on the 12th A.C. came into existence, as also the 13th and 14th A.C., but the 13th took little, and the 14th no part in the first war. Besides the Army Corps there were several Cavalry Divisions.

Soon after the outbreak of hostilities the 1st, 5th and 7th Army Corps were formed into a separate army, under Marshal MacMahon, the remainder constituting the Army of the Rhine, under the Emperor.

The first serious encounter took place on August 4th, near the old disused fortress of Weissenburg, where the Third Army crossed the frontier, and defeated and drove away a Division of the French 1st Army Corps. Two days later, on the 6th, this Army defeated and routed, at Wörth, the Army of Marshal MacMahon, which fled west to Châlons, whilst simultaneously, on the same day, at Spicheren, the French 2nd A.C. was defeated and compelled to retreat by parts of the First and Second Armies. On the 14th, at Columbey, the First Army attacked with success the rear of the main French Army, retiring across the Moselle at Metz. On the 16th the further retreat of the French (now under the command of Marshal Bazaine) westward was intercepted at Vionville by the Second Army, which had crossed the river south of and above the fortress. On the 18th Bazaine's Army was overthrown at Gravelotte by the First and Second Armies, and retired into the fortress and to the protection of its guns. On the 19th Metz was completely invested by the First Army and a portion of the Second Army, the command of the investing forces being given to Prince Frederick Charles. The remainder of the Second Army—three Army Corps and two Cavalry Divisions—were formed into a Fourth Army, the Army of the Meuse, under the Crown Prince of Saxony, and, with the Third Army, which was now well forward on its way to Châlons, moved towards that place, against the reorganised and reinforced Army of MacMahon (1st, 5th, 7th, and 12th Army Corps). During the march it was discovered that this Army had quitted Châlons, and intended to move eastward to the relief of Bazaine in Metz. The Germans now wheeled north, and on the 29th struck on the French flank at Nouart. On the 30th this was followed

CONDITIONS OF THE SECOND WAR 13

up by the defeat at Beaumont. MacMahon now abandoned his eastward advance, and on September 1st was fought the Battle of Sedan. The Baden Field Division had been sent south to watch and lay siege to Strassburg immediately after the Battle of Wörth.

So completely did the changed attitude of the French civil population towards the Germans, during the subsequent operations, alter the conditions under which the invaders had to carry on the campaign, and so greatly did it contribute to the difficulties they encountered in the second war, that it is desirable to contrast the two attitudes somewhat in detail, and to show the results ensuing to the Germans.

Prior to the campaign, universal liability to service did not exist in France: the Army was a sort of caste apart from the rest of the nation, and was not held by it in particularly high esteem. The Army was maintained and paid by the nation for the purpose of carrying on the wars, and fighting the battles for the nation. So, when war was declared, the nation left the war to the Army, as its own special business, with which it had nothing to do; and when King William of Prussia, in an Army Order from Homburg, on August 8th, said, "We are not waging war against the peaceful inhabitants of the country: on the contrary, it is the duty of every honour-loving soldier to protect private property, and not to suffer the good name of our Army to be tarnished, even by isolated instances of indiscipline," the inhabitants willingly accepted the declaration as truthful and sincere, and they determined to stand aside and let the soldiers of both countries fight the war out between themselves. So German cavalry patrols, in search of either the French Army or information as to where it was, rode miles ahead of their own troops, perfectly safe, unless they came upon French soldiers; small parties could sleep in French farmhouses as safely as in their own homes; quarter-masters went forward demanding food and accommodation, which were given without resistance; and in some cases the Germans were received with actual hospitality—as, for instance, at Nancy, where, dinner being ordered by a commander for his squadron, with which he had ridden miles on in front of the rest of the German troops into the town, the dinner was prepared and laid in the square of the city, and ladies waited on the visitors. The opposition offered to the Germans, and the fighting against the Germans, were almost entirely on the battle-fields. But in the second war, patrols and small parties seeking information were held back at every village; they carried their lives in their hands; the patrol would be shot down by a countryman behind a hedge; and to obtain truthful information was extremely difficult. The officer or orderly, carrying a report or an order, sometimes disappeared mysteriously; a small party of soldiers would, perhaps, be surprised at night by a few inhabitants who had noted down their sleeping quarters. When the hostile Armies were so near to each other that their outposts were in contact, the inhabitants lied freely when asked about the position of their own Army; and, observing closely that of the invaders, passed the information on to their own troops. The Germans, therefore, from want of the necessary knowledge, had no true data on which to frame their strategical operations: these were consequently based on guess work only; and large forces were marched off in wrong directions against a foe which was elsewhere, or which existed in imagination only. The supplies of food could be obtained only by threats and force; hospitality ceased, and every man's and every woman's hand was against the intruders. The whole country became a possible battle-field, and from woods, cover, and villages the advanced guards were met by fire, and had to make good their progress by force of arms along roads and paths cut across, barricaded, or partially destroyed by the inhabitants of the district.

And there is one difficulty peculiar to, and encountered in every "People's War," and markedly in this war, namely, the impossibility of ascertaining, except by the test of practical experience, the real worth of the assistance that the population may give to the defence. It may, on the one hand, be merely loud talking and shouting; perhaps incessant sing-

CONDITIONS OF THE SECOND WAR 15

ing of the "Marseillaise," "God Preserve the Emperor," or "Rule, Britannia": on the other hand, it may mean real, patriotic self-devotion, self-sacrifice. The Germans, with a few exceptions, believed that in France it would be of the first kind; to their cost they found is was of the second kind. Disbelieving in its reality, they invested Paris, confident that the inhabitants would insist on its surrender in a few days; the subsequent disposition of their forces was based on the assumption that their corps could now traverse France from one end to the other without let or hindrance. So large detachments found themselves scattered wide apart about the country, just at the time when they were all wanted as a combined force at some point several marches away.

But besides the difficulties from these sources, there was in the conditions one other great change, the disadvantage of which to the Germans can hardly be overrated. They had no longer any Ordre de Bataille of the French Forces; of the hastily-improvised and newly-organised Army.

An Ordre de Bataille, showing the grouping of the smaller units into the larger ones, and giving the names of the commanders and staff-officers, is a necessity in any military force, as much as is a catalogue of a library for the librarian and the frequenters of the library. Without an Ordre de Bataille, command, control, and even the conduct of the ordinary military life would be impossible; but, at the same time, it is a "necessary evil." If a force could but keep the knowledge of its Ordre de Bataille to itself, the existence of documents of this kind would be quite harmless to it; but, unfortunately, the enemy sometimes gets hold of a copy, or he learns the contents, or he even manages to construct one himself; and then the Ordre de Bataille is a great assistance to him in adapting his plans to meet and counteract those of his opponent. The Ordre de Bataille enables him to compare his resources in men and *matériel* with those of his foes. And the capture of even a single private soldier wearing some distinctive button or badge will, perhaps, on reference to the

Ordre de Bataille, reveal to him the brigade, division, or even army corps in front of him.

In the first war the Germans, when entering upon it, and during all the time it lasted, knew the organisation, composition, and strength of the French forces opposed to them. Previous to its outbreak, the Intelligence Branch of the German Army had obtained full information as to the French Army that would take the field. Very few troops had, however, formed part of an army or army corps in peace, but from the newspapers were gathered the numbers of numerous regiments coming from different parts of France, and suppositional combinations of them were formed, based on the grouping of the troops in the peace garrisons. On this data an Ordre de Bataille was compiled, which was communicated to the Army on July 24, and which was afterwards found to require but few unimportant alterations to be perfectly correct. The places where the several corps were collecting were soon known. The names of the different corps commanders, and the strength of their corps in infantry divisions were correctly known. Very few mistakes were made in the names of the division and brigade commanders, and in the numbers of the regiments composing these units. Consequently, the German Staff, knowing where the French Army was, and what it was, were able to forecast its probable lines of advance, its strategy if it took the offensive, and to prepare their own plans to meet it; whilst if the French remained on the defensive, the Germans, knowing beforehand what it was they would have to fight and its position, could arrange their dispositions for attack to the best advantage.

But almost the whole of the French Army that had taken the field at the commencement of the war were now either prisoners or in invested fortresses. One Army Corps, the 13th, which was formed in August, had, after advancing towards Sedan, regained the capital, where had been formed a little later the 14th Army Corps.

In the second war, the French Army in the field was a new army that had not been in existence during the first war. It

CONDITIONS OF THE SECOND WAR 17

was improvised after the Battle of Sedan. From small beginnings it achieved vast proportions; and, notwithstanding all the efforts of the Intelligence Branch of the German Army, very little reliable information as to its strength, composition, and distribution was ever obtained, at all events during the critical period of the second war, the months of October and November, and the first few days of December; so that, contrary to the Germans' experience of the first war, they sometimes were totally ignorant of what they had to fight, or where it was. The errors they committed in consequence were of the gravest character.

The first war had been for the Germans a continuous and uninterrupted series of successes; the path to victory had been, if not easy, at all events very smooth: in the second war the whole scene changes. The first war was, so far as fighting was concerned, finished in little more than a month; the second war dragged on its weary course for nearly five months. So intense and continuous was the fighting in the former that of the total casualties of the whole campaign, close on 130,000, it claimed the larger portion—73,000. The leading in the first war, whether the leading of Armies, Army Corps, or Divisions was plain and simple, since for the leading there was always a definite and recognisable objective, the enemy in front in the field; but in the second war it was not always easy or even possible to select an objective, or even to be sure of the existence of the objective aimed at; so the leading became difficult, and it not infrequently went altogether astray, and to such an extent that even some of the larger units escaped defeat and destruction by a hair's breadth only. And, as was inevitable, there came with the difficulties and dangers, dissensions among the leaders. Also, during the first war, there was in progress but one campaign in the field, that against the Emperor's Army; during the critical period of the second, there were being carried on simultaneously, one in the North-West of France against the Army of the North, one in the South-East against the Army of the East, one to the South against the First Army of the

Loire, and it may be added that the Germans carried out to the West, at the same time, a campaign against an Army of only a very shadowy character, the "Army of the West." Besides these campaigns, they had on their hands the siege of Belfort in the East, and the Investment of Paris. Later on came the campaign of le Mans, in lieu of that on the Loire, but by that time the stress of danger had gone by. The decisive period of the whole campaign was that dealt with here; the ultimate issue of the whole campaign depended on the successful course of the campaign on the Loire, and upon maintaining the Investment of Paris unbroken; failure in one meant, perhaps, failure in the other. Real anxiety hardly existed during the first war, it was absent hardly a day during the second.

Whilst the French Army in the field during the first war had been gradually undergoing the process of almost total extinction, the German Army in France, notwithstanding its losses in the battles, became larger and larger. At the commencement of the campaign it was necessary to make provision for home defence against a possible attack on the North Coast, and also against possible reverses. To provide for these eventualities, the 17th Infantry Division, which originally belonged to the IXth Army Corps, was left in Germany, as were also some Regular Infantry Regiments. The Landwehr were also organised into Divisions, and there were also formed Reserve Divisions; but when the uninterrupted course of success of the German Army rendered the presence of these troops in the Home Country unnecessary they were brought forward into France, thus greatly increasing for further operations the numerical strength of the German Forces in the field. It is necessary now to take stock of the French Forces available for the second war. Of the remnant of the regular organised Army, as it was before the war, an account has already been given.

The Imperial Government had, from the first, done its best to increase its forces to meet the unexpected success of the invader. And the resources, both in men and in material,

CONDITIONS OF THE SECOND WAR

were ample in numbers and quantity, but there lacked that, without which numbers and quantity are of little use, namely, well-considered previous organisation. Under the laws in existence before the war, and those passed in July and August, there were altogether no less than 626,114 men liable for service in the active Army. As regards guns and artillery equipment, there were enough for all the batteries likely to be wanted, even for a very large army, but, necessarily, there was a great deficiency in personnel for the batteries. Of rifles there was a vast quantity. But besides the so-called " active Army," there was another force, only in its infancy, but which was now utilised for service with the active Army: this was the Garde Mobile.

This force was instituted by Marshal Niel in 1868. The institution was the application, territorially, of liability to compulsory personal service to all men, from twenty-one to twenty-six years of age, who had escaped being taken for service in the active Army. It was very unpopular in France, and had made but little progress at the outbreak of the war. The training was of the most meagre character, and the choice of officers was, at one time during the war, left to the men. The military value of the Garde Mobile was determined mainly by the characteristics of the population whence they were drawn. Those of Paris were essentially Parisian; those of the South-East, turbulent and undisciplined; but those of the Loire and Cher were the peasantry, led to battle by their feudal lords: of these it has been said—" The whole of the young nobility of Touraine lie buried before the walls of Beaune-la-Rolande." Hoenig gives the strength of the Garde Mobile at 623,458 men, so the active Army and the Garde Mobile together numbered 1,249,572. Forty thousand marines of no use at sea after the German Fleet had been compelled to retire to safe quarters, and 8,000 men in the Customs and Forest Departments, further increased the total. Of these foregoing bodies of armed men Hoenig estimates that there were 180,000 either wholly or partly trained.

The Republican Government opened, on September 15th, a new source of supply by calling on all civilians from thirty-one to sixty years of age to enrol themselves in the Garde Nationale, subsequently mobilising them, organising them, and placing them at the disposal of the Minister of War. The Garde Nationale was a species of universal service for local defence. From very early times this force had existed in France, but not until the Great Revolution did it receive its designation of Garde Nationale. Being composed of citizens who were not actually soldiers, it played frequently a prominent part in political dissensions. In 1855 it had been almost entirely dissolved; but in 1870, when the people joined in the defence, the nation demanded its revival. Although some of the force took an active part in the defence of Paris, and a whole division was in the Army of the north, it was mainly in the defence of the localities to which they belonged that they were at their best. It was here that they offered real and serious resistance to the invaders. The number available is given by Hoenig at no less than 788,800.

At the disposal of the Minister of War were, at the end of September, placed the Franc-tireurs, some 40,000. The value of these depended mainly on the locality of their origin. Some were a terror to the population; but the Franc-tireurs under Cathelineau were magnificent irregular troops, and did real good service on the Loire. The Corps was from La Vendée, the men were Catholics, their priest recited certain offices of the Church every morning, and on Sundays Mass was celebrated. Their motto was: "For God and the Country," and for God and the country they fought and died.

The Franc-tireurs, the Germans regarded with bitter hatred, and by every means of severity in their power strove to suppress them; and no wonder, for many of them were men of daring and enterprise, and took advantage of any little carelessness or want of caution on the part of small German detachments, or convoy escorts, to inflict damage and

CONDITIONS OF THE SECOND WAR

loss on the invaders. Even while the Army was on its triumphant march from Sedan to Paris, the Franc-tireurs appeared in its rear and recaptured a number of horses from the small German escort. It was Franc-tireurs who, on a night in November, surprised the outposts of the 4th Cavalry Division, obtaining possession of important documents, and nearly capturing the commander of the Division. They were like swarms of wasps round the smaller German detachments. Of these v. Moltke in his correspondence writes, on October 27th: "The audacity of the Franc-tireurs must be punished by severe reprisals, as the war is assuming a horrible aspect. It is bad enough when armies have to tear each other to pieces, but to set nations against each other is not an advance but a lapse into barbarism."

A total of 2,126,372 men nominally available, must yield, except in a nation destitute of all patriotism and all self-respect, a very fair amount of men at the colours. The decrees calling up the several classes of men came into the hands of the Germans; their Intelligence Branch had at hand all the works showing the human statistics of France, so it was easy for them to have estimated correctly the number of defenders available. The result of their studies differed entirely from the actual results of the decrees, and markedly were these under-estimated. It was not that the Germans were bad calculators or bad arithmeticians, but most probably, disbelieving in the practical character of the proud spirit of the French nation, they anticipated that the Frenchmen who, on hearing the call to come to aid in saving their country, would do so, would be but comparatively few.

The Imperial Government, immediately after the disasters of Wörth and Spicheren, had published an appeal to the country. It ran as follows:

"Frenchmen,—We have told you the whole truth; it is now for you to fulfil your duty. Let one single cry issue from the breasts of all—from one end of France to the other. Let the whole people rise quivering, and sworn to fight the great fight. Some of our regiments have succumbed before overwhelming numbers, but our Army has not been vanquished. The same intrepid breath still animates it ; let us support it. To a momentarily successful audacity, we will oppose a union which conquers destiny. Let us fall back upon ourselves, and our invaders shall hurl themselves against a rampart of human breasts. As in 1792 and at Sebastopol, let our reverses be the school of our victories. It would be a crime to doubt for an instant the safety of our country, and a greater still not to do our part to secure it. Up! then, up! and you inhabitants of the Centre, the North and the South, upon whom the burden of the war does not fall, hasten with unanimous enthusiasm to the help of your brethren of the East. Let France, united in success, be more united still under trial ; and may God bless our arms !" These are words and nothing more.

Immediately after the new Government came into power, Gambetta sent to the préfets of the eighty-nine Departments into which France is divided the following communication :

"Our new Republic is a Government of National Defence, a Republic of battle to the last against the intruders. Gather around you citizens who, like yourselves, are animated by the lasting desire to save the country, and are prepared not to shrink from any sacrifices."

What a contrast, as thoroughly practical, compared to the emotional declamation of the Imperial Government! And Gambetta showed, in addressing the préfets, and not the people, that he was both wise and far-seeing.

He approaches the people through the local representatives of the central Government, and reminds these representatives that in the Provinces they are the delegates who will be the instruments of that Government in organising and conducting in the Provinces the National Defence, and he looks forward to the Provinces taking part in the campaign against the invader. The idea embodied in the saying "Paris is France" was acting powerfully at this time in the minds of the leaders

CONDITIONS OF THE SECOND WAR 23

on both sides. The capture of Paris was the one aim of v. Moltke—as of supreme importance. Within Paris itself, the defence of the capital, and the concentration there of the military force of the country, took a strong hold, almost to the complete exclusion of the consideration of any part that the rest of the country could take in the continuation of the struggle. Gambetta was always opposed to these views. He said : " Only one thing was thought of, namely, to defend Paris ; and this idea became so exclusive that nothing was thought of but Paris ; I even found that the rest of the country was somewhat forgotten. It was believed that Paris alone would not only be able to set herself free, but to drive away the invader." General Trochu, who became the head of the Government in Paris, and General Chanzy, who afterwards played a prominent part in the war, also deprecated this attributing to Paris such a monopoly of the National Defence. The new Government determined that it was at Paris it ought to remain. It was decided, therefore, to represent in the Provinces the central Government by means of a delegation of its members, which established itself at Tours, 120 miles from Paris, on the Loire. Mons. Crémieux, a barrister, who was the chief of the delegation, was seventy-four years of age ; Mons. Glais-Bizoin, also a barrister, was seventy years old, and Vice-Admiral Fourichon, who combined the Ministries of Marine and War, was comparatively young, sixty-one years of age. This delegation could hardly possess the physical and mental amount of vigour necessary for governing all France, less Paris, so until Gambetta, escaping from Paris in a balloon, arrived at Tours on October 9th, and practically superseded the delegation, little progress was made in utilising the enormous resources which existed in the Provinces.

As already stated, the march to Paris began on September 4th, and it was on the 19th that the German Army, marching with its front covered by the Cavalry Divisions, arrived before the capital, and took up positions forming a complete circle of investment. To the Army of the Meuse was assigned the northern semicircle ; the Third Army taking charge of the southern semicircle. The Royal Headquarters, and those of the Third Army were very soon established at Versailles—six miles south-west of the enceinte of the fortifications. The artillery park was at Villacoublay, four miles east of Versailles, on the main road. From the Seine below Paris, the Guard and Saxon Cavalry Divisions guarded the rear of the northern semicircle; and, starting from the same point, the 5th, 6th, 4th, and 2nd Cavalry Divisions guarded the southern line.

But September 19th marks the close of a period, of which one of the most prominent characteristics had been the marvellous mobility of the German host that had entered France. Immediately after the battle of Wörth, as has been already mentioned, the Baden Field Division was despatched to Strassburg, and ceased to be a force on the move in the field; the rest of the Germans moved rapidly on; but after the battle of Gravelotte, a very large portion was detached from it and became an immobile force round Metz. From Metz, by Sedan, the remainder tramped on to the capital, and when they had completely formed the investing circle, there was no longer any mobile force of Germans in France —one and all of them had become immobile. For the success of an invasion, no attitude that the invader may assume is more fraught with possible dangers in the future than is the cessation or the suspension of his onward career. Not merely is time afforded to the invaded for fresh preparations for defence, but the prestige inherent in the continued offensive is lost; the invaded have time to recover their self-possession and their *moral;* and they attribute to the invader either exhaustion arising from his previous efforts, or an acknowledgment of inability to pursue his career of victory owing to the numerical weakness of his forces.

Although by degrees the Germans were able to put large forces again into the field, yet, as will appear in the course of this narrative, it was no less a period than ten weeks that France was given to make, undisturbed by the Germans, her

CONDITIONS OF THE SECOND WAR 25

preparations in the Provinces for a renewal of the struggle; and this fact alone, not merely justifies, but compels, us to regard the second phase of the campaign as a new and second war. There was no truce between the belligerents, but in the subjugation of France, there was almost a suspension of arms. Energetically and persistently did the French work at their preparations for defence during the last seven of those ten weeks, but of the nature, character, and extent of those preparations the Germans were able to learn but little. The amount of French territory in actual occupation by the invader was comparatively very small, and the nation did its best to prevent these Germans seeing or learning what was going on outside the limits of the occupied territory; but from the large and extensive unoccupied territory, there was telegraphic communication with the rest of the world through Spain, Switzerland, and Belgium, whilst the outlets along the coast-line were many and open. It seems strange, therefore, not that the Germans on French soil should have been ignorant of what was taking place close at hand, but that the German Government at Berlin should not, by means of spies and similar devices, have obtained from the unoccupied territory itself full information of what was taking place there. When, at the end of September, Strassburg fell, the German troops hitherto employed in the siege took the field, but were compelled to remain in Eastern and South-Eastern France to guard the main German line of communication against attacks from these districts. Under any circumstances, this was their natural sphere of action, but it was later on when, at the end of October, the surrender of Metz set free the First and Second Armies, and in the middle of November, when a large force from the troops investing Paris became available for service in the field, that the want of knowledge told so against the Germans; and some 100,000 men were despatched in directions away from the main scene of the preparations for the National Defence; mistakes only possible to be retrieved through errors and misleading on the French side.

Whether the Germans were wise in determining to continue

at once the invasion after Sedan, or whether Paris should have been selected as the next objective is one of those deep political and military problems which may afford a subject for never-ending discussion among students of war. Mr. O'Connor Morris, in his " Life of v. Moltke," deals with the question with great ability. But, whether the decisions were right or wrong, there cannot be the very slightest doubt that the beliefs on which they were based were absolutely false, and that consequently the Germans soon found themselves confronted by a situation totally unexpected, and they became involved in a prolonged war of a character of which they had no previous experience, and with which they knew not how to deal effectively.

The erroneous views with which v. Moltke entered on the second war were: a disbelief that France, as a nation, would continue the struggle after the terrible defeats inflicted on her, and, therefore, that Paris would surrender as soon as she found herself cut off from the outer world, and with the prospect of hunger before her; further, that as Paris was said to be France, France without Paris would be helpless. But there arose, as regards the future of this campaign, a division of opinion at the Royal Headquarters of the German Army, immediately after Sedan. V. Moltke and his immediate associates disbelieved in French practical patriotism, and anticipated a speedy ending of the war; on the other hand, Bismark, v. Roon the Minister of War, Prince Frederick Charles, and the King himself, greatly doubted that the pride of the French would allow them to yield a speedy submission, and they anticipated therefore a prolongation of the war. Mr. O'Connor Morris says: " Like most soldiers, v. Moltke had little faith in moral power in conflict with material force; he had a rooted dislike and contempt for Frenchmen, and he did not believe that France would make a real effort to vindicate her great name, and to oppose the invader . . . Omniscience is not given to the children of men."

On September 6th, v. Roon wrote : " Whether, old as I am, I shall live to see the end of the war is indeed a matter of

CONDITIONS OF THE SECOND WAR 27

indifference, but I doubt it." But for some time after the investment was completed, the optimist spirit prevailed at Versailles, and there was no anxiety as to the future. Eight days was the limit of endurance first accepted. V. Moltke believed that the Parisians would surrender "if they had no fresh milk"; both he and v. Roon calculated fourteen days as the extremity of endurance; on September 21st, v. Moltke wrote: " Dear Adolph,—I wish that you and yours could spend the winter somewhere in a warmer climate. If possible I will come too. Moreover, I still hope that at the end of October I shall be shooting hares in Creisau," On October 3, Lieut.-Colonel Verdy du Vernois, one of v. Moltke's principal subordinates, wrote : " According to the information at hand, Paris is said to be provisioned for six weeks— fourteen days of that time have now elapsed." But the Parisians belied all expectations, and held the Germans outside her walls for some sixteen times eight days. It was not a mere handful of soldiers, the garrison of Paris, the six line battalions that kept the gates closed ; it was the Parisians, this section of the French People, the French women as well as the French men, that by their endurance of the terrible sufferings due to famine and sickness during that bitter winter kept outside but held close to the walls of the capital —those 120,000 German infantry and their 600 guns, and prevented them carrying devastation into the fair Provinces of France.

And the Provinces, recognising their patriotism, endeavoured to emulate them in their practical excercise of this national virtue, and to render their suffering not in vain. Ere long 800,000 men had flocked to the standards, on which were inscribed the words: " Paris is hungry : come and help her.'

And this obstinacy of the Parisians gave rise outside and near the walls to very serious inconveniences for the Germans. Food, in the early days of the investment, was not too abundant, as the only line of communication to the Third Army was the main railway from Nancy, already broken near

Nanteuil, whilst that of the Army of the Meuse was by ordinary road from Pont-à-Mousson. Requisitioning became, therefore, all-important. When the Germans approached Paris, not only were villages found deserted, but all supplies of food had been carried away ; the French population had already taken the alarm, and the earlier decrees had begun to work, so the requisitioning parties of cavalry that were sent out found themselves everywhere opposed, whether when endeavouring to enter villages or to carry away the supplies dragged from the unwilling owners. Inhabitants armed, men in the uniform of Garde Mobile or Garde Nationale, and Franc-tireurs acted in common against the intruders. But few of the cavalry carried firearms, so detachments of infantry, and even guns, were ere long added to the requisitioning parties. It was mainly in the close and difficult country lying to the west of Paris that the greatest resistance was encountered ; in the open country, which lies a few miles south of Paris, the cavalry were able to obtain better results from their work.

No doubt this requisitioning was not a congenial occupation. In v. Blumenthal's Journal is the following entry of September 27th: "I had to talk severely to the Cavalry Divisions to-day for the very indifferent supplies of provisions they have requisitioned of late, owing to their dread of the Franc-tireurs"; on the 28th: "Again this morning I had so much to do, especially in the matter of the directions which had to be given to the Cavalry Divisions on the subject of requisitioning supplies, that at one o'clock I was nearly dead."

Inasmuch as every day that Paris continued to hold out and to keep the investing Army enchained round the city was a day's gain in the preparations for national defence in the Provinces, the Royal Headquarters had necessarily to take in hand at once the consideration of the possible and probable result of the preparations, to ascertain whence and where the effect of those preparations would first make itself apparent, and what measures, pending the surrender of the capital, it

CONDITIONS OF THE SECOND WAR 29

would be necessary to adopt in view of the future. A mere glance at the map of France would suffice for the identification of the localities most favourable for the preparations.

First and foremost, Central and South-West France, beyond the river Loire, and where, covered by the river, was the great arsenal of France, Bourges, having good railway communication to both the East and North-West of France, and Nevers, the arsenal for naval stores and equipment. Moreover, the importance of this district had been increased by the selection of Tours, on the river, as the seat of the Delegation entrusted by the chief Government in Paris with the conduct of affairs in the Provinces. Far off, in the South-East, in the turbulent district of Lyon, was another probable base for hostile operations. Besançon, and the strong fortress of Belfort, lay on the northern boundary of this district. It was a good starting-point for any operations against the long and thread-like line of communications that connected the Germans round Paris with their own country. But the vulnerability of the German line of communications, and the great results likely to follow from even an unsuccessful attempt against it, do not seem to have received from the Delegation the attention they deserved until too late in the war. As France had command of the sea, the district in the North-West of France, with its fortresses of Douai, Lille, Valenciennes, and others, was another favourable base of operation.

But the district which seems to have had special advantages, not as a centre of preparation by itself, but both as a centre, and as a base of operations in connection with the Loire district, was that to the west of Paris—the lower Seine and the country further south. Through Havre, with its large docks and excellent roadstead, it is connected by sea with the south of France and the rest of the world, while by land there is good railway connection with the Loire district by Alençon, le Mans, and Tours, the connection being protected from the east by the close country already mentioned. It lay, also, opposite to the weakest portion of the investment line, at the numerous bends of the Seine near the capital. Neither of the arms—artillery and cavalry—in which the Germans were so superior to the French, could utilise that superiority to full advantage against an advance from this quarter.

But a knowledge of the mere places of assembly was of little value without a knowledge also of the strength collecting at each, and of the extent of the preparations in progress at each. And here we come to that peculiar characteristic of all People's Wars, and strikingly so of this war— the dense Fog of War which the invader finds encompassing him all round. Sometimes it is a Strategical Fog. He cannot tell what it is behind that Fog; if there is anything behind it, he knows not where it is; and, possibly, there may be nothing behind it at all. So he knows not whence a blow may be suddenly delivered against him; and when he himself is prepared to deliver a blow, he may strike simply *en l'air*. And the very composition of the Fog enables the forces of the invaded country to see through it; in fact, it is one of the instruments of vision as to the movements of the invader. It is the irregular local levies and the able-bodied civilian inhabitants of the locality, with arms in their hands, that give to the Fog, by their stolid resistance, the density of the Fog. But on the invader's side the Fog almost insensibly blends into the population on that side—the population among which lie the invading troops. It is an old saying that ill news flies apace, and what ill news would be of more rapid flight than that in a particular area in the possession of the invader there was a certain body of troops preparing to move off into the Fog in some particular direction? Hence, whilst the defenders have information on which to base their plan of operations, the data on which the invader forms his plans are seldom reliable, and may be entirely, or at all events seriously, misleading. But, on the other hand, a civilian population is apt to form very exaggerated ideas of the strength of the forces that may come to its notice.

Sometimes, again, it is the Tactical Fog, as when the

CONDITIONS OF THE SECOND WAR 31

opponents are actually in contact. The invader knows not aught about his opponent; but his opponent knows all about him.

At the end of September there were in the Loire District the 15th Army Corps, approximately 60,000 strong, but a mere mob under the command of General de la Motte-Rouge. In the Corps were three line regiments; of the rest, two-thirds were Marche Regiments, one-third Gardes Mobiles.

In North-West France the territorial commander, General Fiereck, was assembling battalions of Garde Mobile. General Gudin, with 14,000 armed men, was at Rouen and Elbœuf, on the Lower Seine; General Delarue, with 4,000 men, at Vernon and Dreux, protected the railway communication between Rouen and the South. In the South-East General Cambriels was organising for the protection of Lyon an army at Besançon.

But the German Staff were unable to ascertain the numbers at the several centres. A correct estimate of the response of France in fighting men would, however, not have in any way alarmed them. At the Royal Headquarters was one General v. Podbielski, the Quartermaster-General of the Forces, a bluff, outspoken man, one of that invaluable class of men who, though they may see the darker side of affairs, express themselves in optimistic language and treat difficulties with contemptuous speech. To the new levies he applied a term equivalent to "ragamuffins," and it was easy enough to find arguments to support the optimist views propounded by the general, and accepted, doubtless, by many.

Deficient in training and discipline, and with but few good officers to lead or to staff them, the men could not be of much value either as fighting or marching troops. There were difficulties in organising and equipping the large units into which, for military operations, any great mass of men must be subdivided; there were administrative branches to be organised and provided for these units; there were no generals of knowledge and experience to lead Armies; the Government itself, which had been created by the people, could hardly be regarded as a Government strong enough to hold its own against popular anger in the event of the war going against the new Armies in the field; and a single disaster might wreck all authority; it could be only by some lucky chance that there would exist sufficient unity of thought and action among the new civil and new military leaders to secure unity of aims and purposes in the employment of the new Armies in the forthcoming campaign. So for the present, Versailles took matters very calmly.

CHAPTER III

OCTOBER

In the early days of October, disquieting reports reached Versailles from the direction of the Loire, where the 15th Corps was known to be in course of formation. Considerable activity was apparent on the hither side of the river, and outside the forest which surrounds the city of Orleans for some miles. Orleans is only sixty-five miles from Paris. On October 5th, the French under General Reyau had made, with a force mainly of cavalry, but in which some guns and infantry were included, a reconnaissance northward from Orleans in the neighbourhood of Toury, forty-seven miles from Paris. They were met by the 4th Cavalry Division, under the command of Prince Albrecht of Prussia (father), and after an encounter, the Germans fell back to Etampes, less than thirty miles from the Capital, evacuating the country north of Orleans. It was just at this time that the command of the French troops in Orleans and on the Loire was given to General de la Motte-Rouge, a veteran from the reserve of officers, and who had seen much service in Africa as well as in the Crimea and Italy. At an interview he had had with the Delegation at Tours, one of the Ministers, in bidding him adieu, said to him, "For God's sake do something or other as soon as you possibly can, Public opinion insists on it." On being placed in command he proceeded, therefore, at once to draw his troops forward to Orleans, in view of future operations, and he took up, with some of them, a position north of the forest. On the 7th he visited and inspected the positions taken up, going to Tours the next day in obedience to a summons from the Delegation ;

34 THE PEOPLE'S WAR IN FRANCE, 1870-71

but on his return, on the evening of the 9th, he found on his hands work he had not anticipated.

The advance of Reyau to Toury, and the retreat of the 4th Cavalry Division, had alarmed Versailles, where the successful reconnaissance had been misinterpreted for an advance against the investing Army. It was the Third Army that formed this portion of the line of investment, the 1st Bavarian Corps under General v. d. Tann being the reserve. The Corps was composed of two infantry divisions, each of two brigades, from which several battalions were absent on detached duties, a Cuirassier brigade of eight squadrons, two regiments of divisional cavalry, and 112 guns. The numerical strength was about 16,000 infantry and 1600 cavalry. V. d. Tann was, on the 6th, ordered to meet the threatened advance, which he did by taking up a defensive position across the Orleans road at Arpajon, sixteen miles south of Paris, but as at the same time a sortie from Paris was anticipated, the Corps was at first posted so as to be able to act in either direction. To the force were now added the 22nd Infantry Division, under Major-General v. Wittich, consisting of 5500 infantry, four squadrons of cavalry, and 24 guns from the investing line; and the 4th Cavalry Division, 24 squadrons and 12 guns. The French not advancing, orders were, on the night of the 7th-8th, given to v. d. Tann to take the offensive south. The situation had been curious; for two days the Germans had remained in a defensive position, awaiting an advance of a distant body of an enemy, comparatively very few in number and indifferent in quality, which had not the faintest intention of coming forward to attack. The orders now given to v. d. Tann were to clear the country south to Orleans, and west to Chartres, forty-two miles south-west of Paris, and thirty miles west of the great Paris-Orleans road, to occupy Orleans, and, according to circumstances, to carry on the pursuit as far as Tours. The 2nd Cavalry Division of 24 squadrons and 12 guns under the command of Lieutenant-General Count zu Stolberg, was ordered to co-operate in the intended advance, so v. d. Tann had at his disposal some 21,500 infantry,

6700 cavalry, and 160 guns. General de la Motte-Rouge, on his return from Tours, heard of the approach of the Germans, and at once pushed forward a small force to Artenay, four miles outside the forest, and twelve miles from Orleans. On the 10th, this force was easily driven back by the Germans to the forest, and on the next day, v. d. Tann, following up the French, drove them through the city over the river, and occupied Orleans. The losses of the Germans were not, however, insignificant, some 1200, including 60–70 officers. There was no pursuit beyond Orleans.

The French had not shown any very great resisting power; and it was perhaps in accordance with the sound principle of immediately following up a success, and not allowing a beaten enemy time to recover from a blow, that on the 13th, v. d. Tann received from v. Moltke the following order, which is here given as found in Helvig's work: "Das I. bayerische Armee-Corps von der Tann im Kriege 1870-71." Captain Helvig was an officer of the General Staff on the Staff of the Corps. General v. d. Tann was directed "to extend as far as Bourges" [sixty miles south] "the operations of his army and of the 2nd Cavalry Division, which was now placed under his orders. It appeared to be of the greatest importance, for the further course of the war, to obtain possession of this town and its large gun manufactories, and to render the latter useless.

"Simultaneously with the advance against Bourges, a demonstration was to be made against Tours" [seventy miles down stream from Orleans], "the seat of the Government, and, finally, it was mentioned in the despatches, that the only depôt of military wagons still in the hands of the French was at Chateauroux" [some forty miles south-west of Bourges].

"It was, however, left to General v. d. Tann to act according to his own judgment, as the state of affairs could not be sufficiently well known at Versailles."

The form of this order is that known as a "Directive"; it gives the operation desired or recommended by v. Moltke to be undertaken by the commander, but it leaves, at the same time, full discretion to the latter as to the mode to be adopted, or even as to whether it should be carried out at all.

It was a game with very high stakes that lay before v. d. Tann to play, and v. Moltke had left it to his judgment whether he would play it: it meant not merely the capture and destruction of the enormous main arsenal of the Republic, but, on the way, the destruction of Vierzon, which is forty-seven miles south of Orleans, and is the great railway junction from which ran lines to the north, south, east, and west of France. Major-General v. Columb, the commander of a brigade of the 2nd Cavalry Division, has, in his " Diary of the War," said: " Had the German Army been able to gain possession of Vierzon and Bourges, the vital nerve of the National Defence would have been cut through." There does not seem to have been in v. d. Tann any lack of determination, courage, or enterprise, and yet he decided that the risk of the game rendered it not worth the playing. A brief account of the nature of the risk, as Helvig regards it, will therefore be given.

The strength of the army in infantry had now, owing to casualties and detachments, been reduced to 19,000. Chartres and Chateaudun, only thirty miles west of the road to Orleans from Paris, were occupied by the French; Orleans, therefore, could not be left without a garrison, for which at least a brigade of 4000 men was necessary, thus reducing the active force still further to 15,000 ; the demonstration against Tours could not be by cavalry only. The composition of v. d. Tann's force was peculiar as regards the proportion of the three arms. The number of cavalry and guns was relatively very large, and these arms had found in the open plains north of the forest, and between Orleans and Etampes, full play against the poorly trained troops opposed to them; but this would not be the case in the country south of the Loire. Bourges lay quite five days' march from Orleans. The intervening country is covered with large and small woods, ponds, marshes, and brooks. The general direction of the latter is from east to west, and they form, as it were, so many parallel

OCTOBER

lines of defence. It is unnecessary for an enemy to manœuvre on such ground; he need only make use of its capabilities, and follow the natural instinct of resistance, in order to exhaust his adversary, unless the latter can, at once and permanently, break down his opposition by numerical superiority. In this labyrinth of lakes and woods, and behind numerous brooks, the enemy did not need, for obstinate resistance, troops capable of manœuvring; all that was required was only partly trained men, but plenty of them, and of these the French had more than enough. To mass the German artillery, or to threaten the enemy's flanks by large bodies of cavalry, as at Artenay, was not practicable; an open range was wanting for the one, a sufficient space on which to manœuvre for the other. Both arms were restricted to the roads, and the heaviest task fell on the infantry. The enemy's outposts would be first encountered twelve miles from Orleans, and thence the resistance would be daily and continuous, and the infantry would arrive before Bourges greatly reduced in numbers. It had been ascertained that at Bourges had been already thrown up works for defence, armed with heavy guns; the population and the workmen from the factories were armed and ready to aid the troops in offering resistance, and reinforcements could be brought up every hour by railroad; one hundred and thirty miles would be the length of the German line of communication. So far Helvig. The expedition to Tours (seventy miles) was not very promising, that to Chateauroux impracticable. It is certain, however, that had the attempt against Bourges succeeded, the National Defence must have taken a form totally different from that of the subsequent campaign on the Loire, but it by no means follows that a campaign of some kind in the future would have been rendered impossible; and as, in the opinion of some, the selection of the Loire as a base of operations against the invaders was by no means sound, there might have come about other operations with which the Germans might have found it far more difficult to deal. It was not until the National Defence showed, later on, how powerful it was, that the effect of the non-destruction of

Bourges and Vierzon in October was fully realised. Then it was evident that for the loss of the whole Bavarian Corps in a successful attempt, there would have been something like a full equivalent and perhaps more. But in October, so little did Versailles believe in the National Defence, that the sacrifice would, perhaps, at that time have seemed a useless loss of combatant power. The problem is one of many of the kind, furnishing food for speculation, and nothing more.

In consequence of the decision of v. d. Tann the 22nd Infantry Division and 4th Cavalry Division were withdrawn from Orleans, and sent under the command of v. Wittich by Chateaudun, twenty-seven miles north-west of Orleans, and on the Loir, to Chartres, twenty-six miles north of Chateaudun and on the Upper Eure. In Chateaudun were, under an excellent leader, Lieut.-Colonel Lipowski, 1200 Franc-tireurs and local Gardes Nationales; and when, on the 18th, v. Wittich approached the town, these irregulars, aided by the inhabitants, offered a determined and splendid resistance. It was the first instance in this "People's War" of resistance by what was really a part of the civil population of France. The town had been thoroughly prepared for defence, in fact v. Wittich states that there was a plan of the defensive organisation and a report on it. The fight commenced in the morning; and it was not until 8 A.M. on the morning of the 19th that the defence, which had been of the house-to-house character, ceased, and possession of the town was gained. Terrible were the consequences of this resistance. Much of the town was burnt down and pillage was freely exercised. It is stated that no less than 235 houses were burnt. This was the first essay of the able v. Wittich in the task assigned to him by the Head-quarters of the Third Army, and which is given in the order received by him at Orleans on the 16th, from v. Blumenthal:

" As the neighbourhood of Chateaudun and especially that of Chartres is in the hands of Gardes Mobiles and Franc-tireurs, who are continually threatening the rear of the army before Paris, you are given the duty of clearing the enemy

OCTOBER 39

out of those districts; for this purpose you will, as circumstances may require, form from your Division flying columns, which are to return generally to Paris by Chateaudun, Chartres and Dreux " [on the Blaise, a tributary of the Eure, and twenty miles north of Chartres, and forty miles west of Paris]. " Your departure from Orleans is fixed for the 17th, but you have perfect freedom to halt when you please, and complete liberty in your choice of action. You can go even some miles further west if you consider it desirable to do so. The essential thing is to clear this district entirely of the enemy. To avoid any misunderstanding as to dealing with any prisoners you may take, I have appended to this order directions as regards this matter, and I have, in connection with it, only to remark that localities on which civilians have taken part in a fight are to be punished with the utmost severity, by fines or by being burnt. . . . The population will everywhere be warned that their participation in the war, or their treachery, will always be punished with death, and that they must therefore remain neutral, and comply unhesitatingly with all the necessary requisitions."

V. Wittich does not give the directions mentioned in the letter, but it is probable that as regards dealing with the punishment of the inhabitants they did not differ from those now given, and which also emanated from the Third Army:

" All persons not forming part of the French Army, and not proving their quality as soldiers by outward signs, and who

" (a) Shall serve the enemy as spies ;
" (b) Shall mislead the German troops when charged to act for them as guides ;
" (c) Shall kill, wound, or rob persons belonging to the German troops, or making part of their suite ;
" (d) Shall destroy bridges or canals, damage telegraph lines or railways, render roads impassable, set fire to munitions or provisions of war, or troops' quarters ;
" (e) Shall take up arms against the German troops ;

"will be punished by death. In each case the officer in command will institute a council of war, with authority to try the matter and pronounce sentence. These councils can only condemn to death. Their sentences will be executed immediately. The communes to which the culprits belong, as well as those whose territory may have been the scene of the offence, will be condemned in a penalty for each case equalling the amount of their taxes."

V. Wittich was a soldier who placed duty specially in the foreground, and as his proceedings at Chateaudun painfully showed, he never shrank from any duty however trying to the feelings of humanity, so v. Blumenthal's instructions were always carried out thoroughly. Discount to the full the narratives of the conduct of the Germans in Western France as given by the sufferers, by eyewitnesses, and by French historians, it is impossible to doubt that the severity of the Germans towards the inhabitants was frequently terrible. Hoenig claims for the Second Army in its advance during November from Metz to the south-west, that it was owing to its determination to abstain as much as possible from reprisals that it had to endure much at the hands of the population. No such credit can be claimed for the Third Army. V. Moltke, as has been shown by his letter of October 27th, approved of great severity; v. Blumenthal shared his views on the matter, and as reprisals thus bore the stamp of approbation of the highest authorities, the generals and other commanders followed suit. It would, therefore, be impossible but that when this spirit had permeated down to the lowest ranks, and among the ignorant, these reprisals would verge on barbarism. But in justice to the invaders it must be said that womanhood was respected by them.

West and south-west of Paris it was a real reign of terror that was inaugurated against this "People's War." Helvig writes as follows: "So long as only the hostile armies are fighting each other, the war remains, if the word used does not seem paradoxical, civilised; but from the moment that the population with their brutal hatred and their passions mix in our bloody work, it is 'eye for eye' and 'tooth for tooth.'" Doubtless the reprisals acted frequently as a deterrent to the population in taking their share in the defence of their country, and the people remained neutral. But, as a rule, the endeavour to inspire terror was not effective in this part of France during the months of October and November. And if patriotism be a noble virtue, if *pro Patriâ mori* be a duty, then here French men and French women, and some little more than children, have set posterity an example. Splendid in its self-abnegation, splendid in its sheer heroism, an example, which being little known outside the limits of hearth and home, has never received that recognition and that tribute of deep admiration it so deservedly merits. *Mourir pour la Patrie* is writ large from the Lower Seine to Chateaudun.

On the 20th, v. Wittich resumed his March on Chartres, which was reported to be strongly held. In the city were some 7000 men and half a battery, but the only regular troops were two companies of marines. During the 21st there was a small amount of opposition at various points. The 6th Cavalry Division was now operating from the north, so that the city could be enveloped by thousands of horsemen. What took place after the arrival of v. Wittich at the village of Morancez, three miles short of Chartres, the General himself shall tell.

"Lieut.-Colonel Hendrick brought before me the Curé of the village and the Maires of the localities in front of Chartres. In answer to the requests of the Maires to spare their villages, I replied with the threat to burn down those from which there was any more firing on my troops; and to the Curé, who was interceding for the city of Chartres, I said that I must enter it to-day, either by force of arms or amicably. If it was defended it must expect the fate of Chateaudun. I allowed him to go to Chartres to endeavour to arrange matters. . . . Before one o'clock the Préfet of the Department of the Eure et Loire and the Maire of Chartres came to me. The Préfet, after a vain attempt to take a high tone, undertook that the Gardes Nationales of Chartres should lay down their arms, and that the regular and irregular troops should quit the city, which should be surrendered to me. I gave them until 3 P.M. for the final arrangements; otherwise, I threatened to commence the bombardment at that hour." The General, to show that he meant what he said, deployed his troops and put his guns in position. The Préfet and a member of the municipality came with a white flag before the expiry of the time, and the surrender was concluded, the General remarking that the agreement would be regarded as broken if outside or inside the city a single shot was fired on his men. The city would have to feed the troops and comply with all necessary requisitions. In the event of compliance no money contribution would be imposed. Resistance would have been hopeless and useless; it would, perhaps, have caused the destruction of one of the most glorious cathedrals in the world; so the surrender may be condoned. On the 23rd the 22nd Division received orders the remain at Chartres.

V. d. Tann, at Orleans, had learnt that large bodies of the enemy's troops were concentrated at Gien, thirty-five miles up the Loire, and he asked the Third Army Headquarters that, in case the French attempted to surround and attack Orleans, he should be allowed to abandon the position of Orleans, which, even only from a tactical point of view, was extremely unfavourable for a force with little infantry, but much artillery and cavalry, and to take up a position to the north-east in the neighbourhood of Pithiviers, some twenty-four miles from Orleans, where the ground was better adapted to the use of cavalry and artillery. On October 20th, V. d. Tann received an answer that the continued occupation of Orleans was indispensable, and that the town was only to be evacuated in the presence of far superior forces. It is difficult to see how, Orleans once being occupied, any other answer could have been given. For offensive operations, Orleans was of no value whatever to the Germans; but, having once been taken, the moral effect of abandoning it would have told against them. Moreover, for the French it had no inconsiderable advantages as a bridge head on the right bank of the river.

The first half of October had marked the failure of the forces of the Government of National Defence in their first encounter in the field with the invaders. The defeat seemed almost to show that it was hopeless for France, bereft of her army, to offer, except at Paris, any further resistance to the subjugation of the country. There had been crowds of armed men beyond the Loire, but military discipline had not existed, and organisation was little more than nominal. The Government in Paris expected little from them, nor did it think it necessary to try to obtain from them any real assistance. When General Lefort left Paris for Tours with the Delegation, the Minister of War in Paris said to him : " You will never do anything with the men left to you." General Lefort remarked : " I ought to tell you that, in commencing the organisation of the 15th Corps, I hardly see that the Corps would be called on to take part in any military operation. This army is not perhaps destined to act effectively, but I regard its organisation indispensable ; it will have a considerable moral effect. . . . If, as we all hope, Paris is to be relieved in a few months, well, then we shall have an army which will be able, even if it has never fired a cartridge, to give weight in the balance, if we should be called on to make terms of peace." There was a feeling of disbelief in everything in France except Paris.

The Government of the Provinces had, up to October 9th, been in feeble hands indeed at Tours, but on the 9th, the day before Artenay, there had arrived at Tours, after a journey in a balloon from Paris, Gambetta, the Minister of the Interior. Gambetta at once assumed the authority of a despotic autocrat, and it was Gambetta to whom Germany owed the three or four months of hard and severe campaigning she had to carry through before France lay exhausted at her feet.

Of Gambetta v. d. Goltz writes as follows: " The figure

44 THE PEOPLE'S WAR IN FRANCE, 1870-71

of Gambetta is incontestably one of the most interesting that the great events of 1870-71 have brought into the foreground. Known but a few years, he had made his way rapidly as advocate and deputy during the second Empire, with the result that, after the fall of Napoleon III., it was not with any surprise in his own country or in the rest of the world that he appears as military organiser and General. The part he played has been great enough for his name to live in history for all time. Although he failed to achieve his object, although his dream of becoming the saviour of his country was not realised, his efforts for the salvation of France do not the less deserve our admiration. By the energy of his will he succeeded in animating a country without arms and already tired of resistance, and in drawing it into a struggle which for several months kept the German armies occupied, and taught us to recognise the existence of forces which, without that experience, we should still to-day undervalue. To him sufficed a few weeks to form, out of the chaos of armed men he found available, a well-equipped army of hundreds of thousands." At his right hand, with the title of delegate, and acting as Minister of War, was de Freycinet, a civil engineer, his equal in energy and determination. The magnetic influence that Gambetta showed he possessed over the population of France was a marvel of power.

When Gambetta assumed control At the moment of Gambetta's arrival at Tours, France seemed to be defenceless and helpless beyond the power of recovery. There were in the south beyond the Loire the defeated and dispirited troops of the 15th Army Corps. In the east Cambriel's army was already falling back on Besançon before the newly formed German XIVth Army Corps. There was in Normandy a small body of troops, another in the north, whilst in the west some 30,000 Gardes Mobiles, poorly armed and equipped, and without artillery and cavalry, and without any organisation, but, nevertheless, denominated the "Army of the West," formed a line from Evreux (fifty miles west of Paris and forty miles north of Chartres) to Chartres. At this time France had got together some 40,000 line troops,

the same number of Gardes Mobiles, 5000–6000 cavalry, and 100 guns. Gambetta at once issued a stirring proclamation to the citizens of France. From it some extracts are here given :
" By order of the Government of the Republic I have left Paris to bring you, with the hopes of the people shut up within its walls, the instructions and orders of those who have accepted the mission of delivering France from the foreigner. The situation imposes great duties on you. The first of all is not to allow yourselves to be diverted by any preoccupation that is not war, 'le combat à outrance'; the second is, until peace is secured, to accept, as brethren, the command of the republican power which has come into existence by necessity and right. This power, moreover, could not, without degradation, work to the profit of any ambition. It has only one supreme object, one title to existence : to rescue France from the depths into which the monarchy has plunged it. . . . We have no lack of men ; what has failed us has been resolution, decision, and rapidity in carrying work into execution. . . . We must utilise all our resources, which are immense, shake off the slowness of our campaigns, counteract foolish panics, multiply guerilla warfare, and to an enemy so apt in ambushes and surprises, oppose snares, harass his flanks, surprise him in rear, and, finally, inaugurate the national war. The Republic appeals to all for help ; its Government will avail itself of all zeal, of all forms of capacity. It is its tradition to call to its aid young leaders ; we will do it. Heaven itself will soon cease to be favourable to our adversaries; the autumn rains will set in, and the Prussians, so far from home, disquieted, anxious, worried by our population now awakened, will gradually be decimated by our arms, by hunger, by natural causes. It is impossible that the glory of France shall be quenched for ever, that the great nation will allow its place in the world to be determined by an invasion of five hundred thousand men. Let us rise *en masse* and die rather than submit to the shame of dismemberment."

This proclamation was at once followed by decrees of organisation. The proclamation went home to the heart of the French people, and there flocked to the standards of France the manhood of France. V. d. Goltz says that during each day of the four months Gambetta was in power as Minister of War, 5000 men joined the Levies. In less than six weeks Gambetta created on the Loire alone an army of 180,000 men, provided with all necessaries of war, with a good and numerous artillery, and a force of cavalry almost in excess of requirements. It is stated that by the end of four months 800,000 men were under arms.

Of the many decrees that Gambetta issued, only three need notice here ; the first two are dated October 14th. Of these, one had, and was probably intended to have, a great beneficial moral influence on the newly raised forces now forming part of the active army. All the bodies of Gardes Nationales, Franc-tireurs, or of any kind in arms against the enemy were constituted the " Armée Auxiliare," and this army was placed on exactly the same footing as regards pay and rank and command as the active army, and its officers became interchangeable with those of the active army. The two armies together formed the great " Army of National Defence."

The other decree had a vast effect on the creation of the strategical Fog of War which surrounded the invaders, and also added greatly to its difficulties. It merits being given *in extenso*.

Art. I. Every Department of which the boundary is at any point whatever at a distance of less than 100 kilometres [62½ miles] from the enemy is declared in a state of siege (*etat de guerre*). This declaration is made by the military chief of the Department immediately that he knows the enemy is within the prescribed distance, and it is immediately published through the civil and military authorities. All information respecting the march of the enemy will be sent direct, by the quickest route, to the military chiefs, and to the Préfets of the departments situated within at least a radius of 100 kilometres in the direction of the march of the enemy.

Art. II. The state of siege involves the following consequences: The Military chief of the Department putting aside all other business (*toute affaire cessant*) will convoke a military committee of five members at least, nine at most. The committee will be composed of, besides the Military chief who will preside, an officer of engineers or, in default, of artillery; a staff officer, an engineer of Ponts et Chausées and a mining engineer. In default of these various officials, the members will be selected from among persons who, by reason of their aptitude and antecedents, are best qualified. The committee, after having visited, if necessary, the ground, will determine within forty-eight hours, after the declaration of the state of siege, the points which appear to them best situated to dispute the advance of the enemy.

These points will be immediately strengthened with earth-works and abattis and other means quickly available and not expensive. These works will, according to circumstances, take the character of an entrenched camp of a size sufficient to receive the whole or part of the disposable troops of the Department, and will be provided, if needs be, with artillery (*s'il y a lieu*). Each of the possible lines of advance of the enemy within the limits of the Department will be similarly fortified. The only exception will be when the line of advance is already commanded, in the Department, by a fortress.

Art. III. The Military committee, or the members delegated by it, will have power to requisition direct, persons and materials for the construction of the work mentioned. They will pay by vouchers given by them, which will be discharged from the funds of the Department or communes, as will be laid down later on.

Art. IV. As soon as the Military chief of the Department considers that one of the fortified posts is threatened, he will direct to it the forces necessary for its defence. These forces will be drawn either from the regular or auxiliary troops of the Department not required for the operations of the Army Corps in the field or from the sedentary Garde Nationale. For this purpose, the Military chief will have the power to call out all the Gardes Nationales up to forty years of age, from such communes as he may designate. He will have command of all the forces thus collected, and take the control of the defence. The officer next senior to him will take command at some other point.

Art. V. If a passage is forced by the enemy, endeavours will be made to restore the works as soon as possible, so as to cut off the retreat of the enemy, and the passage will be held until the Military chief considers the enemy far enough away.

Art. VI. During the duration of the state of siege in a Department, the Gardes Nationales called out are subiect to military law ; if they fail to come up, or to do their duty as soldiers, they are liable to be punished according to the military code of the army.

In default of uniform, the Gardes Nationales called up will wear the kepi as a badge showing their status as soldiers.

They should, by means of vouchers, with which they will be provided by the military committee, provide themselves with three days' food, without regard to the supplies of all kinds that the military committee will have been able to collect on the spot.

Art. VII. The vouchers given by the military committee are accepted as currency in the public treasury, and discharged by the means of a loan raised in the name of the Department by the General Council, and, if this has been dissolved, by a departmental commission nominated by the Préfet.

Art. VIII. From the date of publication of this decree, the preparations above described will be taken in hand at once in the Departments included in the zone of war (up to 100 kilometres at least from the enemy), and the Departments beyond this zone will commence the preliminary study of the points eventually to be defended.

OCTOBER 49

The Engineer officers of all ranks, on ordinary service or attached to corps in the field, but not indispensable for the operations of those corps, will immediately report themselves to the delegate of the Minister of War, who will allot them in the Departments, that they may be attached to the military committees, and take in charge the works of defence prescribed by the committee.

Art. IX. The Military Chiefs of the Departments are held personally responsible for the organisation of the defence and the resistance offered to the enemy.

No doubt the Decree is crude, but the circumstances under which it was issued remove it from the sphere of criticism in cold blood. That its actual results in impeding the advance of the invaders fell so much below what might have been hoped for from it, was in part due to want of time to get the system into thorough order. Another cause may have been the absence of sympathy from the regular military authorities with anything outside professional war, or with any efforts by others than professional soldiers, and their dislike to work in concert with the civilian "Commissaires" deputed by the Delegation to represent it in the Departments. The French Official History of the War, now in course of publication, throws light on this matter. In the northern theatre of war the Commissaire was M. Testelin, a medical man at Lille. Of this official the History tells us, " Although his powers were vaguely defined, he knew how to exert his authority and to exercise it with discretion, without interfering in the details of military questions, with which he was not competent to deal." But his first attempt to concert measures with the General who was the Territorial Military Commander was hardly encouraging. Mons. de Freycinet had, as regards the local work in the districts, honestly said that to create the armies must not only everything be produced in the districts, but also the very instruments of production. The General took so pessimistic a view that M. Testelin then turned to Colonel Farre, Director of Fortifications at Lille, a man of

D

great energy, who threw himself heartily into the work. Little, however, was done until Gambetta arrived at Tours on October 9th, and then, so writes the Official Historian, " the conviction of his patriotism, the warmth of his words gave the necessary impulse, and made France conscious of her own strength." General Bourbaki now came to take the command in the north, and he honestly endeavoured to carry on the work begun by Colonel Farre, but differences of opinion soon manifested themselves between him and the civil authorities; and the Government decided to remove him to another scene of action. Of Bourbaki we read, " His professional knowledge had not with it either hope of success or wish to act and to win. Formerly Commander of the Imperial Guard, he inspired but little confidence among some of the population ; his want of accord with the civil authorities complicated the situation." So it may have been elsewhere in the Provinces.

On the 24th, another very important decree was issued, placing on the Sous-Préfets and Maires the duty of obtaining by every means in their power, all information, however unimportant, with regard to the position, numbers and movements of the enemy, and of forwarding it at once to the Préfets for transmission to the Government. The whole administrative work of Gambetta and de Freycinet is a marvel of power, energy and ability.

And here it is desirable to notice how well suited to the national needs at the time of the issue of the decrees, was the system under which Governmental control has always been exercised in France, no matter whether the Government were Imperial, Monarchical, or Republican. This control has taken a form of intense centralisation at the seat of the Government, with the existence of a very numerous body of Government officials, scattered over the country, who receive the orders from the central authority, and ensure their execution. But these officials, Préfets, Sous-Préfets and Maires, powerful as they were locally, when armed with authority to execute a decree, were themselves allowed but little power of initiative. At each city, town or village, they were the representatives of the central authority to see its orders obeyed, but few or no orders could they themselves give without having first obtained its concurrence and approval. It has been said that even for some insignificant repair or alteration to a public building, the local representative of the central Government has first to obtain its sanction from Paris. For generations had this system prevailed, with the result that, on the one hand, there was always in the provinces a feeling of dependence on Paris, and a looking to Paris for guidance ; on the other hand, the orders and decisions received from Paris came invested with all the authority arising from custom and tradition, and were accepted at once without demur. In this sense " Paris was France," but v. Moltke rendered the phrase too literally, and not in the spirit ; and he seems to have believed that by isolating in a great country one large city, the rest of the country would be paralysed in action. He believed rightly that at Paris was a power, but his mistake lay in regarding that power as an attribute of the place itself, instead of that which was inside the place, the central Government. And when, first by ordinary means of locomotion before the investment, a part of that central Government transferred itself to another city, Tours on the Loire ; and when later on, by extra-ordinary means of locomotion, Gambetta also went to that same city and made it the seat of a really powerful central government, to v. Moltke there remained only the shadow of the "Paris that is France"; the substance of the " Paris that is France" had escaped his grasp, slipped through his fingers and was at Tours, exercising its control and influence as powerfully as ever it had done from Paris in the history of the past. The Préfets and the whole army of Government officials now simply looked to the power at Tours, as before they had looked to the power at Paris; and they were as active in the time of war in executing the orders from the former, as when in the days of peace they had executed the orders from the latter. The right objective for the Germans at the time was not the time-honoured Government in Paris; it was the fledgling at Tours, and of this Government, not all, but only two members, Gambetta and de Freycinet. But only by a spirit of divination could this have been known. V. Blumenthal, however, seems from the outset to have believed Tours, and the work at Tours, to have been the right objective. Without Gambetta, all the grand self-devotion and the patriotic spirit, the willing surrender to suffering and death displayed in this war by the people of France might, under any circumstances, have manifested itself in isolated actions, but it would have been of no avail to produce any real effect; it was by the great mind of Gambetta that all forces which would otherwise have run to waste were gathered up together, and their powers concentrated and focused; and thus was given to the rulers of the country from the people of the country, a gift, a weapon so powerful in its nature that only the incapacity of those rulers to wield it saved the invader of "la Patrie," of "la belle France" from humiliation and defeat.

One of the first acts of Gambetta was the deposition of General de la Motte-Rouge, and the appointment of General d'Aurelle de Paladines to the command of the 15th Corps; the formation of a second corps, the 16th, was at once commenced. And to cover this formation and, at the same time, to protect Tours were utilised the irregular levies, and the men whose sole claim to be regarded as soldiers was that they wore some sort of uniform or distinctive badge and carried rifles, and were designated Gardes Mobiles or Gardes Nationales, and also the other inhabitants willing to aid. There was formed a cordon of Franc-tireurs and Gardes Mobiles along the Loir from Cloyes (six miles below Chateaudun) to Morée, and thence south-east along the northern and eastern edges of the Forest of Marchenoir (twenty miles west of Orleans) from Ecoman to Lorges, whence it was prolonged due south to the Loire at Mer (twenty-two miles below Orleans).

And on the 17th the so-called "Army of the West" which

OCTOBER

has been already mentioned, and which was destined to exercise an extraordinary influence on the German strategy to the marked benefit of the preparations for the National Defence, was placed under the command of General Fiereck, the Territorial Commander in the west. It was this "Army of the West," composed of Franc-tireurs, Gardes Mobiles, Gardes Nationales, and armed inhabitants, little more in fact than a population armed, with a very small infusion of troops of the active army, at the most seven battalions of regulars, two of marines, seven mountain guns, and a sapper battalion, that affords such a striking illustration how greatly, in country suitable to its action, the inhabitants may co-operate in the defence of a country against invasion. The "Army of the West" never thought of venturing to fight battles with the invader; that was far beyond its powers; its offensive work was confined strictly to harassing the outlying smaller parties of the invader that came within its reach, and to stopping their progress; and in its defence of localities it created that Fog of War, a Fog so dense that the invader could not ascertain, except by the employment of a small army, what was behind it, where what might be behind it was, or if anything at all was behind it; and yet full knowledge of the actual state of affairs was indispensable to the invader as a preliminary to ulterior operations. Not only had, therefore, the invader to employ force to find out the real state of affairs, but in doing so he spent time urgently needed for other purposes, and eventually he despatched an army, at a time when its presence was pressingly needed elsewhere, to a region where there was nothing to fight. A description of the theatre of war in which this "bogus" army played so valuable a part, and rendered such excellent service to the real armies of France will, therefore, now be given.

The Eastern boundary of the area may be taken as commencing on the North at Pont de l'Arche on the Seine at the junction of the Eure, fifty-five miles below Paris; thence along the Eure for a distance of sixty miles to Chartres. Midway it is only forty miles west of Versailles, and at

Chartres it is thirty miles from the Paris-Orleans road. Here it leaves the Upper Eure which comes from the west, and continuing south strikes the Upper Loir twenty miles distant at Bonneval, and then for ten miles follows the Loir to Chateaudun its southern point. For a breadth of thirty to forty miles westward of this line the country presents the aspect of what may be called a tangle of hills, valleys, rivers and streams which reaches a climax at Nogent-le-Rotrou in the heart of the Perche district. The eastern boundary south of Paris is not very difficult to cross from the East, but it is after crossing that the invader finds his troubles begin. The Blaise and the Avre, tributaries of the Eure confront him to the north-west, the Upper Eure and the Upper Loir with their tributaries confront him to the south-west, whilst to the west he finds the most broken part of the Perche district and the Huisne River barring his advance. The system of defence was the establishment of certain centres or pivots from which the activity started, and the holding with groups of armed men or companies all the roads running in from the east, and all the principal crossings of the rivers and tributaries. The district was thoroughly adapted for guerilla warfare by irregular troops. The troops were constantly shifting, but the three chief centres selected by General Fiereck were on a line facing north-east—the left, being Nogent-le-Rotrou in the valley of the Huisne, where run the railway and high road from Paris by Chartres to le Mans, the centre Brou on the Ozanne a tributary of the Loir, the right Chateaudun.

The principal road junctions, which also were the principal assembly points of the force, were Bonneval, Illiers on the Loir, ten miles above Bonneval, Courville on the Upper Eure, Chateauneuf north-west of Courville, and finally Dreux. At the most important places between these were also posted groups of Gardes Mobiles, supported to the utmost by the population, which, generally, at this time took part in the war. Companies of sappers were employed by the Departmental authorities acting under the decree of

October 14th, to block the roads, or to make entrenchments for the assistance of the defence.

Under these circumstances the German Cavalry were unable to find out what was actually taking place on the important roads from Nogent to Courville and Illiers respectively, and on the important lateral road running through Brou from Nogent to Chateaudun, and the network ramification of roads from these roads to the rear. If the Cavalry tried to get ahead by going round the villages instead of passing through them, they again met with armed resistance. The Cavalry could report what places and woods were held by the French within a semi-circle of three-quarters to one and a-half days march radius; but what they could not find out was where the main body of the enemy was, whether there was any main body, or what this ever active army was intend.ng to do. This restless enemy seemed ubiquitous; now here, now there, appeared bands of armed men which hindered the larger German movements, then disappeared, and appeared again later on to play the same game elsewhere. For the German reconnoitring parties, it was not deducing the direction of the march of a large force, by the general direction of the march of its units; it was nothing more than noting small units marching in every direction of the compass. It must be remembered that by Gambetta's Decree the control was Departmental: and unfortunately there had not been time to combine in the hands of one superior authority central control over the Departmental authorities. This independence was, of course, a very weak point in the general defence. There was an absence of co-operation between Departments, and no unity of purpose or leading. The cordon was continued from the Loir south to the Loire as already described, whilst on the left bank of the latter river, v. d. Tann's vision at Orleans was effectually limited by the character of the country, and the number of hostile troops in that district.

CHAPTER IV

HUMAN NATURE IN WAR, AND THE "PERSONLICHKEIT" OF THE GERMAN LEADERS

AND now to what at first sight may seem to be a somewhat superfluous digression from the narrative, but a digression dealing with matters apt to be overlooked in following the records of campaigns and battles, and of special importance for the understanding of this second war. The possession of a knowledge of the theatre of war being assumed, the other items of information demanded for a full understanding of any operations are, the actual movements of the troops, the orders for those movements, the reasons for which those particular orders were issued, and, finally, the dominant factor of all the operations, the extent to which the judgments of the commanders who issued the orders were influenced, biased, aided, or warped by the fact of those commanders being human beings. For it matters not what are the differences in the social scale among the leaders; it matters not that as in this war, there is on the one side the head of the Hohenzollerns, with his Princes, Grand Dukes, Counts and "Vons," and on the other side a Barrister and a Civil Engineer; they are all the same in one respect, they are men, human beings, with all their little strengths and little weaknesses, moved by the same little or great motives and desires, and the same petty likes and petty dislikes as is he who writes, and he who reads these lines. And sometimes when reading what military leaders have done in the field, and in endeavouring to estimate approximately their work at its real value, we are apt to overlook how the "professionality" of these men is in subjection to their exceeding "human-ness."

HUMAN NATURE IN WAR

We forget that the man is, as a rule—not, however, without some exceptions—the same whatever the clothes he wears, but that this "human-ness" is liable to be somewhat emphasised when the coat is red or of khaki; and, as years go by, the more marked, the more apparent becomes this emphasis, because the older he gets in life, and the higher the rank to which he rises in his profession, the more free becomes the play of self, for the fewer there are in control over him, the greater the number under him who have to acquiesce silently and without comment in his wishes and his orders. The general who is too cautious to risk anything was, it may be assumed, never seen out on even a lovely summer day without an umbrella in his hand. The general who cannot decide quickly between one or more courses of action, never, we may be sure, arranged his railway journey for a long leave until after a prolonged investigation of the railway time-tables to ascertain the relative advantages and disadvantages of various routes and various trains. And these habits, these little harmless habits of peace show themselves at once in another and less harmless form in war. Whilst of no account in peace, in war they have serious consequences, for the qualities most essential to a leader of high position in war are a clear, cool head, the power of forming a correct judgment of the situation, its real needs and requirements, and of quickly arriving at a decision; and, further, there must be in the mind of any man who is a military leader, entire freedom from prejudice against, or jealousy of the officers who have to co-operate with him, or who have to execute his orders. When the mind which is striving to arrive at a correct judgment is obscured by weaknesses inherent in itself, and especially by the weakness of personal likes and dislikes, the judgment cannot possibly be right, so armies and nations suffer. It is difficult to hit off the right English word which signifies the combined personal mental characteristics of the individual. "Personality" has more than one meaning. The German word "personlichkeit," though somewhat untranslatable, seems to indicate the combination best, and it will be employed here. This "personlichkeit" in the enormous influence that it exercised on the German side, as revealed in the Archives now published in Hoenig's work, the prominent part it played, and the evil it wrought, is one of the most striking features of this war. It prevails in all wars, but we are seldom able to unearth it from their records. To the knowledge of the "personlichkeit" of soldiers in command or in positions of influence in a campaign, Hoenig attaches the greatest importance for the understanding of the operations of a campaign ; and a study of the action and effect of it, serves as a warning to those soldiers who may find themselves in these positions. In an introductory chapter to the fifth volume of his work, Hoenig deals with the subject ; of his views a short precis will therefore be given.

The character of the actors affords an extremely important assistance for writing history, but one most difficult to utilise and which can only be employed if thorough and exhaustive data are forthcoming. If the writer has a personal knowledge of the character of the individual he is portraying so much the better. Stringent impartiality is indispensable. Since the greatness of a leader depends mainly on the special qualities of his character, so must the result of all examination of his practical work depend on that character. The greatest power on earth is greatness of mind and the power to exercise it. To examine into this is the first task in an account of the art of war. If one strips men of all their peculiarities, takes from them all the rough angles, all hardness of character, smooths down all their being to one level, all are mere copies of each other. Ignoring individuality leads to mere uniformity in the writing of history. None of the great men, whose deeds we look up to to-day as models, were perfect ; they had their weaknesses, and they made mistakes, so this brings them close to us as men. It would be untrue and most wrong if we praised everything without exception, whatever they did. That is to detract from the credit of others and to deal unfairly with them. There is to-day, unfortunately, little inclination to recount how a great idea and a powerful resolve have failed; who has stood in the way of its realisation, and what great efforts were necessary for its adoption. The feeling is utterly wrong. The commander, alone, cannot, in war, think about and give orders about everything; the work is too many-sided; he needs counsellors and helpers who are at one with him in his spirit as regards the work of the war. But with him alone rests the responsibility. Therefore "personlichkeit" must stand more in the foreground. Why should young people develop their characters, if we paint all individuals, because they are in high positions, as all alike masters of their art and all faultless? If every one is a born hero and a general, then are these descriptions of no value. Surely it is evident that greatness is diminished and is brought to a lower level thereby. " The men whom I have described," writes Hoenig, " are indeed not always geniuses or great characters; but an analysis of them shows that with human weaknesses there is much that is edifying; and perfect men do not exist. A good organisation should so provide in peace that the men who are to be at the head of affairs suit each other."

And there is yet another matter which must be noticed if full profit is to be derived from a study of this war. It is the real meaning of the mystic formula " By Order "; and the conduct of this war we shall understand but little unless we do know its meaning. In the German army will be found on the staff of every division, army corps and army, an officer whose official title may be Generalstabsofficier, Chef des General Stabes or Chef des Stabes, according to the importance of the unit. It will suffice for all practical purposes to designate them by one common title, Chief Staff Officer, provided that it is borne in mind that the officer so designated is in no way the property of the General Officer to whose command he is attached; he is the Chief Staff Officer of the General, but he never ceases to belong to, and to represent at the side of the General that very important body, the general staff of the German army, of which staff during the war, and for long before and after, v. Moltke was the chief.

It is to this fact of belonging to the General Staff that he owes his influence and the high position accorded to him on the staff of any commander. In our own army we have no General Staff, and the resemblance between our Chief Staff Officers and those of the German army is nominal only. In the German army this officer is intended to be the confidante, the adviser of his General, and his *alter ego* ; but sometimes this position is not real but only nominal, owing to a fault in coupling together two incompatibles. Under this system the best presage for the satisfactory exercise of command and control is not *similis similibus*, " like to like," or " like to unlike ;" the Chief Staff Officer should be the mental complement of the commander with whom he serves. With an over-cautious commander, a bold Chief Staff Officer full of daring and enterprise; with an impulsive commander a Chief Staff Officer who is cool-headed ; with a commander who before he acts is prone to weigh and consider long, a Chief Staff Officer prompt in decision ; with a commander difficult owing to temper, a Chief Staff Officer of perfect tact ; with an ignorant commander, mistaking his ignorance for wisdom, a Chief Staff Officer full of knowledge, artful in concealing from his general his superiority in the possession of wisdom, but tactful enough to induce him to accept it as his own. But when the commander is a royal personage, the situation of the Chief Staff Officer is specially delicate and difficult. As a General Officer in the German army who had filled high staff appointments was once heard to remark : " If you want to have your nerves tried, become Chief Staff Officer to a royal personage in war."

It is from the Chief Staff Officer that the "By Order" emanates, but the real authorship of the orders depends in each case on the "personlichkeit" of the Commander and of his Chief Staff Officer respectively. As regards the real meaning of this " By Order " in the second war, it meant at the supreme headquarters almost invariably, v. Moltke and no one else. Not that King William was a mere figure-head ; he was a very wise and far-seeing soldier, and he could take his own line when he chose to do so; but, as a rule, in this second war, he refrained from interfering with the line of action taken on any matter by v. Moltke.

With the Second Army, " By Order " seems to have meant Prince Frederick Charles accentuated and emphasised always by v. Stiehle; or v. Stiehle accentuated and emphasised by him, so the staff of this army seems to have looked too much at one side only of a subject and to have taken one view only of a matter.

As regards the Third Army, Hoenig's History throws no light on this question. Possibly the reticence was intentional; but in the recently published work, giving extracts from the letters and diaries of v. Blumenthal, there is a full revelation of what the " By Order " meant here. V. Blumenthal had acted as Chief Staff Officer to the Crown Prince in the Austro-Prussian War of 1866. He was, no doubt, a very able soldier, and he possessed to a full degree, that self-confidence, and that faith in his own opinions, without which no man is fit for positions of responsibility. But he had also a " temper " which, he tells us, he thinks must have come to him in virtue of hereditariness; and, moreover, he does not appear to have enjoyed the best of health during the war; so, as he admits, he could get into a " real ill humour." Though he recognised v. Moltke's ability, he was by no means disposed to estimate it too highly, and, so far from being a fanatical devotee, as many at Versailles were, he could openly differ from v. Moltke and criticise his measures. As will be apparent in the course of this narrative, it was not only the "personlichkeit" of a man that affected the course of the war, but the mutual attraction or repulsion of each "personlichkeit " on the other or the others, that were potent factors. At this point, however, we have to deal only with the relations between v. Blumenthal and the Prince, and there is no doubt as to who was the predominant partner here. It was not the Prince; charming and fascinating as he was, he had not in him the power to hold under complete control such a strong nature as that of v. Blumenthal, for whom, however,, he had a warm and sincere regard. The independent spirit of v. Blumenthal is well illustrated by the account which v. Blumenthal gives of a remarkable interview between himself and the Prince in the early days of December. An order had come in the night from the King relating to a corps of the Third Army; v. Blumenthal despatched the necessary telegrams.

" In the morning the Crown Prince was very much put out that I had not had him called, as he said he ought to be informed of all orders as soon as they arrive. I said to him that I could not think of waking him for such trifles; moreover, that it came into my province, and not into his, to issue the subsequent order. I told him that I was not in the position of an adjutant who merely had to carry out orders; that I was only too willing to leave him all the honour of the command and do all the work, but that my position could not be reduced to that of a mere adjutant. He saw my point, but he has not a very clear comprehension of his position in the command. With the greatest possible kindness and geniality, he replied that I could do anything I wished, and that he would in no wise hinder me or raise difficulties; but he must be told of everything, especially when an order had come direct from the King. It is not possible for him to feel offended as he is always governed by the very best intentions, but he does not grasp the exact relationship in which I stand to him." And yet most people would think that the commander was quite in the right and the Chief Staff Officer quite in the wrong.

As regards " By Order" in a force collected later on, denominated the "Detachment," and placed under the command of H.R.H. the Grand Duke of Mecklenburg Schwerin, Hoenig in the chapter already referred to remarks, "'The reader will perhaps notice the omission of some character-sketches, for instance, of the officers of the staff of the Grand Duke of Mecklenburg. They were not forgotten, but they could not have been drawn, because it seems to me that the time for doing this has not yet come." So we are left to deduce from the history, our own idea of these matters at the Detachment.. The Grand Duke of Mecklenburg Schwerin, a wilful, determined man, but no great leader, started with a Chief Staff Officer, Colonel v. Krenski, who seems to have been little more than his "man," but, later on at a critical moment, v. Moltke took care that the Grand Duke should temporarily have a Chief Staff Officer who was his " master."

But although, therefore, every care is taken in the German army when selecting officers as Chief Staff Officers for commanders, and to avoid misfits, yet sometimes there come together an ill-assorted pair, and then, either from faults on one side or on both sides, the control gets out of joint, and the troops in the command suffer from bad leading. The following remarks of v. d. Vernois with regard to General v. Steinmetz who, immediately after the Battle of Gravelotte, had been relieved from the command of the First Army and sent to a post at home, are very apposite to this matter.

"The nomination (of v. Steinmetz) certainly aroused some misgivings. The universal and high appreciation of the merits of this gallant fighting General was merited in every respect. But, however high his military capabilities were, his personal qualities and his independence of character were such as to make it difficult for his superiors to deal with him, and made friction probable if he, at the head of an army, were subordinated to a higher command. These doubts, later on, proved to have been not altogether unjustified. The choice of a proper Chief of Staff may, in such cases, do much to smooth matters, and the best possible was made in the person of General v. Sperling, a clear-headed, circumspect and resolute officer. But even his eminent military as well as personal qualities were not able to prevail with such a character as that of General v. Steinmetz." It has seemed desirable to show fully the actual relations of these Commanders and their Chief Staff Officers in this war, because otherwise the reader might be misled into imagining that these relations were the same as those existing between any two officers in similar positions in our own army and bearing similar titles.

The German dualism has been regarded, as in itself it is, a most admirable system for the control and exercise of command. So the announcement of the appointment of Lord Kitchener as Chief Staff Officer to Lord Roberts, when the latter went to take the command in South Africa, was received generally with great satisfaction as a step in the right direction. But, as events showed, this dualism was never adopted at the army headquarters in South Africa; neither Lord Roberts nor Lord Kitchener had in their previous commands employed this system; they do not seem to like it; so Lord Kitchener was never Chief Staff Officer to Lord Roberts in the German sense, nor did Lord Roberts in this sense have any Chief Staff Officer. But in the second, as in the first war of 1870-71, these Chief Staff Officers were living realities, and their existence must always be borne in mind in following the histories.

From this long, but necessary, digression we now return to the situation in the field at the end of October, and shall find ourselves incidentally introduced at Versailles to another of the manifestations of "personlichkeit."

At the end of October and the beginning of November it was known both to v. d. Tann at Orleans, and to Moltke at Versailles, that, on the Loire, there was being displayed great military activity; two corps, the 15th and the 16th, were in course of organisation, and there was a general movement of troops down the Loire towards Tours; the railway that runs from Tours through le Mans to the north was closed to private traffic, and on it trains with troops had been despatched north from Tours. But as to the meaning of these movements, the local General at Orleans, v. d. Tann, and the supreme General at the Royal Head-quarters, v. Moltke, formed completely opposite views. V. d. Tann, on the spot, and in hourly contact with the population of the district, regarded the movement north from Tours as a mere feint, as a blind, to take the attention of the Germans away from

HUMAN NATURE IN WAR 65

Orleans, the repossession of which he believed that the Delegation was determined to obtain. In v. d. Tann's opinion, it was the recapture of Orleans that would be the first objective of the newly-formed Loire army. From Tours, this army, now apparently on its way north, would double back, utilising the railways on the right bank to Vendôme (forty miles west of Orleans), and Blois (thirty-five miles down the Loire), and take up a position of concentration under cover of the forest of Marchenoir, whence, co-operating with a large detachment crossing the Loire at Gien, above Orleans, it would make a convergent attack on him in overwhelming numbers, cutting off at the same time his retreat on Paris.

V. Moltke, on the other hand, took a different view altogether, and he did so because he attributed to the French leaders the intention of doing that which would be most dangerous and inconvenient to their adversary, and the surest and safest for themselves. The weakest and most vulnerable part of the investing line at Paris was, as already explained, that opposite to the western side of the Capital, and on the southern bank of the Seine. Also a sortie from the western side was favoured by the peculiar conformation of the ground, and if carried out simultaneously with the attack of a relieving force, would probably result in the compulsory withdrawal of this section of the investing troops. Moreover, the approach lay farthest from any reinforcements coming to Paris from the First and Second Armies. Besides this, Versailles, the seat of the Royal headquarters and of those of the Third Army were in this section, whilst Villacoubay, the site of the artillery park, was close at hand. Here then was, to v. Moltke's mind, the proper first objective for the French, and few perhaps will disagree with him in this opinion, and he assumed that the French would select it in preference to any other. And it is remarkable how v. Moltke held long and persistently to this belief, to the exclusion of aught else, with the result that the Germans came ere long near to disaster. The difference of views between v. d. Tann and v. Moltke, and the disregard of the latter for the opinion of the former on this occasion, is not the only

E

instance in which in this war v. Moltke misjudged a military situation at a distance from him.

And also it must be remembered that at Versailles v. Moltke was a species of demi-god; he lived surrounded by younger staff-officers whom he had selected and trained for their work; and it would be interesting to learn how often, except by Bismarck, v. Roon, and v. Blumenthal, he was ever contradicted during the whole of the Second War.

It has been said truly that in judging the value of a report received from a distance, it is the signature attached that must be the principal factor in the formation of an estimate of its value. It seems strange, therefore, that v. Moltke should have given so little weight to the reports sent in at this time by v. d. Tann. V. d. Tann was a general of high military reputation, and in this campaign he does not appear to have shown any signs of nervousness or pessimism, yet at Versailles, they apparently did not believe in him. And besides v. Moltke, v. Blumenthal did not agree with v. d. Tann in his diagnosis of the military situation, for on November 4th he believed the 16th Army Corps to be at Blois and the rest of the army, 60,000, at le Mans, where there was hardly a soldier.

CHAPTER V

THE FIRST FORTNIGHT OF NOVEMBER

But it is just at this time, the end of October and the beginning of November, that it is of the greatest importance for v. Moltke to form a correct view of the military situation, and of the views and intentions of the enemy, for there has now come before him a very important question for immediate decision, namely, the disposal and employment of the 100,000 men and 450 guns set free by the fall of Metz on October 28th, for service in the field. In v. Moltke's opinion, it is on the fall of Paris that the course and duration of the war depends. But the capture will not be accelerated by bringing more troops round its walls; there are quite enough there already to keep the French from breaking out through the investing line, and to maintain its continuity round the walls. Every additional man at the investing line means an additional mouth to feed, and the supply of food is neither too certain nor too plentiful. But still there must be no risk; there may be danger to the investing line from without, as well as from within the capital, and it would seem that for the purpose of guarding against this double danger, the forces there are not too large, unless, of course, the danger from without is not in any way serious.

When three weeks ago, on October 5th, General Reyau came north reconnoitring to Toury, drove back the cavalry division, and in triumph carried off 150 head of cattle destined for the German larders; and this minor operation of war had been mistaken for the advance of the enemy to attack the southern line of investment, a certain amount of anxiety as

68 THE PEOPLE'S WAR IN FRANCE, 1870-71

to the adequacy of the number of German troops to keep the enemy breaking out of Paris, and to hold a relieving force at a distance may have been entertained at Versailles. But, probably, the French collapse at Artenay and Orleans may have led v. Moltke to accept v. Podbielski's estimate of the French troops as " ragamuffins," and to determine not to be alarmed in future by mistaking phantoms for corporeal beings. And the reports now made to him by his Intelligence branch were very reassuring; for at the most important hostile centre, the Loire, there were given as between Blois and Salbris, thirty-three miles south of Orleans, on the further side of the river, only 50,000 to 60,000 men, an erroneous estimate, but inevitable in this " People's War " where the invader cannot go and look for himself, and the population either hold their tongues or lie patriotically; erroneous, inasmuch as on the line from Blois below Orleans to Gien above that city, were at least 100,000 men, mostly line or marche troops, of which about 80,000 had completed their organisation in Army Corps, the 15th Corps in three divisions, the 16th Corps in two divisions; whilst preparations were in progress for organising the surplus into a 17th Corps, and a third division for the 16th Corps. But it will be always more or less in the dark that the German leaders will have to work in determining their strategy and their operations during this second war. The simple work in open day of the first war will not come again to v. Moltke on French soil.

To the First Army was assigned the occupation of the north-west of France towards Amiens and Rouen, and looking after the numerous northern fortresses. It would thus protect the northern line of the investment from the hostile army now forming in the north.

The Second Army, under the command of Prince Frederick Charles, with General v. Stiehle as his Chief Staff Officer, consisted of the IIIrd A. C. (v. Alvensleben), the IXth A. C. (v. Manstein), the Xth A. C. (v. Voigts-Rhetz), and the 1st Cavalry Division (v. Hartmann). The strength was approximately as follows:

THE FIRST FORTNIGHT OF NOVEMBER 69

	Inf.	Cav.	Guns.
III. Corps	16,500	1,100	84
IX. ,,	16,600	1,800	90
X. ,,	16,500	1,100	84
1st C.D.	—	3,000	6
Total	49,600	7,000	264

Although the II. Army Corps belonged to this Army, it was now drawn to Paris to strengthen the line there. Paris is one hundred and seventy miles from Metz.

The original order was, that the army should march with the utmost rapidity in the general direction of Troyes on the Seine and the Middle Loire, *i.e.*, into the centre of France. The Prince arranged his programme of march so that on November 10th the Head-quarters, the IXth A.C. and the 1st Cavalry Division should be at Troyes, eighty miles south-east of Paris; the III. A.C. at Vendeuvre, some fifteen miles east of Troyes; and the Xth A. C. with its outermost brigade at Neufchateau, about seventy miles east of Troyes. Troyes is ninety, and Neufchateau one hundred and sixty miles from the great road running from Paris to Orleans.

On November 1st v. Moltke wrote to v. Stiehle a letter, containing a full exposition of the situation as it presented itself to him. It is here given as reproduced by Hoenig from the official archives, and it deserves the most careful attention as giving very fully v. Moltke's view of the future of the war at this time. Emphasis must be laid on the fact of the already mentioned radical difference of the views of the King and v. Moltke as to the spirit which the French nation would display with regard to the continuance of the struggle; so although this letter is a species of " By Order," it gives probably the views and opinions of the Chief Staff Officer at the Royal Head-quarters, rather than those of the supreme Commander. But it will be well, before reading it, to note some of the distances between the places named in it.

Chalons-sur-Saone is distant from Metz one hundred and seventy miles, the fortress of Langres lying on the road connecting them, one hundred and eighty from Paris, one hundred and fifty from Orleans, one hundred and fifteen from Bourges. Bourges is two hundred and ten from Metz, one hundred and twenty-five from Paris; Nevers is on the Loire, thirty-five miles from Bourges, and is at the junction of the railroads from Chalons to Bourges, to Gien and to the south. At Chalons-sur-Saone was a great iron-foundry. Nevers was a centre of supply of naval stores; at Bourges was the main gun factory and small arms ammunition factory.

The letter ran as follows:

" Only the course of events will determine the tasks that will have to be undertaken by the Second Army during its advance. I hardly think that it will be necessary to give support to General v. Werder, who is provisionally in a defensive position on the line Vesoul-Gray-Dijon [in southeastern France]. The south of France will hardly make great efforts on behalf of Paris. On the other hand there are three points on the left flank where the most severe losses to military France can be inflicted, Chalons-sur-Saone, Nevers, and above all, Bourges, where are the great arsenals and the Chassepot cartridge manufactories. . . .

" The main object remains as before, the destruction of the enemy's forces in the field, and the speedy re-inforcing of the forces at Paris, so as to render possible the sending out detachments.

" There appears, therefore, to be no longer any need for the employment of the Second Army troops as an army; one of its corps on each of the named points will be sufficient to overcome all resistance."

With this letter was sent the following estimate of the hostile situation:

1. At Lille, the Northern Army forming under General Bourbaki, and said to be 30,000 strong, and composed of Depôt Troops, Gardes Mobiles and Franc-tireurs.

2. In the West the forces under General Briant at Rouen,

THE FIRST FORTNIGHT OF NOVEMBER 71

Depôt Troops, Gardes Mobiles, mobilised Gardes Nationales, and Franc-tireurs; 16,000 men protecting Rouen and Havre, and harassing the rear of the army investing Paris.

3. The Army of the Loire under d'Aurelle, of 45,000 men, said to have been raised to 60,000, and to contemplate an attack on Orleans; " it is the best organised, the regiments drawn from Africa forming its nucleus."

4. The Army of Lyons under General Cambriels in Besançon. Two divisions of field troops (Depôts and Gardes Mobiles and Garibaldi's Detachment, a brigade of Gardes Mobiles and Franc-tireurs), 35,000; objective, guarding the road to Lyons; eventually advance towards the Vosges. " Besides, during the advance larger bodies of Gardes Mobiles may be encountered."

So no one was wanted at Paris, except one Army Corps, the Second. The total number, 126,000, was fairly correct, the distribution wrong. In one single sentence in this letter we find the source of all the difficulties and all the troubles which soon beset the invaders; the source of the prolongation of the war for three months; the real origin of the campaigns of le Mans and the Lisaine in 1871. That source is the belief of the man in whose hands lay the direction of the war, that " the South of France will hardly make great efforts on behalf of Paris."

Ere long will the three corps, as a united army, be straining every nerve to reach the Paris-Orleans Road, to protect the Investment of Paris against attack from Orleans. Within twenty-eight days will these three corps, as an army, be opposing the first onslaught of a portion of a force of some 200,000 men, whom not only southern France, but central, northern, eastern, and western France have sent to exert their best efforts for the relief of Paris.

From the foregoing it will be seen that v. Moltke, v. Podbielski, and their entourages, were totally in error in their estimate of the *moral* and the spirit of the nation with which their own was at war. To v. Moltke's belief that " Southern France is hardly likely to make great efforts on behalf of Paris " is due the fact that ere long the Germans found themselves in dire straits, from which they escaped, not through the capacity and military genius of v. Moltke and their other chief leaders, but through the errors and misleading of their adversaries.

But in view of the obvious fact that the Army of the Loire was no longer to remain quiescent, v. Moltke determined to take the initiative and thus terminate the period of doubt and suspense. So on November 7th the Second Army received orders by telegraph to hasten the advance of its right wing on Fontainebleau, thirty miles south of Paris and twenty-five east of the Paris-Orleans road, whilst, south of the investing line, a large force, termed a Detachment (Armee-Abtheilung) was formed, the command being given to H.R.H. the Grand Duke of Mecklenburg Schwerin, the Chief Staff Officer, Colonel von Krenski.

The Detachment was formed of the I. Bav. A.C., the 17th Inf. Division (v. Tresckow) from the investing line, the 22nd Inf. Division, and the 4th v. and 6th (v. Schmidt) Cav. Divisions, and was placed under the control of the Commander of the Third Army.

The strength was approximately as follows:

	Inf.	Cav.	Guns.
1st Bav. A.C. . . .	17,500	2,100	118
17th Inf. Div. . . .	9,800	1,200	36*
22nd Inf. Div. . . .	9,000	400	36
4th Cav. Div. . . .	—	2,800	12
6th Cav. Div. . . .	—	2,700	6
Total . . .	36,300	9,200	208

The instructions given to the Duke were as follows: " By order of the King to march on an ' expedition ' to the west." The object given was to " break up the Army of the Loire now in process of formation, and to compel it to retreat by le Mans.

* Including the 17th Cav. Brig.

THE FIRST FORTNIGHT OF NOVEMBER 73

[le Mans is one hundred and ten miles S.W. of Paris.] If the 15th and 16th Army Corps are found north at Blois and le Mans, they may perhaps be driven apart and their re-union be rendered impossible. A further (subsidiary) object would be the destruction of the hostile communications between Tours and Rouen, as well as the utilisation of the occupied territory for the supply of the army. In order to make the communication with the superior command better and quicker, the capture of one or two locomotives would be beneficial. Reports by telegraph to be made frequently to Versailles."

The Detachment was to be on the 12th inst. facing west in the following position of concentration for the subsequent advance. On the right at Chartres the H.Q., the 22nd Inf. Division, and the 4th Cav. Division. On the right rear at Rambouillet, twenty miles from Chartres, the 6th Cav. Division. At Bonneval, the 17th Inf. Division, and at Chateaudun the 1st Bav. A.C., less one Infantry Brigade, with some guns and cavalry, a force to be left at Orleans and which v. Moltke considered sufficient for the protection of that city. But, here again, the King had shown that his view of the situation and his foresight were superior to those of the Chief of the Staff, for later on, as will appear in due course, he said, with reference to the Detachment, "The 22nd Infantry Division was sent to v. d. Tann; I have sent the 17th Infantry Division after it." On the 7th, v. Moltke sent to the Second Army a letter, explaining the reason for his order sent by wire; Hoenig gives from it the following extract. "The fact that the fall of Metz has not induced the French Government to adopt an attitude corresponding to the circumstances, leaves us to conclude that, shortly, a determined attempt will be made to relieve Paris. A more rapid advance of the Second Army with the right wing in the direction of Fontainebleau is therefore desirable . . . and the left wing of the Second Army will remain free for employment according to circumstances." It was no doubt annoying to the Germans that the French Government did not take the same view as they did, of what ought to be done in consequence of the fall of Metz.

In the conduct of all businesses on a large scale, there is bound to be some friction among the principals and chief managers; and in the great business of war this friction will make its appearance, sooner or later. But in war, so long as success in the campaign and on the field of battle attends an army, the friction is comparatively small ; it is regarded as an insignificant annoyance only, and is soon forgotten ; it has done perhaps little serious harm ; but if the tide turns, or is adverse to the army, friction soon makes itself felt, and grows to proportions of evil size. And the reason is not far to seek. Take our own army in South Africa.

Any one who has met and conversed in private with senior officers, staff officers, and others, who were in our army in the long South African War, and has thus been given a peep behind the scenes in that war, must have been struck with the general testimony to the existence of constant and, often, great friction, and, sometimes, of ill-feeling towards each other, among the officers who held important positions in that campaign. It would be difficult to find any one who was really satisfied with the way in which the authority, superior to that authority of which he himself formed a part, exercised its control. Rarely will be met, though sometimes it will be the case, a regimental staff thoroughly satisfied with its brigadier and the brigade staff; this, with its divisional general and his division staff; and these again with the hierarchy at the supreme Head-quarters. Unnecessary interference and blunder-making are common indictments against the superior by the inferior. And then, more unpleasant still, are the imputations of jealousy among the seniors, jealousy that interfered seriously with the success of the operations. The first impression derived from this disagreeable phenomenon is, that war makes men very censorious and queer tempered, and brings the lower nature of man prominently to the front. But this view of the case seems hardly correct. This phenomenon would

THE FIRST FORTNIGHT OF NOVEMBER 75

seem to be due rather to realisation by soldiers actually taking part in a war that the work of war is one of the most serious, one of the gravest kinds of work that can fall to individuals to perform. It is a work of life or death to tens, to hundreds, to thousands of human beings. And on how that work is done, whether it is done the right way or the wrong way, depend consequences fateful to the workers. So when things are going wrong, or seem to be going wrong, it is inevitable that minds become censorious, judgments harsh and severe; mistakes are no longer condoned; blunders neither forgotten nor forgiven. And this disposition of the minds of soldiers is not peculiar to the army of any one country or the army of any one period of history; it prevails in all armies, it has prevailed and will prevail in all periods of history. And so in the second war of 1870-71. The more the inner life of the military hierarchy, or rather hierarchies, is revealed, the more clearly do we see that this war was, in this respect, no exception to the rule. And how different from the first war, when the path to victory, though not easy, was very smooth. Even the cautious v. du Vernois in a remark in his book, when referring to this matter as it was at Versailles in the latter part of November, when difficulties were gathering all round, says:

"It lies in the nature of things that such stirring and difficult times do not pass without friction. Nor did we remain free from it in some respects. . . . The world need not know the dark side of glorious times. There are too many people who love to gloat over this, and who seek to diminish our pride in the great things which have been done, and detract from their well-merited acknowledgment."

But the Editor of v. Blumenthal's Journals does not consider expurgation to this end necessary, so we learn, from the extracts published, a good deal about the tone and temper of mind prevalent in these matters. Even on August 11th v. Blumenthal had written: "I must admit that General v. Moltke has manœuvred very cleverly so that all are concentrated, but I think that he has incorrect notions of what troops are capable of, and of what they can be called upon to do without becoming disorganised."

But so much involved was the Third Army Head-quarters in the control of the first part of this second war, that we owe a debt of gratitude to this editor for having so boldly put before us such a striking picture of the highest staff life at Versailles.

The first thing that seems to have ruffled the equanimity of v. Blumenthal was the transfer of the Royal Head-quarters to Versailles, where those of the Third Army were already established. On September 29th he writes: "I do not mind that" [giving up the present quarters], "but the presence of the King's Head-quarters will be very inconvenient to us, especially for me, as I have not sufficient command over myself to deal with the many unnecessary and sudden questions and bits of advice." On October 16th: "From the presence of the King's Head-quarters arises for me a difficulty which cannot be overrated. Reports are required about everything, and since every moment more or less important reports arrive, I have always to be thinking whither they are to be sent, so that no one can complain that this or that person has received the news not as soon as or even earlier than somebody else."

But beside personal annoyance to the lower staff, there is real evil in this close juxtaposition, for it would seem to be invariably the case that where a superior and a lower military authority are locally near each other, the lower authority loses its power of independent action, and shrinks from the assumption of responsibility. If the two authorities are miles apart, the lower has not the slightest hesitation, when difficult questions come before it, in giving a decision without reference to the distant superior; but the position of the lower authority becomes very difficult when the superior is close at hand, for it deems it often unwise to act when a reference is easy. Moreover, if the lower does act independently, the superior may object, that being within easy reach, it ought to have been consulted. Anyhow the result

THE FIRST FORTNIGHT OF NOVEMBER 77

of this reference to the superior leads to delay and waste of time. On October 22nd v. Blumenthal writes: " This endless sending of news to the Head-quarters is very tiring, especially with matters I can only call trifles. Everything comes to me; something is wanting to be known, something to be better done, and many are simply childish requests. It disgusts me with my good position and often puts me in a real ill humour."

And on the 7th of the same month occurs an entry full of indignation with the people at the Royal Head-quarters. V. Blumenthal had, from the first, been in favour of an active line being taken against the hostile army whilst it was in course of formation, rather than to delay, and so allow the formation to be completed. It is evident that he considered General Reyau's advance on Toury on October 5th ought to have been dealt with by a quick offensive. On the 7th, when v. d. Tann was in a defensive position south of Paris, near Arpajon, he writes: " With regard to v. d. Tann being ordered to take the offensive, Moltke fully agreed and gave his assent, in spite of the protest of various small minds who always try to interfere."

On the same day, with reference to another matter, he writes: "To-day, however, everything again has been altered. Why, I do not know. I fancy that there are many who want to give their opinions, and to have their views adopted, which would not be the case if I had the matter in my hands. It is really most extraordinary that, in spite of the fact that Moltke and I continually come to an agreement on certain points, there almost always step in between us some persons, and the orders are not so drawn up as I had expected. It may be that he is prevented sometimes from acting exactly as he wishes."

To return to the "Expedition." From v. Blumenthal's Journals, it appears that it was with him and not v. Moltke that the idea originated. On October 20th he writes: " A relief [of Paris] by a newly-formed army, we need not fear. It would be months before one could be raised and organised that could attack us with any prospect of success. It is only necessary for us to hinder and render difficult as much as possible the formation of a relieving army. This would be best done if we were not so anxious not to weaken ourselves in front of the fortress, but sent more often distant expeditions as we did to Orleans. I should regard it now as correct, for instance, to send two Army Corps to Tours to drive out the governing body which is there, and break up the force which is being organised."

On the 23rd, evidently referring to this plan, he writes: "The Crown Prince has consented to my plan, and now I have sent Bronsart to General v. Moltke to communicate it to him. He will have no objection whatever to it, but it is to me like a weight on my limbs that I now may not properly do anything more independently, but must always first ascertain and inquire whether anything against it is said in the highest places also. In a word, our wings are cut and paralysed, and if anything serious has to be carried out, it is only our luck and the good God that we have to thank." And at the beginning of November the immobility of the troops round Paris irritates him. In waiting he foresees danger. Had the two Head-quarters been a hundred miles apart, he would have been able to employ his army much as he chose, but here the neighbour next door has to be consulted. On November 4th: "To-day I was once again very angry. Probably my cold was partly to blame, but perhaps also the unsatisfactory manner in which the operations of our armies are being conducted."

But the matter apparently hung fire for a little time, and immediately after the fall of Metz v. Blumenthal again pressed it on v. Moltke. On November 5th he writes "Bronsart drove over to Moltke, and laid before him my request regarding the expedition to le Mans. He was quite of my opinion in the matter, and the Crown Prince promised me, moreover, to plead pressingly with the King for sanction for us to undertake an expedition of the kind under the Grand Duke of Mecklenburg. The Crown Prince returned

THE FIRST FORTNIGHT OF NOVEMBER 79

at 12.30, saying that it was all of no use, as all were against it. . . .

"There is a limit to strength in every man, and it is not at all necessary that I should work night and day and undertake such great responsibility, while a whole crowd of military idlers loaf about in dozens, doing nothing but passing worthless criticisms."

And at last, on November 7th : "This afternoon I heard with gratification that the expedition against the so-called army of the Loire, which I have so long intended and desired, has been sanctioned by the King, and that the command is to be given, as I had wished, to the Grand Duke of Mecklenburg." When v. Blumenthal saw the Duke soon afterwards, he found him so smart and quick in apprehending his task, that he had " the greatest hopes of him."

The fact that it was with v. Blumenthal the intended expedition originated is an illustration of the difficulty of ascertaining who is the real source of a " why " and a " wherefore " in connection with military operations; and seems to show that military hero-worship on the one hand, and scornful condemnation on the other, if indulged in at all, must for fairness' sake be left for exercise by later generations who may get low down into the deep well at the bottom of which Truth lies concealed. But this is not the way of the world; so in the military profession the impostor in high places is less rare than he should be.

As will soon appear the idea of the "expedition" was founded on a totally erroneous, completely mistaken view of the military situation. Hoenig's account was published in 1893. The reader of that work must inevitably assign to v. Moltke any discredit given for a faulty judgment in the matter. V. Blumenthal does not appear in those pages in connection with it; but nine years later, appears v. Blumenthal's Diary, in which we find that it was to v. Blumenthal's repeated importunity that v. Moltke eventually yielded in ordering the expedition. Moreover, in Hoenig's work, v. Blumenthal, during the period that the Detachment was in the field as a part of the Third Army, would seem to have adopted towards the Grand Duke a line which savoured of want of firmness in dealing with a royal personage. As we shall see, however, from v. Blumenthal's Journal, the Grand Duke and the Detachment were, so to speak, v. Blumenthal's *protegés*, and the apparent want of firmness arose from a dislike to have to act as an intermediary between his *protegés* and the Royal Head-quarters when the latter took of the former a less complimentary view than he did. This fact must be borne in mind if we would understand the operations of the fortnight from the 9th to the 23rd of November.

But the mystery that shrouds the Army of the Loire, and the hopelessness of the efforts of the invader to choose the scheme of operations best suited to the realities of the situation in a People's War, where reconnoitring, save in force, is rendered impracticable by the determination of the population to shoot down, somehow or other, any hostile soldier who dares to ride in among them to spy out what is going on, is well illustrated by the work, at this time, of Von Wittich, who, it may be remembered, had, after the occupation of Orleans, gone with his Inf. Division and the 4th Cav. Division to Chartres. Both the 4th and the 6th Cav. Divisions were working in conjunction with v. Wittich's Inf. Division, and the orders for the combined operations were signed by v. Wittich, so that apparently he was in command of the whole force. The General had written to v. Blumenthal asking whether, if occasion arose, he could rely on the cooperation of v. d. Tann (his senior officer) at Orleans. On November 2nd v. Blumenthal, who, at this time was, as we know, pushing the "expedition" scheme through the opposition it was encountering, replied, "Fresh orders as regards v. d. Tann will be sent in a few days." Meantime, on November 3rd, v. Wittich marched the whole force to Courville, twelve miles west of Chartres, and occupied it. Here, however, after dark he received from v. Blumenthal the following telegram :

THE FIRST FORTNIGHT OF NOVEMBER 81

"*November* 3rd, 3.59 P.M.

"According to information, fairly reliable and just received, the hostile army at le Mans is 60,000 strong. I advise you to be very careful. I cannot get good intelligence agents.

" V. BLUMENTHAL."

The stratagem of sending a few trains of troops from Tours to le Mans had thoroughly answered its purpose. Intercepted letters informed v. Wittich that troops of all arms were immediately in front of him to the west, and others referred to a great battle imminent in the neighbourhood; so, by a night march, the General hastily quitted his position and regained the shelter of Chartres; but in front of him there were only parts of the bogus " Army of the West." And v. Blumenthal will not believe that v. d. Tann sees better on the spot what is taking place, than does he himself sixty to seventy miles away, and unable, as he complains, to get good intelligence agents. On November 4th, v. d. Tann is certain that the French are collecting in force near Marchenoir. Patrols and scouts are constantly fired on by the inhabitants of the villages. "These hostilities," says Helvig, "occurring as they did in places where our patrols and detachments had been allowed to pass quietly, were an unmistakable indication of the vicinity of considerable forces of the enemy. The population, become fanatical, and irritated to the utmost by the hard pressure of war, seemed hardly able to restrain the practical expression of its deep and bitter anger, and thus afforded this valuable information to the leaders of the German army."

At the Third Army Head-quarters, however, so Hoenig says, v. d. Tann's reports were regarded unfavourably as exaggerated. V. Blumenthal on the 7th writes: " This afternoon we received information from v. d. Tann that he is expecting to be attacked soon. I do not anticipate any such thing, as the enemy cannot be ready for it yet." Here, again, in view of the actual facts of the situation, is an instance which should serve as a warning to senior officers against that tendency, already mentioned, that seems inherent in the growth towards

F

seniority, to a disparagement of the judgment and opinions of junior ranks. V. Moltke's weakness in this respect has already been mentioned, and here we have v. Blumenthal, who is loudly indignant because his own superiors will not accept his views in preference to their own, exhibiting exactly the same weakness with regard to the value of his own opinions, compared to that of the opinions of a General commanding an Army Corps in his own army.

So, at Versailles, there is a feeling of perfect security so far as any hostile action of the Army of the Loire is concerned. On that staff were three officers, " chiefs of sections," of whom one, Lieutenant-Colonel Bronsart von Schellendorff, was responsible for the movement of the troops, Lieutenant-Colonel Brandenstein for transport and commissariat affairs, Lieutenant-Colonel V. d. Vernois for everything concerning the French army. Every morning v. Moltke held a conference, at which these three officers were present to receive instructions for the day, so permission to be absent would necessarily imply that there was no anxiety as to the immediate future. The diary of Lieutenant-Colonel V. d. Vernois furnishes evidence conclusive on the point.

"VERSAILLES, *November* 8th. Evening.

"To-morrow, Bronsart, Holbein and I intend to pay a visit to the Crown Prince of Saxony [on the north side of Paris]. I hope that nothing will happen meanwhile to prevent our going, although it is not impossible, as an advance of the French Loire Army, and probably also a sortie from Paris are to be expected shortly. Concerning the Army of the Loire, four long days' work has yet to be got through before we are quite ready to cope with the conditions which may result from its advance."

So it might apparently lead to a little inconvenience if the French were prematurely active!

"VERSAILLES, *November* 9th.

"The long intended drive to the Head-quarters of the Meuse Army has at last come off."

THE FIRST FORTNIGHT OF NOVEMBER 83

On the 8th v. Blumenthal had written, "Towards evening a telegram arrived from Tann, saying that strong columns of the enemy are advancing by Beaugency and that he is accordingly taking up a concentrated position at Ormes [five or six miles north-west of the city]." And on the 9th he writes to the Grand Duke, "Captain Lenke has just arrived from Orleans, and I see from his report that the First Bavarian Army Corps views the situation somewhat too gloomily." V. Blumenthal is still obstinately incredulous. And in v. d. Goltz's work we find a curious letter to the Second Army, dated Versailles, November 10th, and signed by v. Moltke, but of which, for the present, only the first part is given here. It commences as follows: "The still continuing resistance of Paris is based on the expectation that the investment will be broken by relief from the Provinces. The reports received make it probable that actually large forces of the enemy have been formed on the Loire into a loosely connected army deficient in equipment; and that this army has already begun its advance from the line Tours-le Mans. The 1st Bavarian Corps in Orleans, and the 22nd Inf. Division in Chartres must therefore be reinforced from the investing line. . . . The 17th Inf. Division was sent yesterday, and the command of all the forces to be employed towards the Loire was given to the Grand Duke of Mecklenburg Schwerin." The letter here breaks off as will appear from the succeeding paragraphs which will be given later on. Of course it by no means follows from the fact that the letter bears the signature of v. Moltke, that therefore he penned it himself; it may have been drafted for him by some Staff Officer, but the date seems clearly wrong, and shows how necessary it is to be careful in dealing with even official letters as reliable records. The Grand Duke was appointed to the command on the 7th (not yesterday, the 9th), and the 17th Inf. Division started on the 8th (also not yesterday, the 9th). That any officer at Versailles penned these paragraphs on the 10th is in the highest degree improbable, for in the evening of the 9th there had fallen at Versailles a veritable bolt from the blue. V. Blumenthal says that on that evening " came a telegram from General v. d. Tann reporting that after a fight which lasted seven hours he had had to retire to St. Peravy." Hoenig states that v. d. Tann at 9.30 P.M. reported to the Third Army that on the 10th he would fall back to Toury to connect with the 22nd Inf. Division. Also during the morning of the 10th, came in another report from v. d. Tann, that the enemy, some 50,000 strong, was at Coulmiers ; and the Third Army in communicating this to the Grand Duke, added that according to another, but not reliable, report, the enemy was much stronger. The lack of belief manifested by v. Blumenthal and v. Moltke in the value of v. d. Tann's views and opinions is extraordinary. As we have seen, v. d. Tann on the 7th tells v. Blumenthal he expects to be attacked ; on the 8th, that he is actually on the move out of Orleans to meet the attack ; yet away go, on the morning of the 9th, three of the Royal Head-quarters Staff for a day's pleasuring ; and on the 9th v. Blumenthal believes v. d. Tann overcoloured the situation at Orleans. Yet v. d. Tann and Versailles are under seventy miles from each other, and the telegraph is at work between them, so there is no difficulty in full and complete exchange of views.

On the 7th a reconnaissance had been made down the right bank of the Loire from Orleans, by a strong force of all arms under zu Stolberg, the commander of the 2nd Cav. Division. The force was driven back with considerable loss. On the same day v. d. Tann accidentally learnt that General d'Aurelle, the Commander of the Army of the Loire, had his Headquarters at Mer. On the 8th, there were signs of a hostile advance. For the Bavarians to have remained in Orleans would have been a tactical absurdity, so on the night of the 8th–9th v. d.Tann, leaving a very small force in Orleans, moved out and took up a position facing west, the centre at Coulmiers, some eleven miles west of Orleans, and in the open country outside the Forest.

V. d. Tann's force numbered 14,543 Infantry, 4450

THE FIRST FORTNIGHT OF NOVEMBER 85

Cavalry, and 110 guns. Early on the 9th, the French army consisting of the 2nd and 3rd divisions of the 15th Corps and the two divisions of the 16th Corps, numbering altogether 72,000 Infantry, 7200 Cavalry and 160 guns advanced to the attack. The Bavarians offered a stubborrn resistance, but at nightfall, were driven off the battlefield; but only just off it, and the faintest semblance of a pursuit would have resulted in the capture of the whole force, so utterly exhausted was it. After a very short rest, the retreat was resumed, and by the night of the 10th the whole force was collected at Toury. The Bavarian losses amounted to 51 officers, 1257 men and two guns. On the 8th, General des Pallières with the 1st Division of the 15th Corps had crossed the Loire above Orleans intending to co-operate in the attack with the main body, but the co-operation miscarried, so that the line of retreat on Toury remained open to v. d. Tann. Another force had advanced on Orleans from the south. V. Moltke's first diagnosis of the strategy of his opponents had now shown itself to be absolutely incorrect.

It was as early as October 25th, that at a conference at Tours, at which Gambetta was present, it had been decided to make Orleans the first objective. Orleans recaptured, was then to be converted into a huge entrenched camp for 150,000 to 200,000 men, to serve as a base for ulterior operations, and as a barrier to any offensive movements on the part of the Germans.

War is, however, full of surprises, and in war, it is the unexpected that happens, so that even the substitution of a defeat for a victorious "expedition" was not likely to disturb the self-possession of a v. Moltke. The first measure to be adopted was blocking the road from Orleans to Paris against the possible advance of the victors in the battle. At 1.30 P.M. on the 10th the Third Army wrote to the Grand Duke, "According to a report of General v. d. Tann the enemy, some 50,000 strong, is at Coulmiers; other information, but not reliable, puts the hostile force much stronger. It is therefore most important for the Detachment to remain for some days on the defensive in quarters as closely concentrated as possible, until the situation becomes more clear ; indeed, it is questionable whether it would not be better to retire somewhat, because it is tolerably certain that on the 14th Prince Frederick Charles will arrive with the IXth A. C. at Fontainebleau, and then a concentric offensive advance would force the enemy to retreat. This is the view of the situation held at the Royal Head-quarters as well as by H.R.H. the Crown Prince." The last sentence, at first sight, reads as if the Crown Prince did not feel strong enough alone to dictate to a brother royalty under his command, as he would have done to a commander of less exalted rank ; but another view of it is that v. Blumenthal, having found his pet scheme shattered and not suited to the situation, wished the Grand Duke to know that also the highest authority thought, that putting it into the background for the present was just as well. To Prince Frederick Charles at Troyes was despatched a telegram at 12.35 P.M : " Strong hostile forces are advancing from the Loire at Orleans. Increased rapidity of advance of the Second Army therefore necessary. IXth A. C. cannot have a rest day on the 11th, and must endeavour to reach Fontainebleau on the 14th." The scribe from whose letter of November 10th, to the Second Army the opening paragraphs have been given, now returned to his interrupted letter, and continues it without break, as follows : " The Bavarian Corps yesterday retired from Orleans after a fight of some hours' duration. A concentration of all the troops under H.R.H. the Grand Duke in the neighbourhood of Angerville-Toury can be effected the day after to-morrow. If, contrary to expectation, the hostile Army of the Loire is able to advance yet further, we shall have to reckon with certainty on sorties in greater strength than hitherto from all sides of Paris, the main attack being against the southern portion of the investment. . . . In a few days we shall be able to determine whether the left wing of the army will not be more usefully employed on the left

THE FIRST FORTNIGHT OF NOVEMBER 87

bank of the Loire than in the country between the river and Paris.—v. MOLTKE."

And here, on this day, we find ourselves on the threshold of a period of the war which, so far as command and staff work were concerned, was a period of discordant views, divergent aims and incessant friction among the higher leaders. It is well known that during the first war this disturbing element had not been altogether absent from the German Staff; but as the progress of that war was one of continuous success these evils mattered little, for their consequences were insignificant, and even disobedience of orders was condoned. The system had worked very fairly, but it had never undergone any great strain, so enthusiasts, judging only from that period, have held it up to admiration as an infallible model for all times and places. But there are exceptions to every rule. More than once even between July and September, directions had been set at defiance and orders disobeyed. "General v. Steinmetz will not obey even my orders," the King is reported to have said, before any of the battles were fought. Even the Crown Prince needed a polite reminder conveyed to him through V. d. Vernois on the eve of Weissenburg. The Crown Prince himself found that General v. Bose preferred to play at the battle of Worth a part of his own choosing, rather than that assigned to him by the Prince. At Gravelotte both v. Manstein and Prince Augustus of Würtemburg, as well as v. Steinmetz, helped to upset the plans of Prince Frederick Charles and v. Moltke.

Had the campaign terminated with Sedan, what heaven-born generals, free from all liability to the weaknesses inherent in human nature would the leaders of the invading hosts have appeared in military history! But now we have left the time when all was plain sailing; we are entering on a period full of difficulty and doubt, and the leaders will stand before us—like all leaders in all wars—as very human indeed.

On the 11th, whilst the various units of the Detachment were on their way to the defensive position, there was a report that the French were moving on Pithiviers, and the Bavarians at once began a further retreat from Toury. The report proved false, and, by order of the Grand Duke, the Bavarians returned to Toury. On the evening of the 11th, v. d. Tann reported strong hostile forces south of Artenay, and that two corps had been engaged against him at Coulmiers.

By the evening of the 12th, the whole Detachment was in a defensive position facing south across the great road from Orleans to Paris, eighteen miles from the former, and forty-seven from the latter. At Toury and Outarville were the Bavarian Corps and the 2nd Cav. Division, with the 17th Inf. Division eight miles in rear of it. At Allaines, seven miles west of Toury, was the 22nd Inf. Division. Five miles to the right rear of this division was the 4th Cav. Division at Ymonville, on the road from Toury to Chartres, whilst at Chartres, twenty-seven miles north-west of Toury, was the 6th Cav. Division. There was an advanced guard three miles south of Toury, at Tivernon. So on this day the actual position of the Germans shows us how completely wrong even wise heads may be in attempting to forecast the plan of a campaign. V. Moltke's far-reaching schemes, extending to operations on a front of two hundred and thirty miles, from Chalons-sur-Saone to le Mans, based on the supposition "that southern France was hardly likely to make great efforts on behalf of Paris," now shrivel up to a pure defensive on one single road—Paris-Orleans. Chalons-sur-Saone, Nevers, and Bourges continued to ply their activities vigorously; the 15th and 16th Corps had not been forced to retreat or been driven apart, but had advanced together to victory; the only waggon depôt at Chateauroux could still send out her supplies of military vehicles for French, not for German use; the great railway line of communication from Vierzon by Tours, le Mans, Alençon to Rouen was untouched, and on it were running the "one or more" locomotives the possession of which would be so useful for speedy communication between Versailles and the Detachment. The three corps, which, separately, were to carry destruction one hundred and seventy to two hundred miles

THE FIRST FORTNIGHT OF NOVEMBER 89

into Central France, were hurrying, as an army, as fast as they could march, to save the investing line at Paris from an attack coming from only sixty-five miles to the south of it; and for the great active expedition to the west was substituted an anxious, passive watching to the south.

The French, on the 9th, had bivouacked on the battlefield, and, as they expected a renewal of the attack, fires were not allowed. On the 10th, the army extended more to the east, the front, about eight miles north of Orleans, running from Tournoisis, twelve miles west of the main road, by Chevilly on the edge of the forest, to Neuville aux Bois, eight miles east of the road. On the 12th, there was a conference, at which both Gambetta and de Freycinet were present, and it was resolved to hold to the original plan of the formation of the entrenched camp at Orleans. The army here certainly numbered on this day 100,000 men.

And now we come to one of the most remarkable and inexplicable incidents of this war. The cavalry at the disposal of the Grand Duke were very numerous, but touch with the French had been completely lost; and on the 12th the cavalry reported concerning this 100,000 men that Artenay was unoccupied (which was true), and that between that place and the Forest of Orleans no enemy was visible. In fact, to German eyes, these 100,000 men had absolutely disappeared. And at once rose at Versailles, and at the Grand Duke's Head-quarters, the belief that these 100,000 men had really marched away on an offensive expedition in another direction; and for some days v. Moltke arranged his strategy on this erroneous supposition. But not only did not a single French soldier go from this neighbourhood, but soon vast reinforcements were poured into it. Rarely has the Fog of War been so dense as here. The French knew well how to keep their secrets, and the population lent its aid.

How this failure of the German cavalry on the 12th can have occurred would be a very interesting problem to solve; no doubt the very peculiar character of the ground had something to do with it; but the solution would require mainly in regimental records, which moreover might be incomplete, an extensive and close study and comparison of the conduct and doings of the smaller cavalry units, such as regiments and squadrons in both forces, and of officer's patrols in the German forces, during the 10th, 11th and 12th of the month. Here we are only able to deal with the general result—touch was lost.

During the 12th the Grand Duke came to the conviction that there was no hostile force towards Orleans, but that the victors at Coulmiers were now moving round behind the screen of the "Army of the West" to unite with the forces in the west, and thence to attack, by Dreux, the western side of the investing line. He therefore issued orders that, on the following day, the whole force should face about, and on its then left, its present right, should wheel up facing northwest towards the line Chartres-Dreux, actually with its back to the enemy; and he communicated to the Third Army his intentions for the morrow. This movement was commenced on the morning of the 13th, and the troops were on the march, when the Grand Duke, to his utter astonishment, received from the Third Army the following communication : "His Majesty the King has, at an audience to-day [the 12th], given orders to the Commander-in-Chief of the Third Army to inform your Royal Highness that His Majesty does not wish your Detachment to take the offensive unless very special reasons not known here should make it necessary. The IXth A.C., under General v. Manstein, has, with special view to this, been so directed that its advanced guard arrives at Fontainebleau on the 14th, crosses the Seine on the 15th, and can connect with you on the 16th. Success seems to be the more certain thereby, as General v. Manstein will perhaps be able to act on the flank of the enemy, who does not expect him." The Grand Duke, when he determined to leave the Orleans road, knew he would be acting against the directions sent to him on the 10th by v. Blumenthal, to remain there for some days in a defensive position; but, as already mentioned, he communicated his intentions to the Third Army. This communication must

THE FIRST FORTNIGHT OF NOVEMBER 91

have been made, probably, not later than midday, for the letter he now received was despatched from Versailles at four P.M., and in the interval there had been an audience with the King. There was telegraphic communication between Versailles and the Grand Duke at Angerville, and as this place is less than forty miles from Versailles, a mounted messenger could have delivered the missive to the Grand Duke that night. The delay in the transmission of the message is unaccountable. The position taken up by the Grand Duke's force was little short of ludicrous, and all owing to the Fog of War. He was marching away from the enemy, and with his back to the direct road by which that enemy could most easily advance, and could in the shortest time disturb the line of investment. The Grand Duke had now to issue orders for the following day, and these orders are remarkable. The first paragraph ran as follows: "According to information received, hostile troops have advanced on the road from Orleans to Etampes as far as Artenay, and on that from Chateaudun to Chartres as far as Bonneval, and have halted there. It is the intention of H.R.H. the Grand Duke that until more full information can be obtained as to the strength and intentions of the enemy, the Detachment will remain in the positions reached to-day ; but to strengthen the occupation of Chartres the 22nd Inf. Division will proceed there to-morrow at daybreak." Hoenig regards the reason given by the Grand Duke for the halt as a deliberate misstatement, the real reason being the orders from Versailles ; nevertheless, it was perfectly true that Artenay and Bonneval had been occupied that day by the French, and strong forces were visible beyond Artenay ; but what the Grand Duke really knew is impossible to ascertain. On the 14th the Detachment with the exception of the 22nd Inf. Division remained stationary.

Here, again, in the exercise of control by the Third Army over the Grand Duke, we have this curious abstention of the Crown Prince from dealing firmly with him. The Crown Prince will not stop the Grand Duke's erratic insubordinate proceedings until he has the concurrence and support of the King, *i.c.*, v. Moltke. And an examination of the entries in v. Blumenthal's diary affords indications that on the 13th the Chief of the Staff of the Third Army held opinions so different from those of its Commander that possibly he left the Crown Prince to deal with the matter by himself.

"In the afternoon a telegram arrived from the Grand Duke saying that to-morrow he will march to Chartres. I forgot to send it to the King—[in the Diary there is no trace of v. Blumenthal being chronically short of memory]—and when the Crown Prince returned in the evening from St. Germains it was very unpleasant for him. It was sent on then. I have become a veritable reporting machine. If this sort of thing goes on we shall have a repetition of the story of the Vienna Council of War at Court."

"'There is a very decided tendency here to dictate every move to the Grand Duke, and this ought to be resisted. If I were in his place I should just report nothing, and cut the telegraph wire."

On the 14th the Grand Duke kept his troops where he had halted them on the 13th, except the 22nd Inf. Division, which moved to Chartres. But the march of the Grand Duke on Chartres was something very much like a defiance to the Crown Prince and to the Royal Head-quarters as well; so at 12.55 P.M. on the 14th the Prince sent to the Grand Duke the following reminder as to his duty : "General v. Manstein can, on the 16th, arrive with the IXth A.C. at Etampes [twenty-eight miles from Paris], to which place he has been directed by the supreme Head-quarters. It is, therefore, only there that the concentration of a large force can be effected most quickly. The road from Orleans to Paris must not be left open, if the enemy advances by Artenay. Frederick William, Crown Prince." To this telegram the Grand Duke wired at 6.30 P.M. the following audacious reply : " Your Royal Highness' despatch of midday to-day received. In order that I may carry out the duty assigned to me of protecting the investment line of Paris against attacks from

Orleans and Chartres, and to have in my own hands the control for the necessary unity in the leading, I request that General v. Manstein may be placed under my orders. The road from Artenay to Etampes will then be protected." It may be mentioned that although v. Manstein's corps belongs to Prince Frederick Charles' Army, he is at this time receiving orders from the supreme Head-quarters, and now a third superior wishes to get hold of him. Fortunately all three are assigning to him the same objective, namely, Etampes.

But in the German Army there are, for even Royal personages, limits to insubordination; and the Grand Duke was, even in these early stages of his career as a leader of an army, for the Detachment was a small army, reminding Versailles of the fact. Hoenig says : " Anyhow, affairs from the 10th to the 14th were not so managed as to raise high expectations from the Detachment, and had there been no special considerations to be taken into account, it would perhaps have been even at that time a question whether it might be advisable upon the whole to allow the Detachment to remain in existence after the arrival of the Second Army on the scene, or at least to consider whether the staff work was in proper hands. These matters were discussed at that time in Versailles and among the General Staff, but no decisive step was taken."

V. d. Vernois writes on the 14th : " We can make nothing of the operations of the Grand Duke, it being not easy at this distance to judge of what is going on on the spot. One of us will probably have to go there." The marginal note in Hoenig is "Friction between the Third Army and the Detachment." But v. Blumenthal took a very different view of the matter, and apparently is, on this occasion, letting the Prince carry on alone his conflict with the Grand Duke ; it is with the Grand Duke that are the sympathies of the Chief of the Staff of the Prince's army. No wonder there is friction.

On this day, the 14th, the entry in v. Blumenthal's Diary is as follows : " Certain news arrived from the Grand Duke which caused great agitation at the King's Head-quarters. . . . The march off of the Grand Duke to Chartres appears inexplicable, though I said to the Crown Prince and to many others also that they could not be judges of what was happening; no doubt the Grand Duke has good reasons for his action, and if he has not reported everything to us he had acted only rightly and wisely. That did not please them. About mid-day came to me Moltke, who looked at things more calmly, but desired that I should give the Grand Duke certain instructions. I could only say that that was entirely against my principles; any one to whom a responsible task is allotted, he must also carry it through. His hands should not be tied. Moltke assented to this, and upon the other points we were also one. Moltke was especially dissatisfied that the Grand Duke should from the outset have disseminated his forces too much. He is right there, but we do not know what were the Grand Duke's reasons for so doing."

CHAPTER VI

THE GRAND DUKE'S DETACHMENT, FROM NOVEMBER 14TH TO 20TH

IT is desirable now to learn the views which v. Moltke himself, on the 14th, took of the general situation and of the future. These are given in his letter of that date to v. Stiehle. In v. d. Goltz's work, the letter is given apparently *in extenso*, and, with the exception of unimportant paragraphs, is reproduced here. It runs as follows:—

"It shows the resources of France and the patriotism of the people, that after the whole army has been captured, yet in a comparatively short time a new army, which is not to be despised, has been put into the field. . . . The retreat [after Coulmiers] was continued on the 10th to Toury, and although there were numbers of cavalry, the touch with the enemy was lost. . . .

"The reconnoitring on the 11th did not obtain sufficient information; on the 12th, Pithiviers was found unoccupied, and beyond Artenay there was no enemy found. According to our estimate, the Orleans army consist of the 15th and 16th corps, numbering 24 line (Marche) regiments, and, with Gardes Mobiles, may be over 60,000 strong. The artillery has presumably been got together from the fortresses; the Algerian troops may be the nucleus of the army. The French give their losses on the 9th as 2000, and the Army of the Loire has, apparently, not considered itself strong enough to advance by more fighting direct on Paris, the only mode by which a real success is to be obtained. It appears that it is endeavouring to turn by the west, our position, which it does not consider advisable to attack. On this march it would be able to unite with the new formations, for which Nogent le Rotrou [seventy-five miles south-west of Paris and fifty-two miles from the Orleans Paris road] is the central point, perhaps even with the 30-40,000 Gardes Nationales, by whom Generals Briant and Bourbaki, on the line Pacy-Vernon-Les Andelys [a line forty miles from Paris *à cheval* the Lower Seine], and as far as Gournay have for a long time held our detachments in check in this direction. It cannot now be doubted that an attack by strong hostile forces from the west would endanger us not less than from the south. The investment could be completely raised for eight days, without the capital being revictualled for longer than half a day; but on the left bank of the Seine we have our siege artillery and the Royal Headquarters, and, above all, we have to take into account the political impression. The Grand Duke has already, therefore, to-day begun his march on Chartres, which place has remained occupied by General von Wittich. In Toury Count Stolberg's Cavalry Division has remained. There is no news from it at present. It is possible, but not probable, that the Army of the Loire is restricting itself to the passive defence of Orleans, and behind the Loire. Gambetta is well aware that Paris cannot hold out without relief. Should, therefore, the departure of that army to the west be confirmed, the Grand Duke will move parallel to this march till the possibility of a decisive attack is offered to him. Then the important place of Rouen will be his next objective. Subject to the foregoing, the protection of the Paris-Orleans road must be undertaken by the Second Army alone. The road cannot be left entirely open for any time, and the Grand Duke cannot be weakened by detachments.

"On the left bank of the Loire the destruction of Bourges is, militarily, the driving the Delegation out of Tours is, politically, important. I have hoped that the Second Army would have been able to march direct on those places, but as, unfortunately, there has been no favourable decision between Paris and Orleans, the only thing to be done is to continue the advance from Fontainebleau and Sens [on the Yonne, a tributary of the Seine, and forty miles west of Troyes, and

THE GRAND DUKE'S DETACHMENT 97

thirty miles south-east of Fontainebleau], first in a westerly direction. Whether the Xth corps shall be directed on Gien on the Loire, will be better determined on the 19th inst. [the day on which the corps was to arrive at Joigny, higher up the Yonne, seventeen miles beyond Sens]. The recapture of Orleans, and the crossing the river by the IInd Army to the left bank will be much facilitated thereby. For the quick approach of H.R.H. Prince Frederick Charles, we are very grateful; it has pulled us through a sort of crisis. '. . . We expect with some certainty a sortie on the 15th inst. on a larger scale than hitherto. We could not dispense just now with the half of the IInd Army Corps. The two Divisions are the only reserve of the extended southern line of the Investment. Fortunately, the enemy continues still quiet in the north-west, otherwise we should have to send detachments there also." Still not the slightest thought of the possible need of concentration in this "People's War"; and, for the long line Châlons-sur-Soane-le Mans, facing south, which had to be abandoned, is substituted another long line one hundred and seventy miles long, Rouen-Bourges, facing west.

This letter reveals two predominant ideas in the mind of v. Moltke; first, a tenacious clinging to the hypothesis he had adopted, at the very first, namely, at the end of October, as to the strategical intentions of the French leaders. The second idea is a determined depreciation of the military value of the resistance that the French nation was organising against him. After the hostile army that the Grand Duke was to meet, but which existed only in the imagination of v. Moltke, had been decisively defeated, the Grand Duke would easily traverse the difficult country along the lower Seine, and possess himself of Rouen some sixty-five miles down the river. V. Moltke thus contemplates directing him to a place one hundred and ten miles from Orleans, the scene of the decisive struggle only a fortnight later. So little able had v. Moltke been to forecast the decisive point that he first had sent the Second Army miles away from it in one direction, and now he is sending the Detachment miles away from it in another direction. That

G

the French had already put into the field two well-equipped army corps, which had proved their fighting power in the open, in no way altered v. Moltke's opinion that the recapture of Orleans, and the capture of Bourges and Tours, would be aught but easy work for the 50,000 Germans of the Second Army. Considering the extremely defensive character of the country this Army would have to traverse, v. Moltke's opinion of French fighting-power must have been poor indeed, and was painfully contradicted by plain facts within a very few days. But there are certainly strong indications that in this war, as will appear hereafter, v. Moltke did not attach to " country " much weight in connection with either strategical or tactical operations.

During the 14th, there came in to the Grand Duke from the Cavalry Divisions a number of reports, and Hoenig says that on these reports he determined, in spite of all the orders he had received to the contrary, to resume on the 15th, his march to the north-west away from the Orleans road that he had received reiterated and specific directions to guard. But although these reports are given to us by Hoenig, it is well to bear in mind that they are not necessarily the whole of the reports received by the Grand Duke; for some may have been lost or mislaid, and, moreover, with every commander there may be certain other sources of information, or there may come to his knowledge certain unrecorded indications of an enemy's movements, all of which, taken in conjunction with the formal reports preserved among the archives, are the real grounds on which he forms his judgment. The general tenour of the reports recorded, was, that towards Orleans the situation was the same as already reported on the previous day, but along the west and south-west lines of observation there were many troops visible. A report from the 6th Cav. Division seems to have had much weight. Beyond Courville, on the high road from Nogent le Rotrou to Paris by Chartres, a closed body of 250 line troops had been seen on the march. The presence of line troops where but few of any troops save Gardes Mobiles and Gardes Nationales had hitherto been

THE GRAND DUKE'S DETACHMENT 99

seen, was a possible indication of the arrival of a fighting force. The troops were really only a part of the already mentioned small infusion of line troops in the " Army of the West." But the reports strengthened the Grand Duke so much in his previous opinion that the attack from the west was now really on its way, that despite orders, he determined to resume the forbidden line of march; but he did not report his intentions until half-past four on the morning of the 15th, when he telegraphed to the Third Army his proceedings, and during the day he brought the Detachment to its prescribed halting-places. The 22nd Inf. Division and the 6th Cav. Division were already at Chartres on the 14th. The 17th Inf. Division went to Rambouillet, twenty miles north-east of Chartres, and on the same road to Paris; the Bavarians to Auneau, ten miles in rear of the centre of the line; the 2nd and 4th Cav. Divisions remained respectively at Toury, and midway between Toury and Chartres at Voves. And this time no one said nay to him, for there was a real " scare" at Versailles. This scare deserves recounting in detail. In the narrow district between Mantes, on the Seine, and Dreux, on a western railway from Paris, on a front of twenty-two miles, there was only the 5th Cav. Division as protection to the rear of this part, the vulnerable part, of the investing line; one brigade was at Mantes, another brigade with a battery of Horse Artillery near Houdan, on the railway, a third at St. Germain en Laye, six miles north of Versailles. On the French side matters had become more lively in front of Mantes; at Dreux the forces, such as they were, had been greatly re-inforced, as also at Illiers and Bonneval; on the 14th, Courville had been occupied by Line Infantry; farther in rear all the villages towards Nogent le Rotrou were held. The important town of Dreux lies some thirty-five miles west of Versailles, and had formed a centre from which guerilla warfare had been carried on for weeks against the 5th Cav. Division. On the 14th, this Division reported that at Bu, a village a few miles northeast of Dreux, were collected 12,000 men, eight squadrons, and eight batteries. This village had already, on the 14th, been bombarded by Horse Artillery, but, as a novelty in this war, the French did not evacuate it but held on. At once, on the 15th, five battalions of the Guard Landwehr, and a heavy reserve battery were hurried from the investing line to support the Cavalry Division, for, presuming the report to be correct, there was much more than a phantom army in this direction, so that when, on this day, the news came that the right of the Detachment was marching in the direction whence the danger was now showing itself, there must have been a great feeling of relief at Versailles, and probably no one asked the question how it was that the Detachment was coming there. But the report was not true; the mountain was but a very small molehill indeed. In the morning of the 14th some Uhlans had approached Bu and had been fired on by Gardes Nationales and Franc-tireurs; two were killed, one was wounded, and one escaped. At eleven o'clock some Uhlans and artillery returned to Bu, but the French commander in the district had brought from Dreux two companies of marines, three battalions of Gardes Mobiles and a section of artillery; he at once advanced to the attack and drove the Germans away. How this force was so marvellously exaggerated in the eyes of the German Cavalry is not explained. At all events little short of a panic was the result. At Versailles, though doubt prevailed whether the attackers were the " Army of the West " only, or whether among them was also a portion of the Army of the Loire, it seemed so certain that an attack was coming that any objections previously entertained to the movement of the Grand Duke lost all their force, and on this day v. Moltke gave the Grand Duke a perfectly free hand, releasing him from the protection of Paris from the south. The letter of release was sent to the Third Army as an instruction to them; its concluding paragraphs ran as follows: " At the same time, and in accordance with the approval of the King, the 5th Cavalry Division is placed under the orders of H.R.H. the Grand Duke of Mecklenburg-Schwerin, to whom is recommended now the concentration of his troops, and the speedy offensive against the hostile forces in march perhaps from Dreux and Chartres."

Then, as if to remind the Grand Duke that his master is still the Crown Prince, and at the same time to reassure the latter that there is no interference with his command, v. Moltke writes: " Direct instructions from here to H.R.H. the Grand Duke are not given." In transmitting the letter, the Third Army did not add anything of importance. On the following day, the 16th, the Duke, still pivoting on Chartres, brought forward his right, the 17th Inf. Division to Nogent le Roi, on the Eure, so that the front faced due west; the left was at Chartres fifteen miles away, the Bavarians were at Gallardon about ten miles in rear of the line and the same distance from each flank. Dreux lay ten miles from Nogent le Roi down the Eure. Up to this time, the Detachment had not met with any opposition, and the work had been one of simple marching. But now, the task before the Grand Duke was one of vast difficulty, and one of which none even of the tried Generals of the German Army had had any experience. With 52 battalions, 110 squadrons, 220 guns, and unweildy and huge trains, he stood on the edge of a tract of broken, close, and wooded country, totally unsuitable for guns or cavalry, seamed with cross roads and lanes, and into which his cavalry scouts could barely penetrate; into this he was to enter and strike a decisive blow on an enemy moving unseen within, an enemy of whose strength, organisation and whereabouts he had not the faintest idea. Not merely to achieve success, but to avoid disaster, two conditions were indispensable; one, the holding the force together well in hand, the other, perfect staff work. But, unfortunately, dissemination, not concentration, was the principle guiding all the operations of the Grand Duke, whilst the Staff work was indifferent. The imaginary enemy before the Grand Duke was the " Army of the West " reinforced possibly by some portion of the Army of the Loire. The actual army was some 35,500 men, the force already described, extended on a front of more than sixty miles from near the Lower Seine down to Bonneval on the Loir. On the extreme left near the Seine were a group of five or six battalions of Gardes Mobiles and Franc-tireurs under the orders of Lieut.-Colonel Thomas. At Dreux was General Temple with seven or eight battalions. Farther south at Châteauneuf, twelve miles from Dreux and fifteen from Chartres, was a similar force under Lieut.-Colonel Marty; other groups continued the line to Bonneval. Not one single piece of artillery was there with the Army. What guns had been there had been withdrawn south.

And it would seem that v. Moltke, a little bit doubtful perhaps that the Grand Duke, as a soldier, could be trusted to walk quite alone, thought it desirable to give him the benefit of a little light and leading; so he penned on the 17th, for his benefit, a memorandum which Hoenig gives us in his book. The Grand Duke did not receive this memorandum, which was sent through the Third Army Head-quarters, until the 20th, when the situation it was intended to meet had passed away; whether it would have been of the slightest use to him will be best judged by a perusal of its contents:

"H.R.H. the Grand Duke has already been informed through the Head-quarters of the IIIrd Army, that from this time he is completely relieved from protecting the Orleans-Paris Road, and that His only duty is to prevent hostile forces advancing on the western roads on the left bank of the Seine. For watching in this direction to learn what is taking place, there is available a very numerous cavalry [probably 10–12,000].

"On the other hand, it is, naturally, not intended that to offer resistance there should be a force on every one of these roads, but only that the advance shall be met on those on which strong hostile forces show themselves. Success on one road will hinder the advance on the others; but to ensure the thorough defeat of the enemy, a close concentration of the force is required. Generally, the Detachment of his Royal

THE GRAND DUKE'S DETACHMENT 103

Highness has to carry out a war not so much of occupation as of movement, by only which means also can the supply of the troops be effected ; and the objectives of the operations are not so much the gaining possession of the larger towns as the destruction of the hostile forces which might have taken refuge in them. I need hardly mention the important *rôle* which consequently falls to the artillery.

" On the 20th, Angerville and Pithiviers will be occupied by two corps of the IInd Army, and the road from Chateaudun will be, thereby, to a certain extent, covered ; so that His attention may now be directed especially towards His right wing. An advance of the enemy by Dreux-Mantes would strike the investing line on its most sensitive point. It was already necessary, therefore, to send from here yesterday a brigade of Guard Landwehr to support General v. Rheinbaben [5th Cav. Division]. . . . The difficulty of His task lies in detecting accurately the decisive point against which a blow is to be delivered with all the concentrated forces ; that this will be effected I am convinced.

"(Signed) v. MOLTKE."

Hoenig remarks that at the Royal Head-quarters they had at this time no conception of the great extent to which the population were taking part in the war, nor did they realise the great difficulties that the topographical conditions of the theatre of war presented to the operations of the Detachment. It so happened that when, on the 20th, the letter came to the Grand Duke, the main body of the enemy was already in full retreat south-west to le Mans. Hoenig's remarks on this letter of v. Moltke's, though severe, are very just.

"If a People's War is carried on on the Cordon system, as was the case here, the enemy has no real decisive point, and this cannot, therefore, be ascertained, and a blow directed against it. Only by an extraordinary gift of divination can, under these circumstances, the best direction be determined ; but even this does not necessarily lead to the retreat of the forces on the flanks, as these are able to get away unendangered in every direction. Anyhow, the formation of the theatre of war in no way lent itself to the v. Moltke Idea. The enemy could be driven back, separated, destroyed at certain points, but there were always open to him roads into 'space,' and by means of the telegraph, and by the help of the population, he everywhere received timely warning of the movements of the Detachment, which was established frontally against the whole cordon. Under these conditions the greatest leader could have done but little." That Hoenig was allowed to publish this letter, which certainly does not add much to the military reputation of v. Moltke, shows how imperative it appeared to the German authorities to put before the officers of the army warnings not to rely blindly on all the strategical and tactical examples furnished in this war.

But v. Blumenthal was getting very irritated at the way in which the Royal Head-quarters were behaving to the Grand Duke. He regarded it as "grandmotherly." On the 16th he writes: "At midday to-day Moltke was with me, and he complained that the Grand Duke reported so little; I ought to order him to take the offensive. But that is not necessary, he will do it of his own accord, and up to now it seems to me he has done perfectly rightly; he stands fairly concentrated between Chartres and Maintenon." And next day he writes even more strongly: he says that some days before there had been a real panic at Versailles, everything packed and ready for a move. It had spread to his own staff without his remarking it, for they did not dare to let him know because they knew his views on such chicken-hearted conduct (Hasenfusslerei). "If only the King, with his Head-quarters and all the Princes, would go away, we could certainly expedite matters, and peace would be near at hand."

From these and the previous extracts will be at once apparent the difficulties which sometimes arise in war in the working of the higher command and of the higher control. The difficulty hardly exists when the scene of operations of

THE GRAND DUKE'S DETACHMENT 105

the armies or large detachments is a considerable distance away from the supreme authority. Prince Frederick Charles at Metz, v. Manteuffel on his way from Metz to the northwest, were left to act for themselves; and v. Werder, in the south-east, though more closely watched by Versailles, was necessarily allowed a certain amount of freedom; but, as we have seen, there was supervision and control exercised over v. d. Tann when only sixty-five miles from Versailles; and now here is the commander of this 50,000 Detachment showing a determined spirit of independence, and wandering about with his troops within a distance of only some thirty miles from the Royal Head-quarters in a manner not at all to their satisfaction. No wonder v. Moltke became impatient; it must have required some self-control to refrain from taking the command into his own hands out of those of the Crown Prince and of the Grand Duke. And the position of v. Moltke was rendered still more unsatisfactory owing to the attitude of v. Blumenthal. V. Blumenthal, under the existing arrangement, was, as Chief Staff Officer of the Third Army, the intermediary between v. Moltke and the Grand Duke; and if v. Blumenthal, differing as he did in this matter with v. Moltke, and favouring the Grand Duke, was not actually obstructive, he seems at all events not to have given support to v. Moltke; and from an incident related by v. d. Vernois, v. Blumenthal was a power that had to be reckoned with even by v. Moltke and v. Podbielski. The Crown Prince might be amenable, but not so the Crown Prince with v. Blumenthal at his elbow. In the early days of August the Royal Headquarters were not satisfied with the state of the preparation of the Third Army for the field. Consequently, a telegram containing a fresh and decided order to advance was drawn up and handed by v. Podbielski to v. d. Vernois to send. V. d. Vernois had been on the Crown Prince's Staff in the war of 1866, when v. Blumenthal was the Prince's Chief Staff Officer. "When I read it," he says, "I said to the General that the telegram ought not to be sent in its present form. I added I knew that staff very well in the last war.

If you wish to create strained relations with them during the whole of this campaign, send it, but I feel perfectly sure they will feel offended, and, I think, not without cause. For a good reason of some kind there must surely be for their not yet fixing the date of starting." So the telegram was not sent, and v. d. Vernois was entrusted with taking personally to the Prince the expression of the wishes of the Headquarters.

On the 16th, the Duke had come to the conclusion that it was at Dreux that the enemy was in force, so he gave orders for a movement in echelon in that direction on the 17th, the attack to take place on the following day, the 18th. On the 16th, the Detachment as already mentioned was facing west, right at Nogent le Roi, left at Chartres. For the morrow, the 5th Cav. Division, on the north, was to advance west and drive the enemy back on Dreux; the 17th Inf. Division from Nogent to advance on Dreux, and if the place were only weakly held, to take it; otherwise, to establish itself in front of Dreux. Fontaine-les-Ribouts lies eight miles up the Blaise; it is eighteen miles from Chartres, whence the 22nd Inf. Division was directed on it. In the event of strong resistance, the division would connect along the Blaise with the 17th Inf. Division on its right. The Bavarians were directed on St. Cheron, ten miles from the Blaise and the same distance from the flanks. On the left the 6th Cav. Division, on a wide front, accompanied the advance, or rather the wheel to the right on the move, as it really was. Probably the Grand Duke believed that there was with the enemy a portion of the army from the Loire, and therefore intended whilst attacking him in front at Dreux, to cut off the retreat of the Loire troops to the south; but, on the other hand, if he believed, as his order stated, that the hostile army was concentrated in strong force at Dreux, this very disseminated disposition exposed his own troops to the risk of destruction in detail. Sometimes in war, the Commander states to his Chief Staff Officer the object of the operation he intends to carry out, and leaves him to work out the details for the units; sometimes the commanders do the work themselves. In this instance, we are unfortunately unable to ascertain who was responsible for the orders for the march on the 17th, the Grand Duke or Colonel v. Krenski. Helvig states that the Bavarians at St. Cheron were to be available not only to support the Divisions in front, but also for employment to the south-west on the left flank, if necessary, as it was not absolutely certain that danger was not threatening from this direction. If this be correct, then, obviously, the Grand Duke, instead of concentrating his efforts on the achievement of one object, was trying to provide for two eventualities, attack to the north-west, defence to the southwest; and it is difficult to see how, had the hostile defence been of an effective character, or the hostile attack serious, success could have been achieved by the Grand Duke in either direction. Hoenig remarks that the Grand Duke disregarded v. Moltke's recommendation for concentration, and that in all operations carried out from a flanking position, concentration is the first thing to be attended to; and that the flanks must be protected by cavalry and infantry pushed forward a day's march; the Infantry, complete and ready to take their part where the encounter is to take place.

The troops met with opposition everywhere in their advance, but as must be apparent from the position and nature of the French forces here, the opposition, though bitter and determined, could not hold out against the highly-trained and well-disciplined Germans. Dreux was easily taken by the 17th Inf. Division, but the 22nd Inf. Division failed to arrive on the Blaise, halting at Marville, some four miles short of its destination. And now, in the mind of v. Moltke, as well as in that of the Grand Duke, the conviction must have begun to dawn, that the ideas that had ruled the strategy since the 12th of the month had been baseless; and that the marching had simply led to an *affaire manquée*. The result was a striking illustration of the difficulties encountered by an invader in a country suited to a " People's

War," a country where the inhabitants and local troops can find scope for their employment, and the exercise of their special powers, and where the population take seriously their part in the National Defence.

The Grand Duke now came to the conclusion, and it was correct, that he had not hit upon the main body even of the nebulous " Army of the West," but on its extreme northern flank ; and as the trend of the retreat of some of the troops encountered was in the direction of le Mans to the southwest by Nogent le Rotrou, he determined to make, on the 18th, a complete change of front from north-west to southwest, and then to advance in the first instance on Nogent le Rotrou. In this determination v. Moltke acquiesced, and from a letter of his of the 18th to the Second Army, given by v. d. Goltz, there can hardly be any doubt that it was on this day that he at last gave up the idea which had dominated his mind since the latter days of October, that the French would attack him on the West ; and also the other idea, that the whole of the Army of the Loire, which had fought at Coulmiers, had gone bodily from the neighbourhood of Orleans.

In his letter he says: " On the question whether the main body of the Army of the Loire is still at Orleans, or perhaps in a more westerly direction at Chateaudun, light will be thrown in a few days, and the information will be at once sent to the Head-quarters of the IInd Army."

It must be mentioned that General Fiereck had, on the 17th, transferred the main body of the " Army of the West," some 16,000 men, from Chateaudun to Nogent le Rotrou ; and the troops from the neighbourhood of Dreux made their way in the same direction with ease. The Detachment had, already, since November 12th, made three wheels in mass, so that, possibly, the Grand Duke imagined, that from the experience acquired, there would be no difficulty in performing the manœuvre a fourth time ; but in this he was doomed to bitter disappintment. The first three had been simply march-manœuvres, undisturbed by the enemy. Against the

THE GRAND DUKE'S DETACHMENT 109

success of the fourth march, the enemy, the elements, and the country formed an offensive alliance of such power as most effectually to stultify the Grand Duke's programme, and to render the 18th a day never to be forgotten by the unfortunate troops that were involved in the operation. Moreover, the Detachment had now thrust himself into a veritable hornet's nest, and there would necessarily be an accompanying sensation of stings. As a warning, as a really profitable example of thoroughly bad leading and bad Staff work, the movements of the 18th are worthy of consideration in detail. In the first place, the shortness of November days must be recalled to mind. On November 18th the sun rises at 7.23 and sets at 4.7; thus giving less than nine hours of daylight for the work in the field. On the day of Wörth when the Bavarians had their first experience of marching and fighting, there had been fifteen hours of daylight. During the whole of November 18th a dense fog, limiting vision to fifty paces and rendering artillery useless, hung over the country, which was very much broken and threaded with cross-lanes and devious paths. The task assigned to the 17th Inf. Division at Dreux was plain and simple, and could meet with no difficulty. It was to march fifteen miles west to Brezolles, clearing the country to the west and north-west, and for the purpose, apparently, of cutting off the enemy's retreat in that direction. But the governing factor in the movement of the rest of the Detachment was the 22nd Inf. Division at Boulay and Marville, some four miles north of Chateauneuf. It was from Chateauneuf that the Division was to move at ten o'clock, and proceed south by the Dreux-Chateauneuf Road to the Eure, about la Loupe, a twelve miles march from Chateauneuf. The Brigade of the 6th Cav. Division, which was to the east at Chêne Chenu, between Chateauneuf and the Bavarians at St. Chéron, was to follow the 22nd Inf. Division; whilst the 1st B.C., leaving at ten A.M., St. Chéron, which is ten miles east of Chateauneuf, was also to move west and proceed to cantonments on both sides of the Chateauneuf-la Loupe road in rear of the 22nd Inf. Division. It would be an interesting War

Game exercise to work out these orders, as a time and space problem of units on full war strength with trains, &c. &c.; but here was not a War Game but practical work in the field, with any amount of possible disturbing conditions. Everything depended on the 22nd Inf. Division being clear of Chateauneuf at exactly the right time.

On the 17th, the enemy that was encountered was not one single body, but was in two bodies; one at Dreux under General Temple, whose line of retreat lay west down the Lower Seine; the other under General Thomas, which, though in the "Army of the West," was part of the 21st Corps, now forming at le Mans; and whose line of retreat ran therefore at right angles to that of General Temple's force. Chateauneuf was practically a defile through which were to pass an Infantry Division, a portion of an Army Corps, and a Cavalry Brigade; the 22nd Inf. Division was to lead, and even if time and space had been accurately calculated, any delay in the passage of this Division in passing the defile at the appointed time must inevitably cause a block in the movements of the other troops; besides which, any portion of the Bavarians that was marching south of Chateauneuf across the road to gain its destination, might bring the 22nd Inf. Division to a halt. And delay at once began at the very first attempt of the Division to move. On the 17th the Division had intruded itself into a country full of hostile inhabitants; and the rightful occupiers, though only too glad to bid "God speed" this morning to their unwelcome guests, were determined to bid it in such a form as to impress it on their memories; so when the Division prepared to move down to Chateauneuf, it found its departure in quiet so strongly opposed that v. Wittich was compelled first to clear the hostile troops from the direction actually opposite to that he was eventually to take. Owing to the fog, the receipt of information, and the transmission of orders was much delayed. Then there was the country between the Division and Chateauneuf to be cleared. Meantime, the Bavarians and the Cavalry Brigade from the west were approaching

Chateauneuf and the road south. General v. Wittich suggested to the Grand Duke that in order to keep his Division together he should let the Bavarians pass across. The Grand Duke refused to accept the suggestion, so part of the Division pushed on; then the Bavarians crossed between it and the rest of the Division, some of which passed the night in Chateauneuf; the head of the Division was unable to get further south than some five miles from the town. The 17th Inf. Division had halted when at five miles from its destination, doubtful, owing to the sound of firing in the south, whether it ought not to move in that direction. Although the marches had been only six or seven miles, the day had been necessarily most trying to the physical endurance and the *moral* of the troops. Nowhere could they move without coming under fire from an enemy quite invisible to them, and possessing a knowledge of which they were absolutely deficient, a knowledge of the country; roads were found broken or barricaded, and every hamlet, farmhouse and village had to be stormed.

The delays and the crossing of the Divisions had been fatiguing. Many detachments had been on the march since the morning; the halts had afforded no real rest, and when, at night, the troops arrived at the shelter assigned to them, it was as likely as not that the shelter was held by the enemy, who had to be driven from it, or it had been abandoned and was in flames. So the troops had to bivouac in the cold without fires. Dropping shots were heard till late at night in the neighbouring woods, creating a feeling of insecurity, and compelling the troops to place outposts all round. As to the train columns, they wandered aimlessly about, not knowing where were the troops to which they were carrying the needful supplies. So hopelessly entangled had the Detachment become, that until disentangled no further advance was possible; the 19th was ordered as a rest-day for this purpose. Either the Grand Duke or Colonel v. Krenski was a master of the art of converting, by well-chosen language, failure into success, so the Detachment order for the 19th runs as follows:

" In to-day's advance the Detachment encountered hostile

resistance everywhere. The advance secured, but chiefly owing to the successful fight of v. Wittich's Division, the attainment of its intended purpose, namely, obtaining more information as to the strength and position of the enemy. It appears that the hostile troops in front of us belong to the Army of the West (General Fiereck), whose head-quarters are at le Mans" [quite wrong]. "His Royal Highness intends to allow the troops to remain to-morrow in their present positions and to give them rest."

The imaginary character of v. Moltke's appreciation of the situation since the 14th had been unpleasantly brought to light by the events of the 17th. The Army, to whose circuitous course the Grand Duke had been moving "parallel," had not been marching at all, for non-existent entities do not walk about the earth. The driving out of Dreux a few thousand irregular troops without a single piece of artillery in their possession, can hardly be regarded as a decisive engagement. Rouen was hardly the next suitable objective, as not the possession of any place, but the destruction of the army in the field was the first aim in all v. Moltke's operations; and so v. Moltke at once accepts the fact that he has followed the red herring so cleverly drawn across the track, and, then occurs to his mind the idea that the lost hostile army may be nearly where it was when he first lost sight of it.

The 19th November was employed by the Detachment in disentangling itself and in preparing for the advance on the morrow to the south-west. The reports received during the day pointed conclusively to a general withdrawal in that direction by the enemy, and also to a strong occupation of Nogent le Rotrou. On the 20th the advance was continued, but for only a very short distance on to the ten miles front—la Loupe-Courville, with the 17th Infantry Division on the right rear at Senonches. It is worthy of notice that the Bavarians had not with them a single map of the country; the Bavarian War Office had been unable in its preparation and despatch of the maps to keep pace with the movements. In this advance, the advantages of cavalry and artillery altogether

THE GRAND DUKE'S DETACHMENT

disappeared, and the large trains were veritable *impedimenta* ; but the district was eminently the theatre for a national war carried on by young untrained soldiers, intelligent enough to utilise the advantages offered by the ground. Although the information obtained on the 20th showed that there were on both flanks of the Detachment not unimportant bodies of troops, yet everything indicated that Nogent le Rotrou was the stronghold where the French would make a determined stand to arrest the further progress of the invaders. And now on the 20th we must leave the Detachment for a time and go to the Second Army to learn what had been taking place there since, in obedience to the orders received at Troyes on November 10th, it commenced its march towards the Paris-Orleans road.

CHAPTER VII

THE SECOND ARMY FROM NOVEMBER 10TH TO 20TH

ON the night of November 10th the front of the army faced south, and extended from Troyes to Neufchateau, a distance of seventy miles. On the 16th the IXth Army Corps, covered by the 1st Cavalry Division, arrived at Méréville, near Angerville, on the Paris-Orleans road. The Army Head-quarters and the IIIrd Army Corps were at and near Sens, on the Yonne, sixty miles from the road; the leading echelon of the Xth Army Corps (one brigade of which was far in rear) had reached Tonnerre, forty miles south-east of Sens, and ninety miles from the road.

On this day v. Stiehle replied to v. Moltke's letter of the 14th; the reply shows how completely, at this time, Prince Frederick Charles concurred in the under-estimate formed by v. Moltke. The writer, when he penned it, little dreamed that in only five days all the ambitious plans for the army would have to be abandoned, and that until the commencement of the following month his chief, overwhelmed by the threatening appearance of the enemy he had bearded in his very den, would adopt in front of Orleans a passive attitude, and hold to it so determinedly, that it would need the express order of the King to move him to the attack.

The letter runs: "His Royal Highness, in conformity with the orders received, and the information communicated, purposes to dispose of the army as follows:

"The IXth Army Corps which, owing to its forced marches must be somewhat exhausted, will close up at Angerville, and pushing forward an advanced guard in support of the 2nd Cavalry Division at Toury will rest from the 18th. On the

21st, the Corps will commence its advance on Artenay and Orleans. . . .

"The IIIrd Army Corps will march from the Loing, where, on the 18th, it arrives at Nemours and Chateau Landon [both places thirty to thirty-five miles from the Paris-Orleans Road], on the 19th to Puiseaux, Beaumont; on the 20th to Pithiviers [fifteen miles from the Paris road and fifteen miles south-east of Angerville]; and on the 21st continue the advance on Orleans in co-operation with the IXth Army Corps, if, as is asserted by a deserter, the enemy, some 30-40,000 strong, is in camp at Chevilly, south of Artenay.

"By the capture of Orleans his Royal Highness believes he can best carry out the duty assigned to him 'protecting the investing army against Orleans.' Afterwards, according to circumstances, his Royal Highness intends to move down the Loire by Blois on Tours, the IXth Army Corps on the right bank, the IIIrd Army Corps on the left bank of the river. There is no risk in the operation, although à cheval the river, because between Orleans and Tours there are exclusive of both places five permanent bridges, and also the IIIrd Army Corps has with it its pontoon train. If a portion of the IInd Army Corps could be employed to occupy Orleans, where all the trains must remain, the operation would be thereby facilitated.

"The Xth Army Corps, now advancing by Tonnerre, will until the 20th march direct to Montargis [twenty-five miles south-east of Pithiviers, forty miles east of Orleans, and twenty miles north of Gien]; thence it can reach the Loire in two marches, and eventually operate against Bourges [forty miles south], render it of no further military importance, and then, perhaps, advance down the Cher against Tours [eighty miles]. If it happens that the enemy is decisively defeated, then, perhaps, from Bourges and Tours, the converging direction on Poitiers [sixty miles from Tours and one hundred from Bourges] may be taken, and all railway communication between northern and southern France thus destroyed.

"His Royal Highness proceeds on this plan, from the conviction that without a decisive victory, the French spirit will not bend, and that we shall force the enemy to fight if we advance direct against his political or military chief centres.

"The IIIrd and IXth Army Corps will, together, be more surely equal to their work, if, before coming into contact with the enemy, they have not suffered from forced marches.

"The Xth Army Corps is, momentarily, only of three Infantry Brigades with seventy-two guns. His Royal Highness will, however, reinforce it with six or seven squadrons of Hessian Cavalry, which are to go to Montgaris, and he will bring up the mixed brigade left behind at Chaumont under Gen. v. Kraatz, and leave only two battalions, one battery, and a squadron watching towards Langres. . . . Since the part of the Army of the Loire which is capable of carrying out operations, and is provided with cavalry, is acting north of the Loire, General v. Voigts-Rhetz will find opposed to him only loose infantry formations, to which he must, with his artillery, be superior; but even if he does not advance rapidly, the direction of this attack would greatly disturb the whole of the hostile operations. . . ."

And, unknown to the Prince, the missing 100,000 men of the Army of the Loire, and more, stood in his path to success.

The march assigned to the Xth Army Corps led it direct into districts, in which, owing to their proximity to the Army of the Loire, the population would be emboldened to take an active part in the defence. The corps had hardly commenced its march towards Orleans than it began to experience the influence on the population of the defeat at Coulmiers, and the evacuation of Orleans. On the 13th, when arriving at Chatillon on the Seine, thirty miles short of Tonnerre, it found unmistakable signs of the "People's War." So evident were these that on this day General v. V. Rhetz sent back word to the 39th Brigade, which was a day's march in rear : " Attitude of the inhabitants of Chatillon hostile; the place evacuated only early this morning by French troops; armed parties in the neighbouring woods; casualties must not be left behind, but be brought on in waggons " (a reversal of a previous order). He also ordered that men coming up to join the Army should march in parties of not less than 3-400. On the 15th the General heard that a surprise by Franc-tireurs was intended for the 16th or following days. Although he knew that this might be a rumour only, he deemed advisable to take special precautions for the further advance.

The march was along one road and in echelon, covering a length of two days' march; the 40th Brigade, far in rear, had to march independently. The 38th Brigade, the General with it, led as advanced guard: to the next, the 37th, was assigned for protection the Corps Artillery and the 1st Train Column; the 39th Brigade with the 2nd Train Column, a light bridge train and a Pontoon Company brought up the rear. With each brigade were two batteries and two squadrons of cavalry. The General determined not to depend on his line of communication for supplies. The leading echelon had to collect supplies on the spot for itself and for those in rear. The daily destination of the troops was kept secret. Each echelon looked after its own security and had to find its own quarters. If necessary, a whole Division and all the Corps Artillery could be concentrated in a day. The packs were now carried on vehicles to save the men in the trying march. Each battalion carried with it three to four days' supplies on waggons, the columns being thereby unfortunately much lengthened. At night the infantry went into cantonments, but the most careful precautions were taken against surprise. It was found impossible to keep up communication uninterruptedly between the Corps and the Army Head-quarters. Infantry escorts were necessary for the field post, and even for the transmission of orders. The country was pretty well deserted by the able-bodied men, as these had gone away south to Auxerre, a centre for the hostile irregular troops. To ascertain how matters stood, an officer with some dragoons was despatched in this direction. They were surprised in Ablis, where they were resting for the night, the officer being killed. The few cavalry in advance were constantly under fire; and the country was so close that the woods on either side of the marching columns had to be cleared by infantry. The road was in many places cut through or barricaded; telegraphs were found broken, bridges destroyed, and all materials for their repair removed. It was in the towns and villages, not in the open country, that the hostility of the population displayed itself. The resistance soon took a more active form, artillery being necessary to drive away the Gardes Mobiles and the Franc-tireurs who now opposed the march of the column. The rapidity of the advance of the Second Army, together with the fighting power of the German columns, had, however, disarranged the departmental plans for resistance, and, consequently, all the hostile troops fell back behind the Loire.

V. d. Goltz writes of this time as follows: "If affairs very soon took a course entirely different from that which had been anticipated, the reason is that the ground on which the anticipations were based—namely, the estimate formed of the enemy—was altered. During the following days, the Army got a glimpse of the difficulties, of which it had regarded even hardly any as possible, and which it soon had to encounter. It could no longer be concealed that against the success of the whole campaign on the Loire, a danger might crop up which could be averted only by the employment of all available forces. Already it had become known through the outspoken remarks of the population which eyed, with a certain amount of contempt, the weak marching columns of the advancing IInd Army that, on the Loire, was assembling an army numbering hundreds of thousands, well equipped, and animated by the highest spirit. The expression *La belle Armée de la Loire* was heard here and there. On the German side, this was at first regarded as mere rhodomontade, as an exaggeration due to the constitutionally excitable temperament."

But, at the very outset, the plan adopted on the 16th was disarranged, owing to the altered views of the population as to the transmission of orders and messages among the invaders; the officer carrying the order, and with a small escort, from Sens to the Xth Army Corps found himself stopped by Franc-tireurs; and it was not until by the chance arrival of a small detachment of the IIIrd Army Corps that the road was cleared, and he could proceed on his mission. The delay in the delivery of the order rendered impossible the arrival of the corps at Montargis at the appointed time. The Prince was at Nemours on the Loing on the 18th, and there in newspapers were found statements that the strength of the Army of the Loire was from 200,000 to 300,000; the Prince also heard there of the fortifications at Orleans, and that the hostile Army was concentrated at Orleans. Another corps, not hitherto mentioned, was also spoken of, the 18th; it was asserted that General Michel of the Army of the East was to take command of the Cavalry Division of the corps. Also it was stated that a body of troops 30–40.000 strong, under General des Pallières, which had not fought at Coulmiers, had arrived from Bourges by Gien. It then occurred to the Prince that, possibly, reinforcements were being drawn from the East by rail to the Loire; and at 4 P.M. on the 18th he wired to Versailles a report in which he said: "Perhaps for the decision troops are being drawn from the Rhone by rail to the Loire, and these will act against our left flank."

On the 19th, the Prince received from v. Moltke the answer, dated 18th, to his letter of the 16th. In it, v. Moltke stated that the King approved the plan of operations proposed on the 16th, and he continued: "a decision, whether the Xth Army Corps should move direct on Bourges cannot yet be given because it cannot yet be foreseen whether the employment of the whole Army towards Chateaudun and Orleans may not be necessary. The question will mainly depend on the result of the advance of the Detachment on le Mans commencing to-day": then come the words already quoted: "On the question whether the main body of the Army of the Loire is still at Orleans, or perhaps in a more westerly direction at Chateaudun, light will be thrown in a few days and the information will be at once sent to the Head-quarters of the Second Army." With this letter came copies of two despatches from London. The first stated that Orleans had been fortified and armed with heavy guns; that a body of 10,000 men had been employed at the work; and that the French Army was massed between Artenay and Orleans. It was alleged that on the Loire, boats had been collected to facilitate crossing the river, as soon as necessity arose for the destruction of the bridges. The second despatch stated that the railways from Vierzon and Blois to Orleans had been restored, and could be used for bringing up reinforcements.

No doubt, the Prince, by his conduct of the operations of this war has laid himself open to much adverse criticism as a Leader; but one indispensable qualification for good leadership he possessed in a marked degree; he knew the importance of information respecting the enemy, and he spared no pains to obtain it from every possible source. Later on, just when assigning its true value to the information obtained was of the utmost importance, he seems sometimes to have allowed, unfortunately, his personal prejudices against the informant to weigh in forming his judgment with consequences that were disastrous; but from the 16th to the end of this month, during which period this particular manifestation of "personlichkeit" had no opportunity of exercising its pernicious influence, the eagerly sought-for information, when obtained, was judicially, though not always satisfactorily, weighed and considered.

On the 17th he had sent west in advance from Sens by Chateau Landon to Boynes near Pithiviers, in order to obtain information, and to provide for the quartering of the IIIrd Army Corps a small flying column of two squadrons with two rifle companies in waggons; cavalry acting alone being useless in these disturbed districts. The detachment marched on a line sweeping far round to the south. The detachment and also the left flank of the corps in its further advance, came frequently into conflict with strong hostile forces. On the

18th, another small flying column with two guns was also sent south towards Joigny. It was this column that came across the officer with the orders for the Xth Army Corps and opened the road for him. On the 20th the IIIrd Army Corps arrived at its destination Pithiviers, and so hostile was the population, that its patrols were fired at from the fields even by country people armed with flint-lock muskets.

All this time, the 2nd Cav. Division and the IXth Army Corps on the Orleans Road, had been unremitting in their efforts to obtain information. The Cavalry Division had on the 13th regained touch with the enemy towards Orleans, and it had been placed under v. Manstein's orders on the 16th. On the 18th, the Prince sent directions to v. Manstein as follows: " It is of the first importance to obtain detailed information respecting the position of the enemy north of Orleans, especially as regards his strength, general dispositions, and the extent and positions towards the flanks. The Commanders of the 1st and 2nd Cav. Divisions are therefore directed to clear up in detail these matters, by reconnaissances which are to be carried out during the following days, preferably round the flanks, and for the same purpose to capture as many prisoners as possible. Your Excellency will, until further orders, send an officer every day (by midday) to my Head-quarters with the information obtained about the enemy, and anything that may have taken place on Your Excellency's right flank." But v. Manstein needed no urging, for he realised the need of information, and at 6.30 P.M. on the 18th he had telegraphed to both Versailles and the Prince : " Enemy's outposts on the line St. Germain le Grand-Ruan-Dambron ; a detachment at Chilleurs aux Bois, bivouac fires on the line Bougy-St. Lyé [a little south] and south of Artenay. According to a consensus of reports, the enemy is preparing a defensive position at St. Lyé and Chevilly." Next day, at 10.15 A.M., he reported that on the outpost line, but with the right a little more forward, are line troops ; there are infantry and artillery at Chilleurs ; bivouac fires as before ; according to a consensus of information received, the line Bougy-St. Lyé is prepared for defence. At St. Lyé, which is on the edge of the forest, and on an old Roman road from Orleans to Etampes on the main road, workmen have been summoned to prepare artillery emplacements in the woods there. On the 20th at 4 P.M. " No change since 17th, but infantry and cavalry are at and south of Orgères [ten miles west of the main road]; strong bodies at Chilleurs aux Bois and further east to Chambon; many bivouac fires south of Artenay. On this day the 2nd Cav. Division reported, " According to statements of prisoners, there are 150,000 men at Orleans, one army corps is at Gidy and another at Chevilly."

On the 19th the Prince sent two of the General Staff Officers of his Army to make personal reconnaissances on both sides of the Paris road. These officers rode through the French outpost line, which was found to be continuous, and the result of the reconnaissance was that the mass of the French Army was reported to be on this road. On the 20th were named in the newspapers as belonging to this Army the 15th, 16th, 17th, and 18th Corps, whose total strength was given as from 150,000 to 200,000 men.

One failure to obtain information deserves recording. The actual text of the Army Order on the 16th from Sens is not given in the works that have been consulted, but v. d. Goltz in his account of it says: "In order to reinforce the Xth Army Corps, and to enable it better to act independently, the Hessian Cavalry Brigade of the IXth Corps was given to it. This Brigade was to march by Pithiviers on Montargis, and arrive at the latter place on the 19th, and seek to connect with the Xth Corps in the direction of Joigny [thirty miles east of Montargis]." A note runs: " General v. Manstein was ordered to give over (abzugeben) 6–7 Squadrons of this Brigade and to send them to Montargis." The strength of the Brigade was eight squadrons. The note is not inconsistent with the Army Order; and its insertion seems as if intended to account in some degree for the subsequent failure in the execution of the Army Order. Hoenig, in his version of the Army Order, adds another duty; the squadrons were

THE SECOND ARMY, NOVEMBER 10-20 123

to march by *Pithiviers* in order to reconnoitre in this direction and to the south, and at the same time conceal from the enemy the approach of the Army Corps; but v. d. Goltz says that this was not alluded to in the order. It is unfortunate that all the order or orders actually received by v. Manstein in connection with this march, and the sources whence they originated cannot be ascertained. The Cavalry Brigade had had very hard work in the March from Troyes, so v. Manstein did not despatch it to Montargis on the 17th, but delayed the new march until the 18th; and he left to the commander, Maj.-Gen. v. Rantzau, the selection of the route to be taken. The distance from Angerville to Montargis by the direct road through Pithiviers is a little over forty miles, so if no opposition were encountered on the march, it was quite practicable for the Brigade to arrive at Montargis on the 19th day named in the Army Orders. V. Rantzau selected, however, a road running north of Pithiviers, and after a march of some twenty miles, halted for the night at Puiseaux, at 2 P.M. On the following day he continued his march, not as ordered by Pithiviers, because the place was reported to be held by 2-3000 Gardes Mobiles, but right across the line of march of the IIIrd Army Corps on its way to Pithiviers, and he halted for the night eight miles short of the place at Préfontaine. The IIIrd Army Corps declining to comply with the request for support, the General on the 20th entered into negotiations with the Maire for the evacuation of the town; and not until noon on the following day, just before the arrival of the leading troops of the Xth Army Corps, did v. Rantzau enter the place. The 2500 Gardes Mobiles had laid down their arms and had dispersed to their homes, but the arms had been removed.

When the account of these proceedings reached the Prince his anger was great. His intention in sending this cavalry had been to hide the flank march of the IIIrd Army Corps by the cavalry moving between it and the enemy, though in the reverse direction, and also by active reconnaissance to obtain that most important information, namely, what was taking place on his exposed flank on the side of the enemy. And yet since neither General v. Manstein nor v. Rantzau regarded the march as anything but an ordinary route-march for the transfer of a force of cavalry, it would seem probable that the Head-quarters of the Army had not made clear its wishes to the corps commander. V. d. Goltz admits that it is doubtful whether, in the state of ferment among the population, this small body of cavalry could have made its way through by Pithiviers.

Of course, it had been only by degrees that the Prince came fully to realise the complete difference between the character of this war and of that which had terminated at Sedan. But the realisation was completed on the 20th, when, whilst shifting his Head-quarters from Puiseaux to Pithiviers, he bent away from the direct road between those places to ascertain personally for himself the character of the theatre of war into which his army was now moving, and also the attitude of the population in this "People's War." He recognised at once, fully, that the whole character of the war had altered; that it was not merely the hostile army that was his enemy, but the whole of the population also, and that from the physical nature of the country both these enemies would derive great assistance. During the ride, the farms and villages were found deserted; in the fields bodies of armed men were visible; bullets fell all round irregularly; prisoners, some of them priests with gloomy faces, bearing expressions of the deepest hatred, came before the Prince; the roads were in many places cut through and destroyed, the sign-posts carried away; and the bells of the churches signalled from church tower to church tower the march of the invaders. By this gloomy November picture the Prince was so deeply impressed that he repeatedly made remarks to those around him about the rising of the Spanish nation against Napoleon I. And the situation could hardly appear otherwise to him, for the French people were in an unmistakable state of frenzy; aloud and openly they declared in the towns that the Germans would be crushed on the Loire by the masses full of deep hatred, and that the decision was close at hand. And there were, indeed, unmistakable indications of a near decision; everything seemed to point to it. Moreover, on the 20th, the Prince had received from the Detachment, a report according to which there were in front of it only troops of the " Army of the West," and there were not there any of the Army of the Loire.

It was the combination of all these items of information from all the various sources mentioned, that led the Prince to telegraph from Pithiviers to v. Moltke at 7.15 P.M. on the 20th the following important message:

" Head-quarters and IIIrd Army Corps have arrived here; the advanced parties drove the enemy to-day out of Nancray and Beaune la Rolande. No news of the Xth Army Corps since the 17th, but no ground for anxiety; its arrival at Montargis is awaited. Our impression is that after the fight at Coulmiers none of the enemy moved away to the North West."

The Prince's message crossed a letter of the 20th from v. Moltke. " Whether he (the Grand Duke) now has in front of him in this direction the Army of the Loire, or this is at Chateaudun (report has just come in that the garrison of Chartres has been 'alarmed') or whether it is at Orleans, or is divided with the 16th Corps still at Orleans, and the 15th further west, is at the present time quite uncertain. From the IIIrd Army has just come in the following report: ' Columns of the enemy have advanced from Illiers and Bonneval (Chateaudun) in the night (19-20) and have compelled the 4th Division Cav. to fall back to the neighbourhood of Chartres. . . . Everywhere on an arc from Verneuil [well to the west of Dreux] round to Bonneval, the enemy, Line Troops and Gardes Mobiles, are encountered.'" The Royal Headquarters had further stated that the strength of the Army of the Loire amounted to 80-90,000 infantry, and that much had been done to augment its artillery."

CHAPTER VIII

THE GRAND DUKE'S DETACHMENT FROM
NOVEMBER 21ST TO 23RD

To return to the Detachment. On the 21st the advance was continued, and for a short distance on this day there was encountered determined resistance, the French, however, everywhere falling back. The view of the situation taken by the Grand Duke on the evening of the 21st, and the orders he issued for the 22nd seem thoroughly sound.

"The enemy, who has been met with on nearly all the roads during the advance to-day, was everywhere driven back, and he retired in the direction of Nogent le Retrou. Since the information from all quarters agree that at this place a defensive position has been prepared, it is to be concluded that the enemy has resolved to offer a determined resistance here. His Royal Highness the Grand Duke intends to attack the position." The plan of operations was to attack Nogent on the west side with the 22nd Infantry Division, and on the east side with the Bavarians. The 17th Infantry Division was sent towards Bellême, ten miles to the north-west of Nogent, to cut off the possible retreat in that direction; to the 6th Cavalry Division was entrusted the interception of the retreat south-west to le Mans. All the troops were to be in position to commence the attack at midday. On the 21st, however, there had occurred an incident, in no way peculiar to a "People's War," but an incident in the higher leading of Armies in the Field, and which merits careful consideration as illustrative of v. Moltke's use of "Directives" in the conduct of the leading in War.

On the 21st, the Grand Duke received from v. Moltke a telegram despatched from Versailles at 10.50 A.M. "Toury

THE GRAND DUKE'S DETACHMENT 127

has been occupied to-day by the IInd Army. Yesterday, the enemy was in its front, on the line Orgères-Artenay and south of Chilleurs aux Bois and Beaune la Rolande [a front of thirty-five miles]; the 4th Cavalry Division [the left Cav. Division of the Detachment] is to establish connection with the IInd Army, and to reconnoitre along the road Chartres-Chateaudun." It seems probable that the telegram of the 20th from the Prince, already given, was the reason for the despatch of this telegram; v. Moltke sent a similar telegram to the 4th Cav. Division also. These telegrams did not affect, in the slightest degree, the Grand Duke's view of the situation, or of the line of action he should adopt. He believed that the "Army of the West," in quest of which he had been with v. Moltke's full approval, was now close at hand, so close, that on the morrow he could deal it a decisive blow. To its destruction, v. Moltke had attached very great importance, and to stop short, just when the prize lay almost within grasp, would seem to be self-stultification. To turn away from it, except by the direct order of v. Moltke himself, would have been to ignore v. Moltke's own wishes and desires, and to help to disarrange his strategical plans. If v. Moltke had in any way altered his views as to the importance of dealing decisively with the "Army of the West," a few additional words in the telegram would have sufficed for the purpose.

But Hoenig takes a totally different view of this matter, and he is strong in his condemnation of the Grand Duke. Hoenig's views are, therefore, given here, not as those simply of a critic, but because from their publication in this semi-official work, it is very probable that they were held at Versailles.

"What impression," he asks, "must be produced on the Detachment? what could v. Moltke have intended by sending the telegram to both the 4th Cav. Division and the Detachment at the same time? Obviously, that at Versailles the situation was regarded in a different way than hitherto, and that there the question had already risen as to a change in the direction in the employment of the Detachment. This direction was here indicated to the Detachment by the mention of the fact, that on the previous day, the enemy was extended from Orgères to Beaune la Rolande: and that the Detachment might, at any moment, be ordered to move in this new direction, was at least probable from the 4th Cav. Division being ordered to connect with the IInd Army. The telegraph being employed for the communication must have given rise at the Detachment to the conviction that time was pressing. In short, this simple telegram of General v. Moltke was a weighty and clear stragetical indication, and had been sent by wire in order that the Detachment might, by proper preparations, be ready for other possibilities that might occur. It must be admitted," he continues, "that for the recognition of the importance of such an intimation, the penetration and intuition of a Leader far-seeing and of clear judgment were necessary. In the telegram the Detachment saw, however, only the order to carry out the duty of connecting with the IInd Army by means of the 4th Cavalry Division; the mere subsidiary mechanical side of it; but the rest of the contents in no way led to the consideration of operative measures, so General v. Moltke remained completely misunderstood. The Detachment held firmly to its view of continuing in the direction hitherto taken, and when entirely different important operations fell to it, it was not prepared for them, and, as will be shown, could not carry them out. The Leader, v. Moltke, could not on the other hand say, in his telegram of the 21st, more than he said; in it there is not a word too many, not a word too few; for, at present, it was essential to be sure whether strong hostile forces had come to Nogent le Rotrou. If this was not the case, then the Detachment must necessarily, to a certain extent, use its thinking power in the spirit of v. Moltke, and at least acknowledge that the military situation indicated a crisis. Then it was advisable to give attention to favorable operative conditions, and indeed in this case probably to the East, for to this direction attention was drawn; above all, *to halt*, to *remain stationary*, to watch the enemy only with cavalry, to advance no further to the south-west, and to wait; but, on the other hand, to think out and prepare all orders for a march off to the east. Only if a command that is far off thinks out matters in this way, and co-operates, can strategical intimations be reckoned on to produce the intended results. This telegram is one of this kind, and on account of its great importance, as well also as a type of the v. Moltke strategical intimations, it deserves this examination ; the more so, because the Detachment soon found itself in a most unfavourable operative situation owing to the telegram not having been understood." So far Hoenig.

But whatever view may be taken of the matter, it does seem remarkable, even on Hoenig's own showing, that as v. Moltke, and the Crown Prince, and Versailles generally, had already formed but a poor opinion of the Grand Duke as a commander and of Colonel v. Krenski as a Chief of the Staff, v. Moltke should have adopted in his communication so enigmatical a mode of expressing his views, a mode suitable enough to big minds like those of v. Manteuffel and v. Goeben, but quite beyond the comprehension of men like the Leaders of the Detachment. Here, the relying on the much-lauded "directive" system of command was a failure.

The truth is that it is doubtful whether during the whole of the Franco-German War there was a day of much greater anxiety at the Royal Head-quarters than this November 21st, 1870. On the evening of the 20th there had been sent from Prince Frederick Charles at Pithiviers the telegram already given. Very threatening was the situation as on the 21st it presented itself to v. Moltke. For the direct protection of the main road from Orleans a force of only two Army Corps (one fatigued by a long march) and two Cavalry Divisions; a third corps missing on the left; the force confronted by a hostile army which had had time not only to complete its preparations, but to be very strongly reinforced; to the south-west, moving farther away day by day from the road, the Detachment, and this might find in front of it the enemy in a strongly prepared position at Nogent, sixty miles away from the road; and he hears also that between the Detachment and the road from Orleans to Paris, the enemy is now advancing so as to separate the two German forces here in the field; whilst everywhere, on the front, flanks, and rear of the Detachment there are hostile troops. It is difficult to see why v. Moltke did not by telegraph give some advice and counsel to the Duke. It would seem as if he himself felt that he could not say what was the best thing to be done, and therefore resigned himself to letting matters take their course uninfluenced by him.

On the 22nd the Grand Duke moved to the attack of Nogent, and, contrary to expectation, the town, which had been one of the chief centres of the "Army of the West," a town in the heart of specially defensible country, was found already evacuated, a general retirement on le Mans having begun on the previous day; and the "Army of the West" disappears from the war just at the place where such an army might have offered strong resistance, just at the time when, to keep the advancing Detachment in the south-west would seem specially desirable. And that short-lived army, in its strength and its weaknesses, offers much subject for thought to those who believe in Home Defence really national in character. This army was composed mainly of civilians whose sole claim to be regarded as soldiers was their wearing a uniform or a distinctive badge and carrying a firearm of some sort in their hands. The younger men bore the title of Gardes Mobiles, and were those Gardes Mobiles for whom no place could be found in the larger organisations, the Army Corps; they formed small independent fighting bodies of men employed irrespective of the locality from which they had been drawn. The elder men bore the title of Gardes Nationales, and to these was, as a rule, entrusted the defence of the localities or districts in which they lived. Time had not permitted the bringing this organisation into thorough working order, and making the regulations that would have ensured the greatest amount of result being obtained from its action in the field. There

THE GRAND DUKE'S DETACHMENT 131

was little cohesion, little combination in the work. But considering the short time that those in this Army had been assisting in the defence of the country, they had carried out admirably and excellently the work of forming a screen, raising a dense Fog of War around the invading army, the only work of war for which such an army is fitted. It was this army that led v. Moltke to carry out strategical operations worse than unsuited to the military situation; it was this army that had helped so greatly in luring 50,000 men and 200 guns away from the Loire, where their presence would have been invaluable, to this district whence no danger threatened; in giving to the Loire Army yet more time for uninterrupted preparations for the field; and in drawing the Detachment so far away from the decisive point, that when the real conflict ensued, and the decisive struggle took place, the fate of the weak force of the Germans hung for hours in the balance; and that the balance did not turn against them was due, not to their wisdom, but to the hopelessly bad leading of their opponents. No wonder that v. Moltke detested unprofessional soldiers, patriotic citizens in uniform and out of uniform. But for acting as anything but a screen, the "Army of the West," as must be all " people in arms," was powerless; for as soon as a " People's Army " encounters on the field of battle a trained army, its fate is sealed. And that a " People's Army " may give its value to the full as a screen in war, most careful organisation and preparation in peace is an absolutely necessary condition. So clearly had the powerlessness of the " Army of the West" in battle shown itself since the 17th, that the authorities at Tours determined, since in it were many fighting men, no longer to sacrifice them uselessly; so, on the 21st, was begun a general retreat to le Mans, where the 21st Corps was in course of organisation, and into which the remnants of the "Army of the West" were to be incorporated. So it had happened that the Grand Duke had to suffer a second time the mortification of dealing a blow *en l'air*, even less hurtful to the enemy than that he had delivered at Dreux.

But although disappointed by having been lured to Nogent by a mirage only, the Grand Duke did not lose heart; for a third time did the decisive point seem to beckon him on; this time it was le Mans, only thirty-five miles distant, a place so important that its abandonment by the enemy without a fight was impossible, and to it the road now lay open; so onwards without delay; he at once pushed forward a Bavarian brigade twelve miles to la Ferté Bernard. At night the Detachment was somewhat scattered, the main body of the Bavarians and the 22nd Inf. Division being in Nogent and the neighbourhood, the 17th Inf. Division ten miles to the west at Bellême. The 6th Cav. Division was at Authon, ten miles east of La Ferté Bernard; the 4th Cav. Division was at least twenty miles east of Nogent, at Illiers and the neighbourhood. Le Mans is nearly eighty miles from Orleans. Truly v. Moltke's intimation had been completely ignored. But there was much to justify the Grand Duke in his independent action, for early in the morning he had received a communication which must have fully confirmed him in the belief that his strategy was correct. At 7 A.M. had come a letter from Prince Frederick Charles, which had been despatched from Pithiviers 3.30 the previous afternoon, the 21st.

"I beg to inform your Royal Highness that the Second Army is with the IXth Army Corps at Angerville, and with the IIIrd Army Corps, and my Head-quarters at Pithiviers; the 1st and 2nd Cavalry Divisions are in touch with the enemy, whose outposts extend from north of Artenay to Chilleurs aux Bois." [This situation certainly does not correspond with that given in v. Moltke's telegram.] "The enemy opposite to us is, according to our impression derived from all the reports received, the entire Army of the Loire. I am awaiting before attacking it the arrival of the Xth Army Corps, of which, by forced marches, the leading troops arrive to-day at Montargis. I hope to attack the enemy in four or five days, and eventually to drive him to the south-west. I suggest to your Royal Highness to co-operate in this purpose by an advance by le Mans on Tours, if the instructions from the Head-

THE GRAND DUKE'S DETACHMENT 133

quarters of his Majesty the King do not require something else."

To this the Grand Duke replied by wire:
"Co-operation in the direction of le Mans, with the projected further advance on Tours, already prepared for by my departure from the Paris-Orleans road. Advance to-day for concentrated attack on Nogent le Rotrou; 4th Cavalry Division remains on the Chartres-Chateaudun road, and is ordered to obtain connection with Stolberg's Division, as ought already yesterday to have been effected." The Third Army received on the evening of the 22nd, by wire, the report from the Grand Duke of his movements for the morrow.

The Grand Duke had fair cause for believing that he had adopted the course of action best suited to the situation. The Royal Head-quarters had informed him that the enemy was in front of the Prince; and by the Prince, who was on the spot, he had been told how best to help him, so the only course to be taken was to comply with his request. But on the 22nd, there came to hand from v. Blumenthal a letter of the same date as that of Prince Frederick Charles, and suggesting a totally opposite course of action.

"For some days I have wished to write to your Royal Highness to offer suggestions as regards the general situation as it appears to us here; but our information is so indefinite, that I have always been afraid of saying something that was incorrect. And even now things are so little clear, that I must restrict my remarks to the following matters. As you will have learnt from the telegram of General v. Moltke, the Army of the Loire, apparently the 15th and 16th Army Corps, was yesterday on the line Orgères-Artenay, opposite General v. Manstein. He was to-day to have advanced under Prince Frederick Charles with the IIIrd Army Corps against Orleans. But it appears as if the Xth Army Corps is still too far away, and, therefore, Prince Frederick Charles will delay for some days making the attack. For your Royal Highness this is inconvenient, because under these circumstances, your line of communication can be threatened through Chartres; but it is to be hoped that the 4th Cav. Division, if rightly handled, will warn you in time so that you will not be taken by surprise. Meantime you may also have in front of you more perhaps than there appears to be. Nogent le Rotrou and also le Mans are said to be fortified, and, as you will see from the newspaper cutting sent herewith, the Army of Brittany, perhaps now 50,000 men, is said to be in an entrenched camp at Conlie (apparently fourteen to nineteen miles north-west of le Mans).

"I think, therefore, that it would be desirable not to advance too quickly on le Mans, but rather to defer the attack for a few days, till you know with certainty about the advance of Prince Frederick Charles.

"His Royal Highness has authorised me to send this letter, and desires to add only, that General v. Rheinbaben may be obliged to advance further towards Evreux, unless the movements of the Army of the Loire compel us to keep him more within reach for the protection of Chartres and the whole line of communication."

And now what a very strange situation has arisen. It was the Crown Prince that was the Grand Duke's superior commander; the Detachment was part of the Third Army, and with any portion of that Army no one but v. Moltke had the slightest right to interfere; yet here we find the commander of another army, Prince Frederick Charles, sending direct to a subordinate commander of the Third Army his wishes as to the line of action he should take, instead of first asking the Commander supreme over both for permission for the co-operation. How was it possible for the King of Prussia to regulate a campaign in which the commander of one of his armies deliberately and independently interfered directly in the operations of another of his armies? And, as a matter of fact, the result of this interference was to disarrange the plan of campaign of the Royal Head-quarters. Again does Hoenig find fault with the Grand Duke for acting in conformity with the Prince's wishes and against the advice

THE GRAND DUKE'S DETACHMENT 135

received from Versailles, but the Grand Duke would have been more than human had he not done so. Moreover, an attack on le Mans must create a panic among the delegation at Tours, who, for their own safety, must at once bring from the Army in front of Prince Frederick Charles strong detachments, and the attack would thus give to the Prince the aid specially asked for by him. In the communications from v. Moltke, the Prince and v. Blumenthal, there was a discrepancy on one very important matter. V. Moltke said that the front of the hostile force extended from Orgères as far east as Beaune-la-Rolande. The Prince gave as the front only the centre third of this line, Chilleurs aux Bois to Artenay; v. Blumenthal gave the western third, Artenay to Orgères; and as the Prince reported from the spot it would be probable that his statement was correct. In this case, the left wing of the Second Army had nothing in front of it, and would be free to attack effectively the Army of the Loire, diminished by the detachments sent in haste to le Mans. Neither the tone nor the contents of v. Blumenthal's letter was calculated to make much impression on a Commander, who had shown that he could take the bit between his teeth if he chose to do so. It had an uncertain sound, was hesitating and painfully apologetic. It was hardly a communication, still less an order, from his commander the Crown Prince, for he had simply approved of it. It seemed to be the expression of opinion of a Staff Officer, of very high degree it is true, but an expression of personal opinion only. And this Staff Officer showed how he misjudged the situation because there was not more, but far less, in front of the Grand Duke than had been anticipated. Nogent was, as v. Blumenthal stated, fortified; but as the fortifications were found destitute of defenders, they were not of a sort to stop an advance. So also the Army of Brittany and the fortifications at le Mans might prove to be of similarly little value. Then, as regards the danger to the line of communications, the anxiety for these was altogether a new feature in the campaign. Gravelotte, Sedan, the advance on Paris, the instructions to v. d. Tann to advance on Bourges and Tours, the despatch of the Second Army to the South of France, all were remarkable in their disregard of lines of communication; but now, suddenly, Versailles appears to be getting nervous on the matter. The Grand Duke had, it is true, asked for a rest-day for the 23rd, but with the fresh prospect of successful operations immediately before him he abandoned the idea; he naturally ignored v. Blumenthal's weakly-framed counsel, and on the 22nd he issued orders that on the 23rd the Detachment should continue the advance on le Mans, but in such a way as to prevent the enemy being able clearly to see the purpose of the movement. The Bavarians were to move forward to la Ferté Bernard on the main road to le Mans; the 17th Infantry Division to St. Cosme ten miles to the right of la Ferté, sending a detachment to Mamers, twenty miles from Nogent on the road to Alençon, to threaten that place, and to draw the attention of the enemy to the north away from le Mans; the 22nd Infantry Division to move to Bellême. The 6th Cavalry Division to go down to the left front to Vibraye, seven or eight miles from the le Mans road. The 4th Cavalry Division was to keep a sharp look-out to the Loir, and destroy the railroad from Bonneval by Châteaudun to Tours; this was the line of advance by which the line of communications was directly threatened. The orders necessarily led to the wide dissemination of the Detachment, which was no longer one single manageable unit, and they placed the bulk of it still further from the scene of operations, the Loire at Orleans. where both v. Moltke and v. Blumenthal anticipated it would be wanted.

On the 23rd the Detachment commenced its march on le Mans, and the Grand Duke, when on the road south of Nogent received, at eleven o'clock, a telegram from v. Blumenthal, dated 9.45 the previous evening, and despatched before the Third Army was aware of the intended advance. It ran as follows: "By order of the King, the pursuit of the enemy toward le Mans is to be carried on by some infantry and

THE GRAND DUKE'S DETACHMENT 137

cavalry only. The Detachment will march forthwith in the direction of Beaugency [on the Loire fifteen miles below Orleans, and between fifty and sixty from La Ferté], where it must arrive on the 25th or 26th. Further particulars will be sent by letter."

It is apparent that, somehow or other, telegrams from Versailles to the Detachment went far more slowly than those going in the opposite direction ; and it would seem that the measures taken at the Detachment for forwarding these messages from the telegraph office were hardly satisfactory. Whether this was intentional or not is difficult to say. The Grand Duke was not more than an hour's gallop from the telegraph office when he received the order, so the delay is inexplicable.

The Grand Duke replied at once to the telegram : " At the conclusion of to-day's march, which cannot be stopped, the Detachment will be between Vibraye, La Ferté Bernard, St. Cosme, Mamers, Bellême. From this position concentration on the line Chateaudun-Vendôme will be the easiest. For this, three days march necessary. All the commanders are desirous of a rest-day. I ask this for to-morrow, because this will be most convenient to the troops, and the direction will also remain concealed."

Meantime, there was at Versailles great anxiety, owing to the non-receipt of any answer from the Grand Duke, so as at 9.21 in the morning there had been no reply, v. Blumenthal again telegraphed : " Has the Detachment moved off towards Beaugency ? " This telegram was also delayed in transmission ; the Grand Duke replied : " Query of 9.20 from Versailles sent on from Nogent to Le Theil just received. The march on Beaugency could not be carried out, because when the telegram came to hand the troops had been on the march for three hours. Order that no rest-day can be given just received." This latter sentence referred to another telegram of 11.20 A.M. from v. Blumenthal : " By order of his Majesty no rest-day can be granted. The march must go on tomorrow, much depends on it."

And here again, for a time, we must leave the Grand Duke, at the conclusion of a series of operations yielding nothing but disappointment to him as the independent commander of as good and effective a force of 50,000 men as ever were put into the field; and we must go to both Pithiviers and Versailles, and we shall then ascertain the reason for the order to march to Beaugency.

CHAPTER IX

THE SECOND ARMY, FROM NOVEMBER 21ST TO 23RD

DURING the night 20th-21st more confirmatory reports came in from the front to the Prince, who now saw that the task before him, which on the 16th had appeared to be so easy, was something very different from what he had anticipated; and he therefore determined to delay the contemplated convergent attack on Orleans for a few days until the three Brigades of the Xth Army Corps should have rejoined the Army. At midday on the 21st v. Stiehle communicated this resolve to v. Moltke in a letter, in which he embodied the information obtained. In the letter he also said: " The great length of the enemy's outpost line is only possible from the wild excitement of the population since the recapture of Orleans. From every place even not occupied by troops, fire opens on the approach of our troops. If we send strong detachments the enemy falls back to the next place and repeats the same game. This is facilitated by the close cultivation. . . . These circumstances taken together have produced in us the conviction that large hostile forces are south of Artenay, on the Paris-Orleans road (16th Corps), and four and three-quarter miles east at St. Lyé, on the Roman road to Orleans (15th Corps). For the present, in view of the presumable strength of the enemy, it would be unwise, before the Xth Army Corps has joined the Second Army, to appeal to a decision of arms, which will influence the whole course of affairs in France. Gen. v. V. Rhetz arrives to-day at Montargis with the head of the corps. But his closing on the left wing of the army, as will be necessary for the fight will, under the most favorable circumstances, require three to four days, because his troops, during their forced marches, have been constantly in fight with the insurgents, and have had no halt-day. . . . In the last report from Gen. v. V. Rhetz from Joigny, which is of the morning of the 19th, he states that his three Infantry Brigades number 12,000 rifles. . . . His Royal Highness hopes to be able to carry out the attack with concentrated forces on the 26th inst., and proposes to drive the enemy towards Tours. Should H.R.H. the Grand Duke advance successfully towards le Mans, our operations would work very well together. Up to that time the Second Army, by concentrating here, and by daily reconnaissances of the enemy, will carry out the duty assigned to it, 'the protection of the road from Orleans to Paris.'" With the letter the Prince sent some addenda, some correct, some incorrect, to the Ordre de Bataille, the German staff were endeavouring to construct as regards the Army of the Loire.

The Prince, in his order of the 16th to the Xth Army Corps directing it on Montargis, had said that it was possible that all three corps might be required for the convergent attack on Orleans, but that it was more probable that, on the arrival of the corps, this would be unnecessary, and the corps would be given the direction of Bourges by Gien. " Reaching this point is of the greatest military importance. It cannot be foreseen whether the corps will meet with any serious opposition in this direction ; but, presumably, even before Gen. v. Kraatz's detachment joins the corps, this, especially owing to its numerous artillery, will be able successfully to deal with much larger hostile forces. It must be left until the 20th, whether the Xth Army Corps goes towards Bourges, and I reserve to myself the details. Meantime I now request Your Excellency to be so good as to communicate to me your opinion on the operation mentioned."

It is not certain whether the answer from v. Voigts Rhetz to this request was received before or after the Prince came to the decision to defer the attack until the 26th, but in either case the answer was conclusive as regards the proposed march on Bourges : the General wrote as follows :

"At the present moment, owing to the absence of all information, I am unable to give a decided opinion as regards an operation against Bourges. I must confine myself therefore to considering the strength I shall have with me available for the purpose." The General then states that he will have to leave behind him to hold certain points and also as escorts to the trains, detachments which will have reduced the corps on its arrival at Gien to fifteen battalions, some sixty guns and ten to twelve squadrons. "It is very probable that with this force I could capture Gien and cross to the left bank if the bridge is not destroyed. But I must take special care, as I have no pontoon train with me, to keep hold of Gien and its bridge whilst I advance beyond. In Gien, therefore, I shall have to leave some three battalions (1500 to 1800 men), and two batteries even if I have the aid of entrenchments. Even if it should be not necessary to leave another detachment at, perhaps, Aubigny, I should have with me, on my arrival at Bourges, some twelve battalions, some 7000 to 8000 rifles and fifty guns. Whether this force would be sufficient, I cannot tell, as I do not know in what strength the enemy is there, or whether the reports which I have read in the newspapers are correct, that Bourges has been put in a state of defence.

"If it had not been necessary to send the Xth Army Corps to Montargis, it would seem to me to have been desirable preparatory to an expedition to Bourges first to clear out Auxerre, and this, as I believe, would have had the effect of quieting the population on my line of march, and then of enabling me to choose a crossing point somewhat higher up the Loire. Gien lies nearer to Orleans which is occupied by the enemy than to Bourges which I shall have to reach."

On the 21st had come to the Prince from the 4th Cav. Division an officer who informed him of the advance of the Grand Duke on Nogent le Rotrou where, according to rumour, it was anticipated the enemy was; and that the enemy who had been in very large force at Dreux had been broken up by the victorious encounter of the 17th Inf. Division with territorial troops. The officer then gave the details of the intended operation. Hence the despatch to the Grand Duke of the communication already given, asking him to continue his advance on le Mans.

The telegram of the 20th from the Prince to v. Moltke, was undoubtedly so brief, that v. Moltke may, perhaps, have regarded it merely as the expression of the personal views of a commander, to whose opinion he did not attach any great weight; but the letter of the 21st which was received on the 22nd must have been conclusive. If, however, any doubt remained, as to the gravity of the situation on the Loire, it must have finally been dissipated by the receipt that day of a despatch from General v. Werder in the south-east stating, that according to reports received, " Michel's Corps had gone on the 16th and 17th in a westerly direction from Autun" near Châlons sur Soane and on the railway line to Gien, Orleans, and Bourges.

On the 21st there had been much anxiety at Versailles with regard to the action of the Grand Duke; strong forces were believed to be in front of him, and the further advance appeared to involve great risk to the line of communications, especially as the 4th Cav. Division on the left flank was not able to hold its own against some hostile force which was pressing forward north, whilst the Detachment moved south-west; and it was believed that v. Blumenthal's recommendation would be regarded by the Grand Duke as an order. There is not in Prince Frederick Charles' letter, as given in Hoenig's words, and which was despatched at midday, any indication that he was going to communicate his wishes to the Grand Duke, as he did at 3.30 P.M., and it does not appear that the Grand Duke cared to be over-communicative to the Third Army; in this, as we have seen, v. Blumenthal regarded him as wise. Had the Prince's message been known to Versailles, its effect on the Grand Duke could have been counteracted; but where two commanders at a distance co-operate with each other and keep

THE SECOND ARMY, NOVEMBER 21-23

their counsel to themselves, the supreme authority is more or less helpless. Without honest, cordial, and thorough co-operation, combined movements in war have little chance of success. At Versailles, it was thought that the only hostile army corps, needing to be dealt with, were the 15th and 16th. They had heard of the 17th, 18th, and the 21st, but where they were and the degree of organisation arrived at by them, was not known. Of the 20th even less had been heard. The Prince's letter of the 21st made, on its receipt, a great impression at Versailles, intensified by the news from v. Werder. It was not known that the Grand Duke had obtained possession of Nogent, but this success, and even a march on to le Mans, v. Moltke could not regard as counter-balancing the danger that must arise for the Second Army if, whilst the enemy opposite the latter was receiving strong reinforcements from the east, the Detachment should be marching away south-west, and be rendering itself every mile more and more useless to the Second Army, as an aid against the increase of hostile strength. Hence the audience with the king, and the peremptory order to give up the march on le Mans and move on Beaugency. At once had been realised the imminent danger in which the Second Army was. With a greatly numerically superior enemy in front and in touch with it, it was extended over a front of forty miles, from Angerville to Montargis, with one of its corps fatigued by long and trying marches, and only the head yet at Montargis, the Detachment sixty miles to the westward and intending to go still further away.

But, unfortunately, v. Moltke and the Prince differed in their views as to the measures to be adopted to minimise the danger. The Prince wished for such a demonstration to the south-west as would force the enemy to send away part of his army to protect Tours, the seat of the government of the Provinces ; v. Moltke determined that a blow should be struck against the left flank of the enemy in his present position by the seizure of a point on the Loire, whence co-operating attacks could be made, either up the right bank against the position, or with a portion of the force on the left bank against the enemy's communications with Tours and the rest of France. This difference in views was fundamental as regards the future strategy of the campaign.

On the 22nd the IXth Army Corps advanced down the Orleans Road as far as Toury; and at Montargis the three brigades of the Xth Army Corps completed their concentration. During the day the Prince received information leading him to believe in a westward movement of the enemy. From the Detachment came the report that the Grand Duke had obtained possession of Nogent and would continue his advance on le Mans the following day. From Versailles came at 10 at night the news of the despatch of Michel's corps from the east to the Loire. The actual situation on the French side was therefore anything but clear.

On the 23rd the 38th Brigade, v. Wedell, the leading brigade of the Xth Army Corps, marched from Montargis to Beaune-la-Rolande and the Prince himself reconnoitred, from Pithiviers to the westward; but the information as to a westward movement of the French was conflicting. A report of the 22nd, received this day, stated that on the 22nd there were 30,000 men in Gien. The Prince determined to remain on the defensive until the arrival of the Detachment, and he communicated to Versailles at midday his intention. Inhabitants reported during the day that troops were marching north from Gien, and it was also asserted that on the 21st General d'Aurelle had his Head-quarters in Gien. The Royal Head-quarters informed the Prince that the attack on Orleans by the Detachment could not be expected before the 28th.

It may be remembered that in the telegram 9.45 P.M. of the 22nd from the Third Army to the Grand Duke, ordering the march on Beaugency, it was stated that a letter would follow. The letter was one from the Royal Head-quarters to those of the Third Army, and it appears from v. Blumenthal's diary, that to the Third Army was left the mode of communicating its contents to the Grand Duke. V. Blumenthal says he received the order at 9 P.M. and he adds: "The order will have to be telegraphed to-night." In the letter, which arrived at the Detachment on the 23rd we read: " It has become probable that the whole of the army of the Loire is opposite F.M. H.R.H. Prince Frederick Charles and is in an entrenched position. The Prince cannot concentrate until the 25th his three Army Corps for an attack on the following day. According to information received, reinforcements have come by railway to the Loire from Autun. Under these circumstances, co-operation of the Detachment of H.R.H. the Grand Duke of Mecklenburg appears to be necessary. As no decisive defeat of the French Army of the West has taken place at Nogent le Rotrou, the pursuit in the direction of le Mans is to be only by cavalry with small detachments of infantry, and His Majesty orders that the Grand Duke with all the remainder of his troops shall at once march in the direction of the Loire. The Detachment will be able to arrive at Orleans or Blois on the day above-named, the 26th, or a little later. For a simultaneous attack, eventually on the left bank of the Loire, the necessary arrangements must be made with the Command of the Second Army. It is desirable, moreover, that the advance shall by surprise gain possession of one of the permanent river-crossings over the Loire; if this does not happen, then the materials lacking for a field bridge must be obtained from the Second Army." In a short addendum to the letter v. Blumenthal remarked: " It would be of great importance if one of the bridges over the Loire at Beaugency or Blois could be captured and kept intact for the operations."

A comparison of the telegram and the letter shows that it was the Third Army and not v. Moltke that definitely determined the exact point on the Loire to which the Grand Duke should direct his march. Hoenig points out also the loss of time arising from its being necessary for the Royal Head-quarters to communicate with the Detachment, not directly, but through the Head-quarters of the Third Army.

It will be desirable, having before us the views of the German Leaders as to the state of affairs on the French side

K

and the basis, therefore, of their plans of operations against the French, to go over to the hostile army, and see how matters really stand there, and what has taken place since the mysterious disappearance of the Army of the Loire on November 12th; but before doing so, as it is Orleans and the vicinity that is to be the scene of the coming decisive struggle, a description of this small theatre of war is necessary, the more so because without a knowledge of its peculiarities we should hardly understand the reluctance of the Prince to take the offensive; nor should we realise how much in this tract of country so admirably suited for defence by inferior troops, the eventual defeat of the French was due to bad leading.

The great Forest of Orleans extends north of the city and on both sides of the Orleans-Paris Road, from Rosieres nine miles to the west, to Gien thirty-five miles to the east; and although not of the same character throughout its extent, yet, generally, it gave cover, so that the Germans were not able to ascertain what was going on within it. The northern edge on the east side ran from five to eight miles south of the position of the Second Army; the southern edge was about three miles from the Loire. Chevilly, eight miles from Orleans, was its northern boundary on the Paris road. On the west side the northern edge lies some three miles farther south, and this portion of the forest consists of separate woods, between which large bodies of all arms can move without difficulty. The woods had been connected by entrenchments, but, from the west and north-west, the ground in front and in rear could be seen, a great advantage to the attack. The real forest extends for a length of twenty miles, and a depth of twelve to thirteen miles on the east side of the Paris road to the Canal d'Orleans, which connects the Loire with the Loing at Montargis. The forest consists of timber trees, with low undergrowth, passable only with some difficulty by infantry in extended order, and rarely in close formation. Artillery could move only on the roads, cavalry only in single file through the wood. The forest was not all of this character; but for

THE SECOND ARMY, NOVEMBER 21-23   147

the Germans it presented a belt of this kind four or five miles broad. The roads giving access to the forest east of the Paris road were : the old Roman road from Etampes passing to the west of St. Germain-le-Grand and Neuville aux Bois, and entering the forest at St. Lyé five miles from the road, and thence to Orleans. The next road comes from Pithiviers, and at eight miles from that place enters the forest at Chilleurs aux Bois five miles to the east, and then running south-west by Loury five miles inside the forest, strikes a road along the bank of the Loire, a mile from Orleans. Near Loury were two large clearings, one on either side of the road ; the third road, coming also from Pithiviers, enters the forest four miles further east at Courcy aux Loges, and bending southwest crosses the Canal, recrossing at Pont aux Moines, where it enters the river road six miles from Orleans. At Fay aux Loges, four and a half miles short of the re-crossing, a branch diverges due south to Jargeau on the Loire, three and a-half miles east of Pont aux Moines. The next point of entry is Chambon, three and a-half miles east by a road running into the third road at three miles south of Courcy aux Loges. There are other roads further east striking the river road, at Chateauneuf, fifteen miles, Sully, twenty miles from Orleans, and at Gien. Lateral communications were few ; all the roads could easily be obstructed and defended. The edge of the forest had been prepared for defence. The whole area east of the Paris road teems with hamlets, farm houses and defensible localities. As regards the entrenchments, a bridge head had been constructed at from half a mile to a mile outside the city walls. About two miles beyond was a sort of intermediate entrenched position with the right flank on the river at St. Loup ; the left at le Grand Orme, on the Chateaudun road. The main position ran along the edge of the forest east of the Paris road ; on the west side it was retired three miles in rear of Chevilly to Cercottes, running thence west to the Chateaudun road eight miles from Orleans. Besides these positions, a strongly entrenched line of localities gave an advanced position. There were plenty of heavy guns in the batteries. Of these entrenchments the Germans knew very little.

It is desirable to give here the impression the country made on the minds of the Staff of the Second Army, as recorded by v. d. Goltz. North of the Forest of Orleans lies a very fruitful level tract of country, offering a wide and apparently a complete view. But between this and the great forest, which consists of large and mostly young timber close together, lies a zone of country with much on its surface, and into which it is impossible to obtain a view. Villages, châteaux, farms, parks, orchards, and vineyards form here a sort of labyrinth which offers a striking contrast to this district of la Beauce close to it. To the east this zone becomes less penetrable to view, and towards Montargis, where, owing to the country being hilly, the difficulty is consequently far greater, the edge of the forest changes into copses, brushwood, gardens, and numerous isolated farms, so that here the limit of the forest can hardly be detected.

La Beauce has also its peculiarities, which must be borne in mind with regard to the military operations. The soil is everywhere rich and soft. In wet weather it soon becomes impassable, vehicles and horses can move only on the roads, and except with great difficulty, only on the Chaussées. But from Orleans to Chartres the soil is better and more gravelly; and the conditions are more favourable. But the impression that this country can be completely seen into is deceptive. The isolated villages lying in the wide fields are certainly visible for great distances. They have neither wood nor gardens near them, and the observer is under the impression that he completely overlooks the intervening ground between the villages; but such is not the case. Everywhere are peculiar depressions, which escape notice from a distance. They are not marked by sharp boundaries, nor by any particular kind of cultivation, and they are, as a rule, not more than eight to ten feet deep. Yet troops camping here completely escape observation, and in the depressions whole divisions can be collected unknown to the enemy, who on the

THE SECOND ARMY, NOVEMBER 21-23

open level ground, on which are the villages and the roads, sees opposite to him a chain of outposts but no masses of troops. This is, of course, to a certain extent an advantage to the attacker, as all his troops can be concentrated unnoticed. . . . On the other hand there are many circumstances which invite the selection of the defensive. By careful choice of artillery positions on the higher ground there can be obtained good and open ranges for guns. If the ground was firm, the numerous cavalry of the Second Army found favourable opportunities for attack against the badly commanded and loosely connected masses of the Army of the Loire. If the ground was heavy through rain, the army could only advance slowly and with difficulty to the attack, and was much hampered in bringing its artillery into action. All these advantages are to the benefit of the Army of the Loire further south towards Orleans, if the Second Army attacks him there; in fact, with every step towards the Loire the attack becomes more difficult.

The student of military history who endeavours to follow the course of the war, and to view it impartially from both standpoints, the French as well as the German, at once encounters great difficulties the moment he changes his position from the latter to the former. In the German Army, the recording on the spot all incidents of a campaign or battle, as these occurred, was a part of the ordinary duty of both staff and regimental officers, and the records were carefully preserved for future reference. Very many officers also kept private diaries, or noted down, from time to time, their own personal experiences. So the German materials for a history of the Franco-German War are well nigh inexhaustible. It has been, hitherto, merely a question of expediency, as to how far these materials should be utilised for publication. But on the French side the case is altogether different. Record keeping was one of the last military requirements which would occur to the officers of any army in course of very hasty formation, and where the stress and extreme urgency of other practical work would lead them to dispense with pen or pencil so far as possible. Moreover, this Army of the Loire was never, save at the outset, on the side of success. It was always striving under the adverse circumstances of defeat and disaster. It was the present, not the future, that occupied the minds and thoughts of the French officers ; of little importance, therefore, seemed the noting down of times and places for some possible reference hereafter. It was not to the memorandum book, but simply to the memory, that were committed the details of action, the conduct of individuals, the movements of troops, the words and the expressed wishes, intentions and opinions of actors in the drama. Moreover, it is notorious that the French temperament does not lend itself to a judicial description of any events of which the surroundings are those of excitement and emotion. Then, again, there is the loss of records that ensues when defeat and disorder occur. So the French records of this war are incomplete and frequently contradictory. Many were destroyed in the time of the Commune. Of one French historian of the campaign, whose style is very sensational and dramatic, it has been said, " If you already know what really took place, read him, for you will be able to distinguish the truth from the imaginary and the former is valuable ; if you do not know what actually happened leave him on one side, for you will mix up the one with the other." Hoenig goes very fully into this matter in the preface to his fifth volume. He has examined and compared the various sources of information, probably more closely and carefully than any one else, and he states that even that gigantic official work, " Les Actes du Gouvernment de la Defense National," teems with misstatements, and the works written by the chief French actors in the war, de Freycinet, d'Aurelle, Chanzy, Crouzat, and others are full of contradictions. There is no doubt also that the non-employment of pen and pencil at important conferences or interviews led to misunderstanding of views and intentions, to misinterpretations of orders and of wishes, and therefore to disastrous results. There is, however, no difficulty in following the movements of the larger bodies of troops such as brigades, etc ; the accounting for the movements and fixing the responsibility for them is, however, for the reasons given, not always possible. It is mainly the statements of Hoenig and Lehautcourt, a French writer, that will be accepted in this narrative.

After the fight at Coulmiers, the troops remained on the ground north of Orleans, and not a moment had been lost by Gambetta in organising into manageable military bodies the huge crowd of men who, moved by the spirit he had awakened in them, came flocking to the standards of France in obedience to his summons. For the 16th Corps a third division was organised. The formation of the 17th Corps was commenced at Mer and Blois, below Orleans; that of the 18th Corps at Nevers and Gien above Orleans; and that of the 21st Corps a little later at le Mans; whilst on November 15th or 16th, some 40,000 men of the Army of the East were taken to form the 20th Corps and to complete the 18th Corps. The troops were brought from Chagny to Gien by rail on the 18th and 19th. Of course it was the earlier formations that had secured the better trained men, and to them had been posted the officers remaining available after the catastrophes of the first war; so that for the later formations there were but few well-trained men or efficient officers. The military value of the corps diminished in the order of their formation; the 15th was an excellent corps, and numerically nearly double that of an ordinary army corps; the 16th nearly equalled it in efficiency, but the others were indifferent. The larger a force in the field, the more essential it is that the staff should be both competent and experienced; but it was impossible to find for the large Army of the Loire the number of qualified officers for the provision of the correspondingly large and numerous staffs. Large masses of men collected for fighting purposes are of no use standing still. They have to move from one place to another, and whilst on the move, the supply of food and ammunition must be provided for, and the mode in which they are moved, and the provision for the supply, falls to the Staff Officers. The mechanism of the movements of troops in large bodies, the amount of supplies required for them, and the mechanism of securing the conveyance and the distribution of these supplies, do not enter into the professional knowledge of the regimental officer. It is sometimes said that a smart adjutant makes the best Staff Officer; this may be to a great extent true, but the best adjutant in an army will be an incompetent Staff Officer until he has learnt what staff work is, and has mastered its working. Not the least influential factor in securing the success of the German Army in the campaign of 1870-71 was the immeasurable superiority of its staff over that of the French Army.

Captain Aube, a naval officer who commanded the 1st brigade of the 2nd division of the 20th corps, has given in the *Revue des Deux Mondes*, a very interesting account of the corps; its General, Crouzat, in a small pamphlet, also has given his view of his command.

The corps was for the most part composed of Gardes Mobiles drawn from various parts of France—the Upper Loire, Jura, Garonne, Eastern Pyrénées, Upper Rhine, Vosges, Meurthe, and Corsica.

In the Gardes Mobiles and the Franc-tireurs there were many officers and even in the ranks men belonging to the highest classes of society, some bearing the greatest names in France, who had left behind them everything—fortune, comfort, families, young wives, little children—to hasten to the defence of their country. They were brave fellows, facing cheerfully all the discomforts, all the dangers of war, always ready for any sacrifice, and deeply loving their country. The corps was brave, disciplined, and patriotic. Officers and soldiers had the simple and one idea—duty. The cadres, especially in the lower grades, were very insufficient, and in the Gardes Mobiles had not had time to learn their work. It was this failure of cadres of companies, indispensable for leading and for controlling young soldiers under fire, that was the chief cause of their reverses.

The corps had all the good qualities, and all the faults, of young, intelligent troops, often full of ardour, but without any

THE SECOND ARMY, NOVEMBER 21-23

experience. The Mobiles invariably obeyed orders, and endured uncomplainingly the fatigues of incessant marching; their patient forgetfulness of self, their devotion, were always equal to the numberless privations they had to endure; but, whilst obeying, they reasoned, asked the why and the wherefore, and discussed the orders given, all the more, because the authority which issued them did not, in the eyes of either the men or the officers, possess the sanction of experience nor the prestige of rank long possessed. Had not this General, who commanded a division, been only a non-commissioned officer and become a General, from having served his apprenticeship for command in the ranks of the Southerners in America? Another was only a captain when the war commenced, or before that, perhaps, in the ranks of the army, where they had known him. That these improvised Generals were fit for their new position by their bravery and patriotism was not the question. Were they, by their knowledge of their profession, equal to the command given them?

Of the staff of the corps there were only two that belonged, or had belonged, to the staff of the regular army. Nearly all the others had been taken from a daring band of young men known as *les Quarante*, who had made an unsuccessful attempt to blow up the bridge at Saverne. Some of the newly-made Generals were conspicuous by their numerous escorts, and the eagerness with which their aides-de-camp got hold of, for their Head-quarters, châteaux and farms, which could have served as cantonments for a whole battalion, the army being obliged to bivouac often without shelter, straw or wood in the snow and mud. The physical privations the corps had already endured in the Vosges were very great; some of the men had no shoes; very few possessed gaiters, cartridge-boxes, knapsacks, or camp equipment. In a canvas (*toile*) bag were stowed away promiscuously spare things, food, and cartridges. The men received four days' supply of biscuit at a time, and could only carry them by passing a string through them and wearing this as a sort of bandolier. The biscuits crumbled away on the march owing to the rain or snow, and the men were consequently without bread. Even worse was the fact that in the bags the cartridges became too damp for use. The firearms were of the most varied kind, from a simple rifle (model of 1815 converted) to the American Remington; this was another source of trouble and confusion.

At the conference between the Delegation and the Generals that was held on the 12th November, three days after the victory of Coulmiers, it was agreed that a position should be taken up at Orleans as a base for future operations. General d'Aurelle did not, however, regard the position with much favour. On the same day General Crouzat, the Commander of the Army of the East, received orders to form out of that a corps of three Divisions, the 20th Corps, and a Brigade for the 18th Corps, forming at Nevers. At Orleans the work of preparing the position was pushed on with great energy so that by the 19th the position was nearly completed. On this day the disposition of the Army of the Loire was as follows:

At Gien the whole of the 20th Corps and the greater portion of the 18th Corps, the remainder of the latter being at Nevers. Close to and on the east of the Paris road was the 1st Division of the 15th Corps, the other two Divisions were west of the road; the line was continued westward by the 16th Corps, to the Conie Brook which joins the Loir between Chateaudun and Bonneval; the 17th Corps was between Meung on the Loire and Chateaudun on the Loir, whilst the troops of the Army of the West were falling back towards Chateaudun and Nogent le Retrou to form the 21st Corps, of which the rendezvous was le Mans. Nominally therefore the Army of the Loire consisted of some 200,000 men in six corps, but of these there were five fairly completed in formation, one not completed; the front was over forty miles and was covered, so far as the 20th and 18th Corps were concerned, by detachments thrown forward on the roads to the front; and for the rest of the Army by a strong line of outposts from Neuville aux Bois, through Artenay to the Conie Brook.

It was on the 19th that the Delegation intimated to d'Aurelle their opinion that the purely defensive attitude must be exchanged for active operations for the relief of Paris. The success of any operations of the Army of the Loire was, however, from the first, very doubtful, independently of the inefficiency of the Army, owing to the vital differences of opinion, which, on military questions, existed between the civil government of the provinces, the Delegation, and the commander-in-chief of its army, General d'Aurelle. That amongst the generals themselves there was not always unanimity of opinion was only in the ordinary course of affairs; but the strong counter-influence of General Chanzy, the advocate of active measures, must have told much against d'Aurelle. The cause of the great differences of the views held by the Delegation and by d'Aurelle lay in the fact that the former looked at the military situation from the national point of view, whilst the latter regarded it from the military standpoint only. To the Delegation, the relief of Paris was the supreme object to be accomplished for the salvation of the country, the only purpose of the military operations of the army; and inasmuch as the duration of the resistance of which Paris was capable was necessarily limited, it desired the speedy initiation of measures for its relief. Even if, owing to time being wanting, the army could not attain the degree of efficiency desirable for the purpose, it was better to make the attempt with it as it was, rather than not at all, or too late.

On the other hand, d'Aurelle looked mainly to the capability of the newly raised army as determining the operations to be undertaken; and instead of recognising the fact that the Delegation represented the Government of the country, and as such its directions must be accepted and complied with, he assumed an attitude of inertia, which had the lamentable result of causing, almost of compelling the Delegation to take command of the Army, and not only to decide what operations should be undertaken, but also to direct how they should be carried out. There can be little doubt that, in this matter, d'Aurelle's judgment failed him, and that, instead of remaining at the head of the army, in an attitude of non-assistance to the Government, he should have resigned his command, and have left the Government free to appoint another general in his place. D'Aurelle, unfortunately, did not realise that even if a faulty plan of operations was to be adopted, it would be far better to accept it, and, as a soldier of experience and knowledge, do the best he could with it, rather than let it be controlled by civilians, absolutely ignorant of the working of the machine they were setting in motion.

On the 19th de Freycinet wrote to d'Aurelle " We cannot remain at Orleans for ever. Paris is hungry and is calling to us. Study the line of march to be taken to enable us to give a hand to Trochu who would come to meet us with 150,000 men, whilst at the same time a demonstration would be made towards the north. We are considering here a plan of operations. Let me know as soon as your ideas have taken shape, and we will meet at Tours or your Head-quarters to discuss the plan." To this fair suggestion d'Aurelle replied on the 20th that his army was not 250,000 strong as alleged, that if he was to lend a hand to Trochu he must first of all know Trochu's intentions; and, instead of making any suggestion himself as to the plan of operations, he adopted the extraordinary and suicidal course of assuring de Freycinet that he was quite willing to consider any plan that the Delegation themselves might suggest. As Lehautcourt rightly says, this was taking a singular view of the duty of a Commander-in-Chief and such an exchange of duties presaged no good for the future. Naturally, this unexpected reply greatly irritated Gambetta, who on the 20th in a severe letter directed d'Aurelle to prepare at once a plan of operations for the relief of Paris. He pointed out that owing to the difficulty of communicating with Trochu, to delay until Trochu's plans were known was to wait for what might never be obtained, and he gave to d'Aurelle as the principles on which the operations were to be based :

(1) The best troops must be on the flank.
(2) The available forces numbered 250,000 men.
(3) Paris must be the objective, and d'Aurelle must draw up a plan of operations accordingly.

To this letter d'Aurelle did not vouchsafe a reply until the 23rd, when he wrote as follows: "The solution of the problem (the march on Paris) is not the least of the matters I have to consider. To solve it demands the co-operation and mutual understanding between the Government and the Army as represented by the chiefs to whom you have given your confidence. So far as I am personally concerned you may rely on my complete devotion. May God make my strength equal to my devotion."

But the Delegation, impatient at his delay, had already taken the control into their own hands. Trochu had said that Paris could hold out to the end of the year, but the relief must be effected much sooner; and in a letter of November 19th from Jules Favre in Paris, that Minister had said that December 15th was the limit of holding out. The Delegation knew also that Trochu contemplated a sortie about November 26th, so something must be done at once to prepare for co-operation.

De Freycinet assumed that the Army of Paris would move up to Melun along the right bank of the Seine, which river would thus protect its right flank. The Delegation determined, therefore, on the 21st, that the Army of the Loire should advance on Fontainebleau; the preliminary step being an advance of the 18th and 20th Corps and a Division of the 15th Corps on Pithiviers and Beaune la Rolande, thus clearing the way for an advance of the whole army. This line is parallel to and twenty miles from the Loire, and its flanks are on good roads leading north-east to Fontainebleau. For the intended operation the Delegation sent the orders for the movements of the several bodies of troops to d'Aurelle for transmission to the commanders. The 18th and 20th Corps had been constituted into an army under Crouzat, but he was subordinated to d'Aurelle. Against the orders sent d'Aurelle submitted some objections, many of considerable weight; so de Freycinet modified them to a certain extent, sending to d'Aurelle a reply that was both fair and dignified.

"If you gave me a better plan than mine, or even if you gave me some plan or other, I would give up my own plan and recall my orders. But during the twelve days that you have been at Orleans you have not, notwithstanding the repeated requests of M. Gambetta and myself, given us any plan at all. You have confined yourself to fortifying Orleans according to our recommendations after you had declared the position to be untenable. I am glad to find that you have greatly modified your opinion on this point, since you no longer wish to abandon your position. . . . Something must be done. . . . Paris is hungry and desires to be helped." But now there was a dual authority exercising control in the Army. The Delegation issued its orders for the movements of Corps or Divisions, sometimes direct to the commanders, sometimes through d'Aurelle; the commanders naturally turned to d'Aurelle for directions, but d'Aurelle was not in the counsels of the Delegation, so orders and counter-orders succeeded each other in rapid succession; there was no unity of purpose or action in the movements. On the 23rd the 20th Corps had advanced from Gien to about eight or nine miles south of Beaune la Rolande, the 18th Corps was still at Gien, the 15th and 16th Corps were very much in their old positions from the Paris-Orleans road to the Conie, whilst on the extreme left the leading troops of the 17th Corps were as far north as Bonneval and Chateaudun on the Loir. The troops of the Army of the West were falling back towards Chateaudun and from Nogent le Rotrou to be incorporated in the 21st Corps forming at le Mans, and it had been the intention of the Delegation to oppose the advance of the Detachment frontally with the 21st Corps, threatening with the 17th its line of communications. This project came to naught.

Up to the present the movements of the two forces, the Second Army and the Detachment, have been followed separately; this has been convenient as they had separate objects, separate aims. Now, from the 23rd, they are to co-operate in accordance with general instructions from one source. The operations of both on each day will therefore be so narrated, that it may be seen to what extent the co-operation was real or was only nominal. But it is well to bear in mind that, as is evident from the extracts of correspondence already quoted, neither Versailles, Prince Frederick Charles, nor the Grand Duke had any but the vaguest idea of the real position, strength, and intentions of that Army against which they were about to operate—the Army of the Loire.

CHAPTER X

NOVEMBER 24TH

V. MOLTKE has now taken in hand the control of the operations against the Army of the Loire. The Prince is to attack, but is not required to do so before November 28th, by which time the movement of the Grand Duke against the left flank of the Army of the Loire will be producing its effect. The situation was very similar to that of the commencement of the campaign in Bohemia in the Prussian-Austrian War of 1866. Then v. Moltke remained at Berlin, whence by telegraph he moved the armies of the Crown Prince and Prince Frederick Charles until the time arrived when he considered it necessary to go to the theatre of war. This method of control did succeed, though the caution and slowness of movement of Prince Frederick Charles were very noticeable. And now v. Moltke is at Versailles at the apex of the triangle, and is connected by wire with the Prince at Pithiviers, forty-five miles distant at one angle, and with the Grand Duke at la Ferté Bernard eighty miles distant at the other angle; these two leaders being seventy-five miles apart. But there is a difference, namely, that the " personlichkeit " of these leaders is far more marked than was the case in 1866: each has already shown the possession of a will of his own; and with Prince Frederick Charles, v. Moltke's own relations and those of the Grand Duke are somewhat strained. V. Moltke is somewhat in the position of the driver of a pair of steeds, one a kicker, the other a jibber, and neither of the pair is inclined to run in double harness with its companion on this occasion. As on the 24th, the Prince's Army is the predominant partner in the scheme of co-operation, the proceedings of this Army on this day will be

NOVEMBER 24

considered first. The two Brigades of the Xth Army Corps at Montargis marched to Beaune la Rolande by different roads, the 39th (v. Valentini) by a northern road, the 37th (v. Lehmann) with the Divisional General (v. Woyna) by a southern road through Ladon. Here, however, this Brigade met with opposition from strong hostile forces, the 20th Corps and a Division of the 18th marching north, which, after a short but sharp engagement, were driven back, and the three Brigades were concentrated at Beaune in the evening.

The Prince, ever eager to obtain every scrap of information procurable respecting the enemy, had, on the 23rd, ordered reconnaissances along his whole front for the 24th. From the right, the 2nd Cav. Division and the IXth Army Corps came in reports of the presence of very strong forces in front, and of the arrival, at Chevilly, of railway trains from the south, apparently carrying troops. At Chevilly were some 10,000 men, with some batteries of artillery; there were no signs of any march to the west; on the contrary there was a movement (as was the fact) of large bodies of troops towards the east. Further, v. Manstein reported the ground west of the Paris road to be favourable for purposes of attack. No prisoners were taken. On the east of the Paris road, and near to it, the IIIrd Army Corps had, with a force of four battalions, two squadrons, and two batteries, reconnoitred towards Neuville aux Bois, where is an important junction of roads. Here, however, the Germans were repulsed, losing 9 officers, 162 men, and 17 horses. It appears that the reconnaissance had been made contrary to the warnings given by the Corps Commander and his chief Staff Officer, Col. v. V. Rhetz. The Prince had been persuaded by v. Stiehle to give the order; and when he learnt of the disaster, and that not even one prisoner had been taken, there was a lively interchange of remarks between him and v. Stiehle. The Corps Staff had always a poor opinion of the Army Staff, and this incident increased the ill-feeling existing between the former and v. Stiehle.

From the Xth Army Corps had been sent out from Beaune

three small reconnoitring parties in different directions. Two of them found strong hostile forces close in front, but did not succeed in taking any prisoners. The third party was directed towards Boiscommun, only three miles south-west of Beaune, and its work was productive of most important results. The troops here employed were three squadrons and two companies, and they were accompanied by two of the Staff Officers of the Corps, Captain Seebeck and Lieut. v. Kotze. Of this reconnaissance Hoenig gives in the " Volkskrieg " the chief incidents, but in a small pamphlet he has narrated it in detail; and so instructive is the narrative that an abstract of it is here put before the reader.

The Commander of the detachment was Major v. Schoeler, but although senior to Capt. Seebeck he had to act in conformity to the wishes of his junior officer, who, as Staff Officer, represented the General Commanding the Corps. Before the detachment moved off from Beaune the officers were assembled, and Capt. Seebeck explained to them the situation as follows: " Of the strength, position, and intentions of the enemy, whose main body is presumed to be behind the Forest of Orleans, there is uncertainty; but in the neighbourhood of Bellegarde [six miles south of Beaune] are strong forces, so that a hostile offensive on the line Bellegarde–Boiscommun may be expected. The front of the Second Army is such that the Xth Army Corps forms its left flank; the main body of the Corps is to-day concentrated in the neighbourhood of Beaune; one Brigade is still away east of Montargis. Paris can hold out at the longest only three to four weeks. Apparently, an Italian Division of irregular troops under Garibaldi's son has joined the Army of the Loire. To clear up the state of uncertainty, reconnaissances have been ordered by the Second Army for the 24th from all units of the Army. From the Xth Army Corps there will be to-day one on Boiscommun, a second on Bellegarde, a third on Ladon (Lorris) [six miles south-east of Beaune]. If fire is heard in those directions, it is at the reconnoitring detachments." Then Seebeck continued: "So, gentlemen, the cavalry has to carry out the reconnoitring; the companies will eventually take up a position of support. The main and chief business is to take prisoners; for every officer captured there will be given an 'Iron Cross.' Be so good as to communicate this to the men." What an incentive! The most coveted decoration in the German Army, the Iron Cross.

With the Cavalry at the head, the detachment moved off at 8 A.M. Short of Boiscommun, the leading zug [or troop], under the command of Lieut. v. Riedesel, came on a hostile cavalry lancer piquet dismounted; this was driven back and pursued to the entrance to the village. V. Riedesel now sent scouts into and around the village, to reconnoitre, and as their reports on their return did not fully satisfy him, he determined to trot into the village and ascertain for himself how matters stood. At the entrance was standing a peasant, of whom v. Riedesel inquired whether in the village were any more troops than the Lancers who had just gone into it. The peasant replied that there were none. V. Riedesel now caught sight of Lancers in the village, and at once ordered the attack, and riding in with his men, soon found himself in a real trap. A half-squadron of the 2nd Marche Lancer Regiment was there, and Lieut.-Col. de Brasserie, the commander of the regiment, was just entering from the south with the main body. Not only did the Lancers open fire, but also from the houses fire was opened on the Germans; and as these went forward, the inhabitants, after the last trooper had gone by, drew carts into the street to prevent their escape. The Germans were soon overpowered, v. Riedesel was wounded and taken prisoner, but the greater part of the troopers got back towards Montbarrois, about a mile in rear, where the Infantry had now taken up a position of support. Meantime, Colonel de Brasserie had arrived from Bellegarde with the remainder of the regimemt, and he had intended to give his squadrons a rest after their long trot. His first object was to restore order in the village, but the commander of the leading squadron, seeing an opportunity for pursuit, had taken the initiative upon himself, and was now following up the retreating Germans. The colonel rode after them to recall them, but the horse got the better of the rider, and ran away with him to the front. Naturally, the other squadrons followed the commander, and, consequently, a considerable body of Lancers, in more or less disorderly fashion, were galloping out of the village northward, whilst, from the opposite direction, were coming forward the main body of the German Cavalry; and close at hand to the latter was a small group of the Staff Officers and orderlies. A determined *mêlée* now took place, the Lancers eventually being driven back; de Brasserie was severely wounded, and fell, a most valuable prize, into the hands of the Germans. The value, however, lay not in de Brasserie's rank, but was owing to a mental disqualification in him as a soldier—he was deficient in reticence. So in reply to questions which he should have declined to answer, he said that he had come out to reconnoitre the Germans, that the main body of the enemy was behind him, and that probably there would be a battle next day; that they wished to get round the Xth Army Corps, and therefore Garibaldi had come. He said that he belonged to " Polignac's Corps," which had come from Besançon [Polignac was only a Divisional Commander in the 20th Corps, originally under Michel, and now under Crouzat].

Seebeck had constantly sent reports to the Corps Headquarters at Beaune. Col. v. Caprivi, the Chief Staff Officer, possessed, to a remarkable degree, aptitude for comparing and piecing together information derived from different sources, and by noon he had mastered all the results obtained from the Boiscommun expedition. Some one newly-arrived Corps was in front here, but whether it was Michel's or Crouzat's, or what number it bore, had not been ascertained. At all events it was neither the 15th nor the 16th.

And further east at Ladon, some eight miles from Boiscommun, more information was being obtained, not by reconnoitring, but by an almost dramatic chance of war; but information which, so far from enlightening the Prince, further thickened the Fog of War which now tactically, as well as strategically, was rapidly enveloping him. At the eastern entrance to Ladon, the scene of the engagement of the 37th Brigade, had been picked up by Trumpeter Brosig of the 9th Dragoons, a pocket-book, which he at once gave to his superiors, and which was sent on the same day to the Corps Head-quarters. The pocket-book was the property of an Englishman, Captain Ogilvy, who, serving on the side of the French, had fallen in the fight. In the pocket-book were three papers, all of great value, but as they stood they increased the confusion of mind at the Army Head-quarters. The least important was a document giving the orders for the march of some army corps for the 24th. Of the others, one was a letter in the handwriting of Gambetta; it ran as follows:

"THE FRENCH REPUBLIC.
" LIBERTY, EQUALITY, FRATERNITY.
" THE GOVERNMENT OF NATIONAL DEFENCE.

" The Member of the Government of National Defence, Minister of the Interior and of War.

" In virtue of the powers delegated to him by the Government, by Decree dated Paris, October 1st, 1870.

" Accredits to General Crouzat, commanding the forces assembled at Gien, Captain Ogilvy of the Engineers, attached to the staff of the 18th Corps, and temporarily detached from it.

" Captain Ogilvy enjoys my fullest confidence. I have long been in consultation with him on the military operations. Gien is clearly the key of our position on the Loire; I know that it is safe in the brave hands of General Crouzat; I send Mons. Ogilvy to him to assist him in his work, and I request that he may be present with a vote at the meetings of the council.

"(Signed) LÉON GAMBETTA.
" TOURS, *November* 19th, 1870."

The third document was an *ordre de bataille* of some army corps, but it bore no heading indicating any particular corps. During the day, there came in from other sources, from newspapers, deserters, prisoners, and ordinary wayfarers, information which rendered indubitable the conclusion that in front of the Second Army had been collected a very large hostile force; that this force intended to take the offensive immediately; and, lastly, that the whole country for miles round Orleans had been very strongly prepared as a defensive position.

But from the documents of Captain Ogilvy arose other serious matters for consideration. The delegation regarded Gien as "the key of our position on the Loire;" it might be the base for offensive operations; and there were opposite the extreme left of the Second Army, or rather beyond it and outflanking it, large forces assembled under the command of Crouzat. As a matter of fact, it was these forces on their way from Gien towards Beaune that had been encountered this day. That Pithiviers was now directly threatened from both south-east and south-west did not admit of doubt. As regards the accession of strength to the enemy in front of the Second Army, the evidence seemed to show that this was the 18th Corps named in the newspapers of November 20th. And at once had to be considered the several strategical operations, any one or more of which the enemy starting from his very long base, might select for an advance for the relief of Paris. There were four possible lines of advance: one from the right by Gien, Montargis, and thence direct north between the rivers Loing and Yonne; the second against the centre of the Second Army at Pithiviers, and thence either to Fontainebleau, or to the Paris road at Etampes; the third from the French centre along the main road to Paris, the fourth from the left flank by Chateaudun and Chartres on Versailles. Opposed to this enemy, now, was the Second Army on a front of twenty-five miles, with the Detachment some fifty miles distant.

And it was the letter from Gambetta to Crouzat, and the reference in it to Gien, that determined the whole of the strategy of the Prince in the immediate future. V. d. Goltz says: "If he [Gambetta] looked on Gien as the most im-

NOVEMBER 24   167

portant point on the Loire, whilst up to this time Orleans had been regarded as such, the intention was apparent that the attack was to be commenced with the right wing of the Army of the Loire. This emphasised, that the oft-promised relief of Paris would not be carried out along the great road from Orleans to Paris, but down the Loing towards Fontainebleau. A number of advantages told in favour of this direction, and soon it acquired more and more probability."

The orders of the Prince for the 25th drew the Army a little to the east, but it still held on to the Paris road. Each corps was directed to be so concentrated as to be in readiness for any attack by the enemy. If no combat was audible before 2 P.M. the corps could then commence to go into their cantonments. It seems from Hoenig that these orders may be taken as the commencement of the divergence of views that existed between v. Moltke and the Prince as to the strategy to be employed against the Army of the Loire. On the 14th v. Moltke had told the Prince that it devolved on the Second Army to protect the investment from the South, and that the Orleans road must not be "left entirely open for any length of time;" but at that date the Detachment was moving away to the north-west, and so the defence of the road fell to the Second Army alone. This defence the Prince originally had intended to carry out offensively by a bold converging attack on Orleans irrespective of the Detachment. Subsequently the Prince had found himself reduced to a purely passive defence; v. Moltke, whilst acquiescing in the change at the time, desired that it should be exchanged for the offensive as soon as possible : and in his view the right course for the Prince to adopt now for the defence of the road was not the posting on it a portion of the army as a direct physical obstacle in the path of a hostile advance, but the concentration of the whole army more to the east in some position whence, by manœuvring against the flank of an advancing enemy, it could arrest the advance, whether from the east or the west of the enemy's long line; where it could, in collected force, directly repel an advance from the centre, and where the troops, being well in hand, a bold offensive could be taken should opportunity offer. V. Moltke held that now for the defence of the Paris Road there was not merely one army, the Second, but two armies, that and the Detachment, so that the strategy adopted should be the co-operation of convergent forces from different bases. The Prince would, however, for the present, have direct passive defence only, and this on a long front out of all proportion to the small strength of his Army. Besides which, he detested strategy of the co-operative kind. Hoenig says: " He had no opinion of combined operations, at least, unless the combination was on such a small scale that it could be worked by one of the two commanders. He disliked any tactical stroke, unless previously assured that there would be at hand for it all forces within reach."

The widely scattered Detachment was, on this day, moving somewhat slowly to what might be called a preparatory position for the march on Beaugency ; but one important matter had come to the knowledge of the Grand Duke before he issued his orders for the 24th, namely, that a considerable hostile force [the 17th Corps] was now moving up the Loir by Chateaudun interposing between him and the Second Army, and directly threatening his line of communications, as he had been warned by v. Blumenthal. Strangely enough, the Grand Duke, when on the 23rd he sent his reports to Versailles did not mention this hostile advance. Here is another instance of the powerlessness of v. Moltke to deal with the situation ; powerlessness due in this case to the carelessness or reticence of one of the chief commanders. It is possible that the *moral* of the Grand Duke may have been somewhat disturbed by the order to march on Beaugency. Hoenig suggests that in the order, the Grand Duke perhaps foresaw the possibility of the Detachment ceasing to be an independent command, and of his being placed under the orders of the Prince; or even of the Detachment ceasing to exist as a unit, and its corps being incorporated in the Second Army: there may have therefore been no great excess of zeal on his part in contributing a share to the compulsory co-operation.

On the French side it had been found impossible to move the 20th Corps (30,000) to the positions assigned to it for this day. The 18th Corps was now on the march from Gien to Montargis to create a diversion on the German left, whilst des Paillières with the 30,000 men of the 1st Division, 15th Corps was, in conformity to orders from Tours, struggling along bad roads from Chevilly towards Crouzat; the three groups were still a day's march apart, but the 24th is marked by what was practically the abandonment by d'Aurelle of the functions of chief executive military commander. Crouzat in a despatch to d'Aurelle concluded with the words: "I await your orders." D'Aurelle forwarded the despatch to Tours with the following addition:

"Since I do not know fully the object of the movements, it is difficult for me to give detailed orders: Generals des Paillières and Crouzat are a long day's march apart, and could not therefore support each other. It is doubtful whether General Crouzat will be able to continue his movement to-morrow. Are the two corps to concentrate and where? For fear that General Crouzat may not receive his orders sufficiently early through me, I request that they may be sent to him by telegraph direct to Bellegarde, and that I may know what they are." As Hoenig says, d'Aurelle by this letter proved to the Delegation his want of independence; it was an abdication of his leadership; Gambetta took him at his word.

The actual military situation on the evening of the 24th is one of paralysing over-extension everywhere. With the Germans, there are two bodies of troops each so widely extended that each is unfit for any immediate strategical operation, and they are separated from each other by an intervening hostile corps; whilst in front of them is a very large hostile force intent on at once taking the offensive against them, but unable to do so, owing to the same cause, incomplete concentration.

On this day, the 24th, there comes before us an incident in the inner life of German command and control, of a remarkable character, and which is also yet one more illustration of the breakdown, in periods of doubt and difficulty, of that system of mutual confidence and co-operation among the higher leaders, which, as a rule, was a characteristic of the first war.

Readers of the German Official History of the War (v. Moltke's own work) may have noted, that although v. Moltke was the real chief commander of the German Armies during the campaign, it is to the King of Prussia that is given all the credit for the conduct of the war; and they may recall to mind one remarkable passage in which the King and the Emperor Napoleon III. are contrasted as supreme commanders of the opposing armies.

"The Monarch, at whose disposition lies the State with its resources, is only entitled to be at the head of the Field Army, when competent to command the troops in person, and take upon his own shoulders the weighty responsibility of all that may happen. Failing these conditions, his presence with the army cannot but have a paralysing influence. . . . For by *one* will alone must the operations be controlled; when influenced by several counsels, no matter how well meant, this will must always lose in clearness and decision, and the leading of the army which depends on it will become uncertain."

The inference intended to be drawn from this passage is clear, namely, that it was King William alone that commanded the host of Germans in this great campaign. Now to another view of the matter.

At Versailles the old King stood, as the leader, above and apart from all around him, whoever they might be, and though he rarely interfered, yet he had his own views on all matters that came under his cognisance ; and if need be, he could act on those views. For some time the King had been dissatisfied with the state of affairs at both the Second Army and the Detachment, and with the small amount of information he received concerning them; yet the political situation made it necessary that he should understand fully and clearly what was taking place. So he determined to find out the truth for himself. It was the Second Army that appeared to be the pivot of the combined operations, so to this army he decided to send some one whom he could trust to obtain for him the information he desired. The selection of the emissary was difficult, for on the one hand he must be an officer of great professional capacity: yet, on the other hand, he must not be of so senior a rank as to lead the Prince to suspect that there was any dissatisfaction with the leading, or that the officer sent was to exercise control either alongside him or over him. That tact must be a gift innate in the emissary, goes without saying. The officer to whom the King entrusted this most delicate mission was one of his personal aides-de-camp, thirty-eight years of age, Lt.-Col. Count v. Waldersee, lately the Commander-in-Chief of the allied expedition to China. It seems that on the 23rd the King had already determined to send an officer, but not until the following day did he carry his resolve into effect; and then, through Colonel v. Albedyll, the chief of the Military Cabinet, which corresponds to our own Military Secretarial Department, he summoned v. Waldersee to his presence and addressed him as follows: " We are on the eve of a decisive moment of the war. The French Army of the Loire has gradually been more and more reinforced, and better organised. I have foreseen that a long time and have said so to many; but these gentlemen always know everything better than I do, and they maintain that the real war is at an end. The position of v. d. Tann's troops in and around Orleans did not correspond to my views; his position was too dangerous, and he was obliged to retire with loss. The 22nd Division was sent there, and I despatched afterwards the 17th Division, and it is clear that the Grand Duke, with all these troops, has not become equal to dealing with the enemy. Much about the same time Metz fell, and now we have succeeded in bringing up the Second Army. But it is very weak, and it numbers not much more than 40,000 rifles; the enemy is estimated at from 150,000 to 200,000 men. I know well that my troops are better than the French, but that does not deceive me into supposing that we have not a crisis before us. If Prince Frederick Charles is beaten, we must give up the Investment of Paris. . . . I have explained in this letter, which you will give to the Prince, the serious character of the situation; repeat to him that I have the most thorough confidence in his leading and in his practical knowledge of war. Start at once, for there will be a fight soon. You will report to me daily, and you will remain with the Prince until I recall you."

Entrusted with this remarkable mission, which was unknown to v. Moltke, the Count at once started for Pithiviers, where he arrived on the 25th, and delivered the letter to the Prince. He was received most courteously, and was a guest at the Prince's table. v. Waldersee rode about the army, conversed with the Generals and the Staffs, learnt their views, and daily sent his letter to the King. Substitute for these personages respectively our own Sovereign, H.R.H. the Duke of Connaught, Earl Roberts, and say, Col. Douglas Haig, A.D.C., and we realise the curious ways of the German Army.

CHAPTER XI

NOVEMBER 25TH

ON the 25th the slight movements ordered by the Prince were carried out ; the Xth Army Corps was directed to undertake the protection of the left flank of the Second Army; and to v. V. Rhetz was it left to determine how far eastward the Corps should extend, and also the sending detachments to Montargis or Chateau Landon. From the IIIrd Army Corps was sent to Nemours a detachment of two companies and a squadron.

Opposite the Second Army the main body of the 18th Corps was pursuing its march on Montargis ; the 20th Corps with a portion of the 18th Corps, remained in an entrenched position about Boiscommun ; des Paillières' Division has reached Chilleurs aux Bois.

The Detachment, on the 25th, after a short march of nine or ten miles, was pointing to the Loire, the Bavarians leading and being at Montdoubleau, on the road by Vendôme to Blois; the two Inf. Divisions were respectively ten and fifteen miles in rear ; the 6th Cav. Division was in front ; whilst, strangely enough, the 4th Cav. Division had been withdrawn from touch with the enemy, and was brought close in to la Bazoche Gouet, on the east flank of the rear of the long column. From the leading cavalry to the rear-guard at Nogent le Rotrou, the Detachment was extended over thirty miles. The shortness of the march was viewed with disfavour at Versailles, but it is probable that this shortness was not due to any remissness on the part of the Grand Duke, but was owing to his experiencing the need of sparing his tired troops, for whom a rest-day, pleaded for by their commanding officers, and asked for by the Grand Duke, had been refused. But, on the 25th, owing partly to reports received during the day, and partly to the non-receipt of a delayed report, the Grand Duke found himself compelled to determine whether he should continue to act strategically as ordered by v. Moltke, or act according to his own judgment to meet the requirements of a completely new situation, in which he now, suddenly, found himself.

The Bavarians, during the last few days, had been marching on the arc of a circle, and on the 25th their ammunition column and some bridge trains were moving to rejoin them by its chord from Montlandon through Brou to Arville. This road had been reported to v. d. Tann as quite safe; but at Brou the column was suddenly attacked by strong forces of hostile infantry. With the aid of the 4th Cav. Division, the escort succeeded in extricating the convoy, but the French, the advanced troops of the 17th Corps, remained in possession of Brou. To the Grand Duke it was now evident that the enemy had not only interposed between the Detachment and the Second Army, but was moving across his line of communications, and that v. Blumenthal's warning was not groundless. He therefore determined to abandon the march to the Loire, and on the next day to turn against the threatening enemy on his flank and left rear; but, unfortunately, he selected as his objective the most northerly point of the enemy's advance, Brou, so that instead of moving south-east, or even east, he will move north-east. Not merely did this involve a change of about ninety degrees in the direction of the line of march of his 50,000 men and 200 guns, with the delays, impedings and blockings, its necessary accompaniments, but, as will appear later on, this selection was strategically a mistake; for this, however, the Grand Duke was not solely responsible; a cavalry subaltern must share the responsibility. Unfortunately, there had not come on the 24th to the Grand Duke, a most important piece of information. On that day Lieut. v. Busse, with ten troopers, had been sent from the 6th Cav. Division to reconnoitre Chateaudun. He crossed the Loir by a ford south of the town, and entering from that direction, found it full of hostile regular troops, infantry, cavalry, and artillery, and also Gardes Mobiles. Returning, he found that the ford had meanwhile been blocked ; he swam the river elsewhere with his little party, but his own horse was so injured that he had to be extricated by his troopers, the horse being left behind. Through the nearest village, losing four men and their horses, he forced his way under a severe fire from Franc-tireurs. He then took shelter in a neighbouring wood for the night, reconnoitred Chateaudun again the next day, and afterwards returned to his Division. For his courage and conduct v. Busse received great commendation in Army Orders, and as a brave soldier he had done his duty well, but as a reconnoitring officer he had let slip from his memory how much the value of information obtained depends on its speedy receipt by those who may have to act upon it. The Grand Duke, on the 25th, knew that some French were already as far north-east as Brou, and that was all he knew about this alarming hostile advance ; but the cavalry subaltern had learnt a great deal more about the enemy, namely, that due east of the Detachment was a hostile force of all arms, and, including regular troops, a force which, from its composition, was probably the main body or a portion of it ; and owing to a little forgetfulness, this young officer did not at once communicate to the Grand Duke this invaluable strategical information, but kept it to himself, thereby contributing a share to the erroneous selection of an operation of strategy. So the Duke struck a blow against the point of a spear instead of endeavouring to break the shaft. The relative situation of the Detachment and of the French 17th Corps recalls to mind Hamley's remark, that when two armies at the same time threaten each other's line of communications, that army which fears most for its own will give way. How far General de Sonis, the French commander, knew the exact position of the Detachment we do not know, so it cannot be ascertained how he regarded the danger to his own line of communications ; but, at all events, the Grand Duke believed the situation to be perilous to the Detachment, for he forthwith gave way and abandoned his own advance. It is impos- to say, except *ex post facto*, whether the Grand Duke was right or wrong ; he could not have known that the enemy was one of the least efficient corps of those in the Army of the Loire. Perhaps nine out of ten commanders would have acted as he did, whilst the tenth, a man of enterprise and decision, relying on his 50,000 well-trained troops and their able eaders—for in the Detachment the divisional commanders were good soldiers—would have pushed on boldly, risking all on this one chance of war, and knowing that at one and the same time he was threatening both the Government of National Defence at Tours and its army at Orleans. The result of such a stroke cannot be determined, as so much would have depended on the moral effect produced among the French Leaders, both military and civil.

So far as mere movements are concerned, November 25th is in no way interesting or instructive, but otherwise it is one of the most interesting days of the campaign, and certainly instructive. It was one of the days, too many by far, of alteration in the strategy, but as regards drawing on the past for lessons for the future we must go to Beaune la Rolande and Pithiviers.

At these two places the need of the moment was to ascertain what this newly arrived hostile force in front really was. V. Caprivi at Beaune was hard at work endeavouring to solve the conundrum. How different from those August days at Vionville in the first war, when a glance at the button on the coat of a prisoner or a dead enemy lying on the ground may have sufficed to tell him, by a simple reference to the *ordre de bataille*, whether it was le Bœuf's corps or Canrobert's corps, or some other corps that was in front of his own, which then was exhausted by battle, as now it was wearied by hard marching and continuous fighting. Priceless now for the Second Army, and especially for the Xth Army Corps, was a true *ordre de bataille* of the Army of the Loire on November 25. How easy would its possession have rendered the laying down on the chart the course to be steered by the Corps and the Army.

Most unexpectedly, however, there came to v. Caprivi a stroke of real good luck. The wounded prisoner, Colonel de Brasserie, had by his manner as a chivalrous soldier and gentleman, so impressed the German staff, that they had exercised considerable delicacy in trying to elicit information from him ; but the Colonel allowed his affection for his wife to get the better of his discretion, and he wrote to her a letter, in which he told her that he belonged to the 20th Corps (General Crouzat). This letter having necessarily to go through the German Military Post Office was opened and read before transmission to Madame de Brasserie, and it gave to v. Caprivi the information he was seeking for in vain elsewhere, namely, the numerical designation of the corps that had been engaged at Boiscommun ; moreover, it supplied the heading missing from the *ordre de bataille* found in Captain Ogilvy's pocket-book for, in that *ordre de bataille* was named among the "1st Division, General de Polignac," the 2nd Lancer Regiment, the one engaged at Boiscommun the previous day, and commanded by de Brasserie. V. Caprivi was, however, not satisfied with only the information that in front was one particular corps ; he believed that the force that had been encountered, or whose presence had been reported on the previous day, was far larger than a single army corps could be ; and at 9.30 A.M. he reported : "The hostile troops with which the Second Army was engaged yesterday belong partly to Michel's Corps (earlier combined with Garibaldi), partly to three Divisions, which were on the march from Gien, and according to an order found, were yesterday to arrive at Beaune, St. Loup and Juranville." On the 25th 146 prisoners were brought into the Army Head-quarters at Pithiviers, and were closely interrogated. In drawing inferences from their statements, the Head-quarters had before them v. Caprivi's report that the strength of the French was one

Army Corps, and, besides, three Divisions. Owing to de Brasserie's indiscretion, it was clear that the corps was the 20th. But among the prisoners were men from the 44th Marche Regiment and the 73rd Gardes Mobiles, neither of which appeared in the *ordre de bataille* ; they belonged, therefore, not to the 20th, but to another corps ; so it was evident that there were larger forces than only one corps in front. Not, however, that the Head-quarters accepted this conclusion.

The examination of the prisoners, many of them very voluble and excited, increased the confusion of thought. They had been taken in the fight not at Boiscommun, but at Ladon. Some said they belonged to the 20th Corps commanded by General Crouzat, others that they belonged to the 18th Corps, commanded by General Michel. To these assertions were added others that they had come by train from the east to Gien. But the places of formation of the 18th Corps were known not to have been in the east. But from the east, as already mentioned, had come a brigade for this corps ; and as parts of both the 18th and 20th Corps had fought at Ladon, all these statements, though apparently irreconcilable, were true. The reference to Crouzat at Gien, the mention of Ogilvy being detached from the 18th Corps, the uncertainty as to the names of the commanders, and the original statement of v. Werder, that it was Michel's corps that had gone west, combined to increase the difficulty of drawing the true deduction from the information gathered. The Prince, however, believed that the prisoners were either trying to deceive him, or were ignorant of the actual organisation of their army. And he did not believe that there was more than one corps in front of him.

During the 25th, and apparently in the forenoon, v. Stiehle had written one of his long letters to v. Moltke giving his view of the situation, but it is of little interest, except in the concluding portion ; and here we find one of the saddest illustrations of " personlichkeit " we meet with in this war. The Prince had always, and not unnaturally, felt deeply being deprived after Gravelotte of the 5th and 6th Cavalry Divisions, which had originally belonged to his army, and which had played so prominent a part in his successes in the earlier period of the campaign. They had been taken from his army, given to the Army of the Meuse, and had led the advance to Sedan. On the day of Sedan, however, they were with the Third Army, and here any prestige they had gained was certainly diminished by their neglect in allowing General Vinoy with Blanshard's Division of the French 13th Corps, to pass through them and make his way back to Paris. With the Third and Fourth Armies they went on to Paris and did good work in covering towards the west and south-west the line of investment. When the much diminished Second Army marched from Metz there was given to it the 1st Cavalry Division under General v. Hartmann. The Prince regarded v. Hartmann as an indifferent cavalry leader, and it is certainly possible that he was justified in his opinion. The Prince, in his advance from Metz, placed this Division on the right flank of the army, a position in which it could be of the least value to the army, but it was the nearest to Paris; and persistently, in season and out of season, he inserted in his communications to v. Moltke a request for an exchange of this Division with the 5th and 6th.

On this matter, however, v. Moltke had been firm, for compliance with the requests was simply impracticable. And now again, on the morning of the 25th, crops up the same demand, a demand which, made as it was under the existing circumstances, renders it difficult to avoid attributing to the Prince some smallness of mind as a leader. The demand ran as follows: "The 2nd Cavalry Division provides for the important and difficult task of watching the enemy on the right flank of the Second Army. For estimating correctly the value of the reports received a thorough knowledge of the individuals from whom they come is necessary: this is the principal reason why his Royal Highness Prince Frederick Charles again and pressingly requests that the 6th Cavalry Division now nearing the Second Army may be again part of it, because the regiments and their officers, and their mode of doing their work in the field, are fully known to his Royal Highness." The 2nd Cavalry Division under Count v. Stolberg had, since the 13th, been closely watching the Army of the Loire, and had acquired a knowledge of the country north and west of Orleans; there is no trace of inefficiency in the Division. Far away to the west and north-west have been with the Grand Duke the 6th Cavalry Division, under the command of Major-General v. Schmidt, the best Cavalry General in the German Army. This Division, like the 2nd, had also acquired an intimate knowledge of the tract of country over which it had been working; that knowledge so important for cavalry in all its operations. Yet now at this crisis, the Prince, himself a cavalry officer, asks that they may exchange duties, exchange spheres of operations, each go from country they know to country they do not know, and where they will be comparatively inefficient, until they have had time to learn and understand the new country.

For both the Prince and the Grand Duke there was a very great surprise in store this day, as agreeable to the former as it must undoubtedly have been disagreeable to the latter. At about one o'clock in the afternoon had been written at Pithiviers a letter for the Duke, or it was being written; it informed the Grand Duke of what had taken place on the 24th, and also of the arrival from the east at Gien on the Loire of a Corps 30,500 strong; and that, exclusive of this Corps, the Army of the Loire is some 120,000 strong. The Prince will therefore defer active operations until he has the co-operation of the Detachment. At ten minutes after the hour there arrived from v. Moltke a telegram to the following effect: " His Majesty the King has ordered : The Detachment of his Royal Highness the Grand Duke of Mecklenburg is placed, until further orders, under the command of Prince Frederick Charles. The Detachment is to watch by Cavalry

NOVEMBER 25

with Infantry supports the roads from Tours and le Mans to Paris, and is to march as rapidly as possible in the direction of Beaugency until further orders. The March programme, as proposed for the following days at the Head-quarters of his Royal Highness the Grand Duke, is to be sent as quickly as possible by wire to the Head-quarters of the Second Army, which is to-day at Pithiviers, and here also." A similar telegram was sent from Versailles to the Grand Duke.

Here we see v. Moltke suddenly giving up the control of a strategical operation which he had himself taken in hand only three days previously. At first sight it seems incredible that he should have counselled the King to take this step. The Prince had already shown that he differed from v. Moltke in the strategical employment of the Detachment; v. Moltke knew already the difficulty of making the Grand Duke obey the orders even of the King, and he must have foreseen the improbability of his being more amenable to one who was only a Royal Prince; he must probably have been also aware of the ill-feeling between the Grand Duke and his new commander. Putting the reins into the hands of the Prince would seem therefore equivalent to letting the operations against the Army of the Loire go to the wall. But although there is no record of the actual reason, the circumstances of the moment seem to furnish grounds for an hypothesis, which is now submitted for consideration as, not improbably, correct.

The task of giving the necessary amount of time and thought required for the control of the operations against the Army of the Loire at this period must have been, mentally and physically, beyond the power of any human being in the position of v. Moltke—a position in which the strain, already enormous, was increasing hourly. The quarter from which came least anxiety was the north, where v. Manteuffel with the First Army was now commencing operations. V. Manteuffel was a soldier of the highest ability; with him was, as a corps commander, v. Goeben, the idol of the German

182 THE PEOPLE'S WAR IN FRANCE, 1870-71

soldiers, so that in the leading of that army v. Moltke justifiably had the fullest confidence. There was an anxious time as regards the south-east of France where v. Werder, a soldier not apparently of special military ability, was in command; it was from this quarter that the German line of communications was most open to attack. But it was Paris itself that demanded now the closest, and at the same time, unremitting watchfulness. Here Trochu was preparing for the great effort, known afterwards as " Ducrot's sortie." If this were to succeed the consequences might be of a very serious character. No wonder then that v. Moltke relieved himself, for a time, of some portion of his arduous work; but this relief was to be only for a season, inasmuch as, the danger over, he, a week later, again took the reins into his own hands from those into which he now surrendered them. The surrender was somewhat akin to making of necessity a virtue.

The unsatisfactory leading of the Detachment and the difficulty already experienced by v. Moltke in controlling the commander may further have made the operations on the Loire a burden to v. Moltke. The Grand Duke's order of the 24th for the 25th had given great dissatisfaction at Versailles; so much so, that the authorities were compelled to consider what action should be taken in the matter. It was seriously discussed on the 24th, but the decision was left over for the morning conference at the Royal Head-quarters on the following day. Very early on the 25th, before the decision was arrived at, v. Blumenthal, at 9.55 A.M., wired to the Grand Duke that thunder was in the air: " It is of the utmost importance that the Detachment should move forward." The decisive telegram already given was sent at 1.10 P.M. to the Grand Duke, by whom it was received at 6.16 P.M.

At Pithiviers the Prince at once made use of the freedom given him to act contrary to v. Moltke's wishes, and he added to the almost finished letter to the Grand Duke, before despatching it: " I may tell your Royal Highness, in consequence of this telegram, that I can only assume that the March programme to be sent to me will give, for the movement in the direction of Beaugency, the right wing at the utmost." The letter did not reach its destination until the evening of the 26th.

CHAPTER XII

NOVEMBER 26TH

ON the 26th nothing of importance occurred at the Second Army. The Prince held to the opinion, and v. Waldersee seems to have shared his belief, that only one corps, the 20th, Crouzat's, was immediately in front. At the Xth Army Corps v. V. Rhetz carried out his duty of protecting the left of the Army by sending away to Chateau Landon six companies, two squadrons, and two guns from his already weakened corps. In a slight engagement at Lorcy, arising out of a hostile reconnaissance, the participation of the population in the defence again displayed itself. To the German outposts came men who, apparently, were well-disposed peasants, and who offered for sale bread and other articles of food. Conversation naturally ensued, with the stereotyped question, " Are there any French troops near ? " and the equally stereotyped falsehood, " None." The bargains concluded, and the vendors having disappeared, out burst a French battalion. Among the peasants had been officers and men, with one eye on the bargains, and the other on the numbers and badges of the German troops.

On the French side the 18th Corps arrived at Montargis ; the 20th remained in position, occupying Ladon on its right, St. Loup on its left, while des Paillières' division, of which the centre was at Chilleurs, was guarding the edge of the forest on a front of nearly twenty miles, Cathelineau's Franc-tireurs connecting it with Crouzat.

The 26th was, however, a great day for letter-writing at Pithiviers, but before dealing with this most interesting and important correspondence, the operative work of the day must be given. Early in the morning the Prince had heard from the Grand Duke of his intended march north-east on Brou ; so, now freed from control, he shook off from his feet the last particle of the Beaugency dust of Versailles, and, at 11.16 A.M., wired to the Grand Duke, " Your Royal Highness is ordered, attacking the enemy by way of Chateaudun and Bonneval, to march without loss of time to unite with the Second Army, of which the right flank is at Janville " [west of and near Toury]. The Detachment meanwhile pursued its way north-east, and, in the evening, extended from Brou on the north (22nd Inf. Division) to Droué on the south (Bavarians), fifteen miles ; but as the rear corps of the previous day was now the leading corps and *vice versâ*, there could not fail to be again march complications. There was not, however, any fighting ; for de Sonis, alarmed by false reports to the effect that the Second and Third Armies and the 4th Cav. Division were closing round him, retired on the 26th to Chateaudun. A somewhat alarming report had come to the Germans from three prisoners, that a force of 75,000 men, including three battalions from Chateaudun and ten from Bonneval were on the march in a direction they could only indicate as " to the north." The Grand Duke, although he knew that he was now under the Prince, had not, during the day, received any orders from him, so in a communication to Versailles, he mentioned this fact, and, later on, asked by telegraph the Third Army, " Have I anything to do with the Third Army ? " But now the Grand Duke was to receive a serious shock to his feelings and his pride, for there came from v. Moltke the following telegram :

" His Majesty the King has, at a personal audience to-day, been pleased to command, on account of the special importance which now attaches to the operations of the Detachment under the orders of your Royal Highness, that Lieutenant-General v. Stosch, to whom has been communicated his Majesty's views, shall act, until further orders, as Chief of the General Staff of the Detachment. I must not omit to inform your Royal Highness, with the deepest respect, that a special superior order will follow."

The step taken by v. Moltke—for of course it was his doing—was altogether exceptional in the conduct of control, and this case was beset with difficulties requiring to be treated with the greatest delicacy. Nominally, it was merely substitution, temporarily, of one Staff Officer for another. But as the Commander is the superior of the Staff Officer, and as, up to the present time, the Duke does not appear to have had, or made, any complaint against Col. v. Krenski, he was indirectly responsible for the continued failure of the staff work; so the change was necessarily somewhat of a reproof to him, and an expression of dissatisfaction at the way in which this work had been done. But in the selection of the substitute, two points had to be taken into consideration : he must be, professionally, of great ability, he must be of rank that in itself must carry influence. The choice was, therefore, very limited, and seems to have lain between v. Podbielski, the Quartermaster-General, and v. Stosch, the head of the Intendance Branch. After having undergone a certain amount of preliminary sounding, v. Stosch, on the 26th, accepted the post, but as he could not leave the Royal Head-quarters without the sanction of his chief, v. Roon, the Minister of War, v. Moltke had to ask personally for this. V. Roon saw the necessity of the case and gave the required permission, saying that he would keep v. Stosch's appointment open, provided that he was not away too long.

But, possibly, it was not merely to get better staff work that it was v. Stosch who was chosen for this mission. V. Moltke knew that he had now on the Loire two obstinate personalities, over whom he had voluntarily given up control. V. Stosch was an excellent soldier, a large-minded man, but in view of the situation he was a good deal more. Owing to his high position on the supreme staff of the German forces, and his close professional connection with v. Moltke, the chief Staff Officer of those forces, he was, on the Loire, little less than v. Moltke present by proxy. The Grand Duke must now be aware that if he rebelled against his new Chief Staff Officer he would be rebelling against v. Moltke, whilst the Prince knew similarly, that although he might be determined to act in future in disregard of v. Moltke's expressed views and wishes, there was present only a few miles away from him in the theatre of war, v. Moltke's personal representative, endeavouring to hold him in check. Nevertheless the Prince regarded the change as decidedly for the better. V. Stosch quitted Versailles on the 26th and arrived at the Detachment on the following day. And now to the letter-writing.

From Pithviers at midday v. Stiehle reported to v. Moltke the views and intentions of the Second Army with respect to the Detachment; he wrote also that owing to the heavy character of the country, due to the rain, it was impossible for the French to advance to the attack ; the French would, therefore, remain quiescent, hoping that the Second Army would take the initiative, attack them in their well-chosen and well-prepared positions in the Forest of Orleans, and become engaged in a many days' fight on a wide front ; then the numerical inferiority of the Germans would enable some of the French forces, not engaged, to advance, compelling the attackers to give up the fight and march after them ; the French would not fail to claim this as a victory. So the Prince would wait until the Detachment came near enough for effective co-operation, and then he would determine whether the right wing could secure a crossing over the Loire below Orleans, whence masses of cavalry could be sent into the country on the other side. An attack on Orleans from the north-west would be thereby greatly facilitated. The success of this plan, he added, depended, however, on whether the Xth Army Corps could hold in check for several days the right wing of the enemy, and also on the enemy not pushing forward large bodies of troops between the Loing and the Yonne. People travelling reported the force opposite the Xth Army Corps to be 60,000, but this he believed to be an exaggeration. The French corps opposite the army were, he said, the 20th, 15th, and 16th. The 18th [at Montargis] under Bourbaki [Billot was in command, as Bourbaki had not yet arrived] was he said at Tours [some eighty miles away] ; the 17th [at Chateaudun] was at le Mans. A Fog of War indeed; the French people in their war kept their secrets well.

On this day the Prince replied as follows to the letter he had received from the King:

"I am fully of opinion that I must not run any risk at this period of the war, where the fall of Paris has to be considered. Looking at my position, twenty-eight miles long, opposite a far numerically stronger enemy, with whose outposts I am in touch at several points, many would consider it dangerous. But it must be borne in mind that the enemy over-estimates my strength very much, and that the bad ground away from main roads can hardly, or only with great difficulty, be used for manœuvring, so this protects me; and this sort of position deceives the enemy; so it must be admitted that I can remain here until the enemy learns the truth, and until the ground improves. I do not see any danger to myself, only a little inconvenience.

"The concentration of the main body of the hostile regular troops in the Forest of Orleans, if my impression is correct, has been well considered and well carried out.

"Does the enemy contemplate the relief of Paris?

"Certainly this was his intention. That it is so now, I doubt. Somewhere about the 15th, orders were already given for an advance on Etampes, but were recalled on the same day when the approach of '200,000 men from Metz' was heard of." [This was not the case; no such orders were given.] "But in this campaign we have had already some wonderful experiences. I mean the order from Paris to MacMahon for the relief of Metz, which led eventually to Sedan. So may now, also Lawyers' orders decree that the Army of the Loire shall under any circumstances go to relieve Paris.

"Will the enemy advance on the broad front, as his outposts stand now, or from one or both flanks?

"I believe that he would specially prefer the direction by Pusieaux" [due north of Beaune] "to Fontainebleau, especially if he still wishes to take the offensive, because the ground is there on the whole most favourable for him, the direction is straight, and because he will march past my left flank, and this direction leads away from the approaching Detachment of the Grand Duke. I own that it would give me much pleasure to have to deal with such an advance, because the operation would be new to me. I should endeavour to manœuvre with the centre corps (the IIIrd Army Corps) as Napoleon did against Blucher's Army on the Marne in 1814. I presume, of course, that the enemy, in order to deceive me, shows the heads of columns on all the roads to Paris, without prejudice to the main body which marches off to the right. I would pledge myself that the enemy, at the most, advances only four or five miles a day.

" But far more difficult than this question is that of driving the enemy out of the Forest of Orleans. If the Emperor Napoleon III. said with truth he had never been able, owing to the numerous cavalry which covered my advance to the Moselle, to find out where the main body was, so can I say the same as respects my own situation now. I know only, with certainty, that this or that village or farm house is occupied; where some large bodies of troops are is also occasionally known ; where the main body of the army is, whether at Orleans, or on the line Gien-Bellegarde, I do not know. We have not been successful in taking prisoners at many places.

" I hope that I shall know more about the enemy when the Grand Duke arrives, whom, under the existing circumstances, I must employ tactically, not strategically, against the Army of the Loire."

This was an honest statement of his refusal to adopt v. Moltke's strategy.

It must here be remarked that v. Moltke was in complete ignorance of the correspondence carried on between the Prince and the King, so later on, in discussions with the latter, he was somewhat surprised to find his Majesty meeting him with the very same arguments that had been put forward to himself by v. Stiehle. The letter continues : " I know nothing of the condition of the Grand Duke's troops, nor details of the length of their marches, but I have no great objection to their being given a rest day" [when v. Stosch was on his way to hurry them on]. "The arrival of this Detachment in front of Orleans, even without this rest-day, is not concealed from the enemy, who must be in touch with it; and if I am compelled to make an attack, which I could not have carried out before to-day, but would carry out to-day, little is lost if I wait yet one day longer, and delay it to the 29th.

"The fight against Orleans will probably last many days, and be very bloody; but I will undertake it unless I receive other orders.

"One must do in war what is most inconvenient to the enemy, not that which he likes. To me it seems clear that the enemy wishes me to attack, and wherever I may make the attack I shall come on a series of small strong localities prepared for defence. Since I must always so arrange as to be able to get in front of an enemy who, when I am engaged with him, may march past my flank on Paris, I am unfortunately more restricted in the choice of the direction * of my attack than I should be after the fall of Paris. Then there would be disposable for Orleans, so many troops, that perhaps the enemy might be again invested. How far the capture of Orleans will "throw the enemy over the Loire" [apparently a quotation from the King's letter] I cannot say; for that will be only one part of the enemy's army. How far it will hasten the development of matters at Paris I do not know. Whether it can be postponed until after that catastrophe is beyond my judgment. But what I can be sure of is that I will do my best for both, to hold the enemy as far from Paris as possible, or to wrest Orleans from him. The loving and gracious God grant that this object may be attained without too severe loss." [And then peeps out after piety, practical

---

* In the letter as given by Hoenig and v. d. Goltz respectively there is a remarkable difference here. The latter uses (p. 101) the word "Angriffsrichtungen"; the former (vol. i. p. 366), the word "Angriffsbewegungen," a serious difference.

tactics.] "In all cases the artillery shall prepare the way thoroughly for the infantry.

"To day's daily state gives 48,000 men ; but from this total must be deducted, per Army Corps, at least one battalion for escorts to trains and baggage, etc., against Franc-tireurs, and also every day some sick. In this total are included also footsore men and small commands of all sorts, which have been left behind on the march ; so that 40,000 rifles are certainly not exceeded. But the troops are splendid, and already many wounded officers and men are again to the front.

"When the war is over the infantry must have a better fire-arm—that is the general desire."

The value of this letter lies in its giving us the views of the leader of 100,000 men, on the strategical and tactical aspects of a military operation, on the issues of which depended whether the tide of conquest had come to the full, and henceforth must exchange the flow for the ebb ; or whether the last remaining barrier to its onward course should now be swept away, and the deluge of invasion spread over the whole land. Whether v. d. Golz has given the letter *in extenso*, we do not know, but certain it is, that from his position as one of the staff of the Prince, he has done justice to his commander. Taken then, as a fair representation of the mind of the Prince, the letter is hardly that of a really great soldier ; there is in it somewhat more of the student of war, than of the soldier in the field.

That the French had over-estimated in an extraordinary degree the Germans opposed to them, was a fact ; for on the 23rd d'Aurelle, in a report to Tours, estimated the combined strength of the Second Army and of the Detachment at 200,000, and stated his belief that at Pithiviers (where there were only 16,000), there were 80,000 men ; but at any moment it was possible that the real numerical inferiority of the Germans might have been discovered. As regards the possibillity of working over the country, the Prince was quite mistaken, as he found to his cost two days later ; so the justification for the great extension of his position was based on very weak reasoning. As regards the tactical aspect of an attack on Orleans, the Prince was, on the other hand, thoroughly correct in his views. Although he sarcastically spoke of Lawyers' orders as governing the French operations, he could not possibly know that, as was actually the case, Gambetta and de Freycinet, and not d'Aurelle gave the most important orders; he was bound to presume that the defence of this most defensible position round Orleans would remain in the hands of the military Leader; and a visit to the ground cannot fail to impress on the mind, the almost hopeless character of any attack on it with a numerical inferiority of infantry if it is defended by troops even not wholly regulars, but who are numerous and are utilised in accordance with the simplest principles of military leading. With respect to the Prince's strategy, as revealed in the letter, there seems to be a want of unison between theory and practice; the student of war states the case fairly, the soldier fails in the application to practi&e. The Prince gives correctly the strategical operations open to the enemy for adoption; and he is equally correct as to the only way in which it is possible to deal effectually with them, and he quotes as an exemplar Napoleon and the Marne; but he seems to overlook the fact that the mode in which he is dealing tactically with the situation, this vast extension of front, will render in the highest degree difficult, that close concentration of all available forces, which is the foundation-stone for the subsequent strategical manœuvring operations. To place himself in a situation analogous to that of the great Napoleon, much time will be required, and the enemy will certainly not allow the concentration to be carried out undisturbed; but the " heads of the columns on all roads " will do a good deal more than merely " show " themselves; they will engage and hold to their ground no small portion of the troops which the Prince will be trying to draw together away from them for the strategic movement on which so much depends, and for the success of which rapidity in execution is essential.

NOVEMBER 26

It was on this day that the Prince had finally thrown aside the operation of convergent strategy initiated by v. Moltke on the 22nd and handed over by him on the 25th to the Prince to carry out; and for it the latter now substitutes an operation of convergent tactics. It is possible that v. Moltke's scheme might have succeeded, but owing to causes, of the existence of which it is in the highest degree improbable that v. Moltke was aware. These were the virtual abandonment by d'Aurelle of the chief military command, and the assumption of this command by Gambetta and de Freycinet; the diversity of views between d'Aurelle and Chanzy, the chief commander on the western side of the great road; the rawness of the left flank corps, the 17th, the little value of the 21st Corps at le Mans; the nervousness of the Delegation for the safety of Tours, the exaggerated estimate of the German forces, and the erroneous notions as to the positions, views and intentions of the invading forces in this theatre of war. The Prince's tactical operation, however, involved an attack on a very strong and well-prepared position, held by a numerically superior enemy. Had the Army of the Loire, before it was actually attacked, not been previously weakened by the overthrows on November 28th and December 2nd, and had it received that attack, not outside, but secure in the position itself, it is very questionable that the attack would have been successful. But, nevertheless, in the preference for the strategical attack v. Moltke seems to have grasped the situation far better than did the Prince. In the first war the first French Army had proved its stubbornness in defence, and had revealed its weakness in manœuvring. Whilst it was likely that the second French Army, animated by the highest spirit of patriotism, would rival its predecessor in endeavouring to hold its ground when attacked by the invaders, it was most improbable that it would reach even the former low standard of manœuvring power, and it was almost certain that its generals and staffs would be even still less capable of utilising the little of that power it possessed. That d'Aurelle, with the materials at his disposal, would be able effectively to meet a hostile strategic operation coming on him by surprise at some unexpected point in the long front of seventy miles from Gien to le Mans is in the highest degree unlikely. V. Moltke wished to take advantage of a weakness, the Prince ignored the weakness and preferred to attack under conditions the most favourable to the enemy. Mechanically worked tactics were to be substituted for art-like strategy.

CHAPTER XIII

NOVEMBER 27TH

THE period from November 27th to December 2nd is the decisive period not only of this " People's War," or of the campaign on the Loire, but it may be regarded as the decisive period of the whole Franco-German campaign of the Second War; for during it the French Army in Paris made its greatest effort to break through the investing line, whilst from the south the Army of the Loire made its two great attempts to force the investing Army to release the capital from its grip. But it was on the result of any decisive encounter on the Loire, and not on Ducrot's forcing his way through the investing line with some 50,000 or 60,000 men that for the Germans the future depended. If the French Army of the Loire were thoroughly defeated, these 50,000 or 60,000 men would be aimless wanderers, easily dealt with; but if Prince Frederick Charles were defeated, and the Army of the Loire victorious and free to move, immediate concentration of nearly all the remaining German forces in France became at once a necessity for self-preservation, and this would involve the abandonment of the investment. Thereby the practical sympathy of the whole of Europe could not fail to have been enlisted in the cause of a nation that had endured such prolonged suffering, and had by such endurance emerged successfully from disaster and defeat; and it is possible that from political considerations, Germany might have hesitated to embark on a new campaign against France. Hence, at this time, the importance of the campaign on the Loire. That the crisis on the Loire lasted so long was due to the Fog of War, which now hid from the contending commanders on both sides what was in front of them; so that instead of rapidly carrying out movements which must have brought the crisis to a climax, there was cautious refraining from activity, because any movement seemed fraught with danger.

It is impossible to relate here all the details of the proceedings on these days, and of them only a general account can be given, attention being drawn also to some matters in them specially deserving notice. But even this account may raise in the mind of the reader some not altogether satisfactory reflections on the value of the study of the Art of War; and this feeling would be intensified by a careful perusal of the large amount of recorded details. *Cui bono*, the study of war, if leaders blundering and giving wrong orders, and if troops fighting blindfolded, can thus win in campaigns and battles? The elements of chance, of luck, and fortune, seem to have had here far more weight and influence on the results than did study, thought, and brains.

It is impossible not to sympathise with the Prince in the anxiety he felt from the earliest hours of the 27th. The reports had told him that during the previous day, the enemy in front of him had gained ground, slowly and not much, but still, ground had been gained; and the number of the hostile forces in front of the 9000 or 10,000 men of the Xth Army Corps must at the lowest estimate be 55,000.

On the previous day he had viewed, without any disquietude or disapproval a rest-day for the Detachment; but now, as the storm was certainly gathering, and might burst on him at any moment, the sooner the Detachment came to his aid the better; but there arrived a telegram sent early by the Grand Duke saying that he would reach the Loir that day, but must take a rest-day on the 28th; and at 8 P.M. came from v. Stosch a confirmatory telegram; so no help could be looked for in that direction; and also from many sources came reports that the French Army was massing to the right at Montargis,* beyond the German left. In Ladon, had been

* As the incidents are now becoming localised at and near Beaune, it

found letters from French soldiers, at the camp at Montargis, all referring to the march on Paris, and the certainty of success. " It is evident," said most of the writers, "that now at last it is to be an advance, for at the places where only a few days ago there were Prussians, they [the French] are now advancing victoriously." Reading the reports, it is impossible to doubt that the Prince was fully justified in drawing from them the conclusion, that the strategical advance selected by Gambetta was to be up the valley of the Loing. He therefore determined for the morrow to carry out a general movement towards the East, so that the army would front towards Montargis. And yet the conclusion he drew was the opposite of the truth, for the French had no intention whatever of taking this line of advance; and they had not, on the 27th, massed forces at Montargis. The 18th Corps had been there on the 26th, but on the 27th it was drawn west, leaving only a brigade to cover the right of the delayed attack on Beaune and Pithiviers, for which the final preparations were completed by Crouzat this day. It will appear later on that the orders given by the Prince, and an order given by v. V. Rhetz, to meet a situation that did not exist, led to the successful dealing by the Germans with the situation that did exist.

And now to the Detachment, which, owing to the retirement of de Sonis and the 17th Corps on the night of the 26th, entered Chateaudun and Bonneval on the 27th, encountering but little opposition. Some of the inhabitants resisted to the last, and being taken with arms in their hands were at once shot.

V. Stosch, in the course of his journey to Chateaudun, where he expected to find the Head-quarters of the Detachment, struck first on the 4th Cav. Division and the 22nd Inf. Division, north of Bonneval; and by his own personal observation, as well as from conversation with some of the senior officers, found how widely different was the actual condition of an army that

seems desirable to warn the reader that in this book the name "Montargis" indicates *invariably* the town on the Loing, and *never* the little village four miles east of Beaune.

had been struggling continuously for a fortnight against a people in arms, from the idea formed of its condition, by Staff Officers of high degree, including perhaps himself, who had all the time been comfortably fed and lodged at Versailles. The whole Detachment, including its staff, was in a state of moral depression. As the officers he met told him, this depression was not due to the mere physical exertions, to the marching off before dawn, the haltings, delays and crossings on the roads; the arrival after dark into quarters, or into no quarters at all, but into wet and cold bivouacs: these trials and discomforts would not have told on the men if only there had been some tangible result, one battle, one real encounter; but instead of this, there had been only a perpetual irritating skirmishing with guerilla bands. One big battle, and the Detachment would still have been fit for any work. V. Stosch soon became convinced that a rest-day was absolutely necessary, and he forthwith obtained leave for it from Versailles.

The Duke received v. Stosch with a somewhat distant manner; the change of Chief Staff Officer without consultation with him was a departure from rule, and he might fairly suspect that v. Stosch had been sent to keep a watch on him. But soon v. Stosch discovered that the discontent of the Grand Duke arose from the same cause as did the general depression, hard work with no result. Employing, therefore, the utmost tact, and constantly nourishing in the mind of his commander the prospect of a battle in the near future, and one worthy of the Detachment, v. Stosch succeeded in establishing himself in the position he had been sent to occupy, namely, accepted and trusted adviser and counsellor, and, not improbably, as a sort of protection against the idiosyncrasies of the Prince, whose behests the Grand Duke had now to obey.

V. Stosch, turning to the investigation of the way in which the staff work had been carried on, found a state of things that fully accounted for much of the unsatisfactory leading, and for the meagreness of the information that from time to time had been furnished to Versailles. To his surprise there was no Field Bureau, the records were in disorder, *précis* of information received were not forthcoming, there was no proper subdivision and distribution of Staff Duties; in short, there was not at the Head-quarters any proper Staff Organisation. All this, v. Stosch at once reformed, and he put the staff work on a right footing.

The 17th Corps had now quite disappeared from the neighbourhood. On the 26th, de Sonis, at Chateaudun, had received permission from d'Aurelle to retire on Orleans. But in Tours a real panic had arisen on the receipt of the news from de Sonis, that he believed two armies and a Cavalry Division to be closing on him. Orders were at once sent to d'Aurelle to provide for the protection of the Delegation, so he ordered de Sonis not to retire on Orleans, but due south on Marchenoir, and he suggested a night march; a dangerous form of retreat even with good soldiers, but full of risk for those here. Some hostile cavalry patrols, a few stray shots, and the 17th Corps broke and fled; a large number rallied at St. Laurent des Bois, not far from Marchenoir, some did not stop until they had got to the Loire at Beaugency. On the 27th, from the country far and wide, the scattered troops were gradually collected south of the Forest of Marchenoir.

On this night of the 27th, whilst the Detachment is looking forward to the well-earned rest of the morrow, and the Prince is full of the strategic movement north from Montargis that he is to thwart, Crouzat, within a few miles of him, is at work at his plan of battle for the morrow, and has drawn up his orders for the decisive stroke which, within four and twenty hours shall, he hopes, have crushed at all events the Xth A.C., the left of the Second German Army. During the day the 18th Corps, with the exception of a brigade that remained at Montargis, had been brought to Ladon. The plan for the battle was good, and in devising it Crouzat possessed an advantage not usually found with an attacking force; he knew in detail the positions of all the troops of the Xth Army Corps on the night before the battle; whereas the defenders could only surmise in the vaguest way the dispositions of even the largest units of the attacking force, and were actually doubtful what those units really were. Nor could it be otherwise. The area over which the Xth Army Corps was scattered in the neighbourhood of the battlefield is some twenty-five square miles in extent. On it are a large number of villages and hamlets, and roads and tracks are in profusion; the line of German outposts was ten miles in length, and, in front of Beaune, but 500 or 600 yards distant from that of the French. It was, therefore, impossible for the Germans to prevent the population collecting information as to the disposition of the troops over the whole area, and then transmitting it to the French outposts, whence it went to Crouzat. During the battle there were confined in the church of Beaune, forty civilians who had been captured whilst taking part in the previous fights, or whilst obtaining information. Amongst them was the Curé of Lorcy, the Sous-Maire of Montargis, and the Maire of a small village. Crouzat's plan was to envelop the Xth Army Corps, to cut it off from the rest of the Second Army, and to crush it. Crouzat considered that the key of the position he was to endeavour to hold after its capture was the village of Beaune; v. V. Rhetz seemed to consider it also the key of his own position, though that it was so, as the key of a position protecting the left flank of the Second Army, his special duty, is not at all certain; so whilst he disposed his corps specially for its protection, Crouzat made its capture the special object of the battle. Crouzat determined that after the German outposts had been driven in, the 18th Corps from Ladon should advance on the east side of the village, whilst the 20th Corps advanced simultaneously against its front and its west side; the Germans would thus find themselves enveloped on both flanks and their line of retreat threatened. If they retired, Beaune must be left to its fate; if they did not retire, they would find themselves surrounded by overwhelming forces. On the left of the 20th Corps were Cathelineau's Franc-tireurs, who were maintaining connection between that corps and the 1st Division (des Pallières') of the 15th Corps, which Division, on a very wide front, was guarding the entries to the Forest of Orleans east of the Paris Road. It was intended that the troops on the left of the 20th Corps should deal with any German reinforcements arriving from Pithiviers. As on the 27th des Pallières had been informed both by Crouzat on his right, and by Chanzy on his left, that they expected to be attacked, he considered it to be his duty to remain in his present position, to look both ways, help in either direction and also prevent the enemy breaking in between the two corps. It must be mentioned that owing to orders being sent from both Tours and d'Aurelle, there was great doubt at times in the minds of the Generals as to what they were expected to do.

CHAPTER XIV

NOVEMBER 28TH—BATTLE OF BEAUNE LA ROLANDE

AT eight o'clock on the morning of November 28th, there fell into Beaune from the south near St. Loup, two miles south of Beaune and four west of Juranville, a few shells, of which one struck the house in which were the Head-quarters of the Xth Army Corps. The battle of Beaune la Rolande, the effort to accomplish the first stage of the advance of the Army of the Loire to the relief of Paris, had begun. It was the first of the three battles which in one week were fought on the Loire. A detailed narrative of the battle would be beyond the scope of this work, so only a general account of it will here be given.

The 2400 men forming the ten miles line of German outposts were soon driven in, but the 18th Corps in advancing from Ladon towards the east side of Beaune by Juranville and Venouille, encountered unexpectedly strong hostile forces in the way. At the time when Crouzat allotted this task to the corps he knew that the Germans were not in force here; but unknown to him, v. V. Rhetz, in accordance with the directions from the Prince to watch towards Montargis, had drawn in the early morning to this flank his one reserve Brigade and the Corps Artillery, so these were at once utilised to stop the advance. The main body of the Xth Army Corps was collected here about Long Cour, which is two miles east of Beaune. General Billot, who was in command of the 18th Corps, endeavoured in vain, after having captured the advanced German posts, to drive the Germans from the main position; but at 2 P.M. he abandoned the attempt, and leaving some troops in front of the enemy, he marched, concealed by the close country, with the

NOVEMBER 28

remainder to Beaune, and took part in the unsuccessful attacks there later on in the afternoon. Against the German right, Crouzat, with the 20th Corps, had been at first decidedly successful, though the splendid attack of this Garde Mobile Corps on the south-west and west side of the village of Beaune failed against the well-disciplined resistance of the 38th Infantry Brigade (v. Wedell). But by an enveloping attack from the west the Germans were forced back on the north side of the village, the defenders of which thus became isolated from the rest of the corps. So bad was the outlook towards 2 P.M., that v. V. Rhetz, on the receipt of an erroneous report from a Staff Officer that Beaune had fallen into the hands of the French, ordered a general retreat. But at the suggestion of Colonel v. Caprivi the issue of the order was suspended, as reinforcements were on their way from Pithiviers. It was about 3 P.M. that the troops of the 5th Infantry Division arrived near enough to influence the course of the fight, and then a counterstroke against the left flank of the attack drove the French back. The garrison in Beaune had held out against the earlier attacks of the 20th Corps and the later ones when the 18th Corps also entered on the eastern side of the village into the fray. The battle was prolonged into the darkness, and then the French were driven finally off the battlefield, leaving the defenders of the position, however, worn out and exhausted.

The initial operation for the relief of Paris had failed. Rarely has an attacking force been so completely overthrown and rendered so thoroughly incapable for either defence or offence: rarely has the demoralisation resulting from a single defeat in one theatre of war so greatly influenced the course of a subsequent renewal of the struggle in another theatre of war. Beaune la Rolande made itself felt on the Lisaine. Usually after a battle the victor knows that he has won, but here, strangely enough, whilst the losers fully realised the completeness of their own defeat, the victor not only did not realise his victory, but he completely misunderstood what had happened; he believed that his victory was only a narrow escape from actual defeat, and that he would have to undergo a similar ordeal next day. So the fruits of victory remained ungarnered. And this was owing to a very great extent to the fact that the war of which this battle was an incident, was a "People's War" in a tract of country singularly adapted to a war of this character. It was by the aid of the people that Crouzat had been able to lie hidden close to his enemy, and to place, unknown to him, his troops in position whence they could burst out on him unexpectedly; it was with the aid of the people that when he had failed and was forced to abandon the attack, he found again the safe shelter from which he had emerged, a haven of security and rest. On the night following the battle, all that the Prince knew was the bare fact that an attack had been made on the Xth Army Corps, and had been repulsed.

No doubt to judge correctly the result of a battle, even if it be a victory, is often a matter of great difficulty, and it is only the commander, possessing a real military *coup d'œil*, who can see below the surface of that which lies before him; but it is certain that a leader less cautious and more physically active than the Prince would have found out something of how matters stood. Until there is given to the world the views and reasons of action of the Prince other than those to be found in official or semi-official publications, it would be both unjust and unfair to form any final opinion on his capacity as the German leader of the operations against the Army of the Loire; and that this information is not available is the more to be regretted because his line of action and his conduct during the week commencing November 28th appear to be, to say the least, somewhat strange.

For the 28th, three possible courses of action that the enemy might take on this day were in the mind of the Prince in the early morning; and whichever of the three Crouzat might select, an attack on the Xth Army Corps at Beaune on that day was certain. Crouzat might elect to commence operations by throwing his whole force on the corps and crushing it; or whilst attacking the corps for this purpose he might

NOVEMBER 28

simultaneously advance from Montargis down the Loing ; or if this advance was the main operation of the day, he must at the same time attack the corps strongly enough to hold it at Beaune, thus preventing it either attacking him on his left flank during the advance, or retiring quickly to the north-east to intercept the advance short of Fontainebleau. On the early discovery of the real meaning of the indispensable attack on the corps, the right and successful subsequent employment of the whole of the Prince's command depended. The Prince had told v. V. Rhetz that the mission of the corps was to protect the left flank of the Second Army, but to regard this as its only function, would be to take a very limited view of the situation and its requirements, for on the corps the future course of the campaign depended ; it was the pivot on which the future strategy turned. If the corps were defeated at Beaune and had to fall back, it gave to Crouzat another starting-point towards the capital, for from Beaune he could make not only north-east to Fontainebleau, but north-west to Toury or Etampes on the Orleans-Paris road ; besides which the Prince with his two unbeaten corps could not expect to hold his own against a now certain general advance of the whole Army of the Loire. If, concurrently, Crouzat with a real attack on the corps, was sending forces north from Montargis, it was indispensable to maintain the corps on its present line for a time to cover the flank march of the two other corps towards the east, or to enable them to concentrate ; if Crouzat, really marching from Montargis, was only demonstrating against the corps, every man and gun unnecessarily detained in the present position was a sheer waste of power urgently needed elsewhere. On November 28th it was at Beaune la Rolande that the Oracle had established itself, and there only could it be consulted as to the future. Yet the personal behaviour of the Prince seems to throw great doubts on his having realised the fact.

The sound of guns at Beaune was heard so plainly at Pithiviers in the early morning that v. Waldersee, who was engaged in writing his daily letter to the King, brought it abruptly to a close, mounted his horse and rode off towards Beaune. The firing had aroused the inhabitants of Pithiviers to a high pitch of excitement. At street corners, doors of houses, and in market places and open spaces, they gathered discussing among themselves the course affairs were taking, and openly speaking of this firing as the commencement of the expected decisive battle. Meanwhile the telegraph wires from Beaune to Pithiviers were conveying to the Prince information and reports false as well as true. Apparently about 8.30 A.M. came from v. V. Rhetz at Beaune a message dated 7.4 A.M., stating that the general had, during the night, been informed that on the previous evening the enemy had occupied Fontenay on the Loing, four miles south of Chateau Landon, and eight miles north of Montargis. The general was therefore shifting his corps artillery and his reserve brigade nearer to his left wing. It seems probable that the French in Fontenay were only foraging parties, and yet it was this erroneous information that caused this shifting and led to the failure of the attack of the 18th Corps. A little earlier had arrived at Pithiviers from the neighbourhood of Nemours a sanitary column which reported that on the previous evening Nemours, which is twenty miles north of Montargis and only eight miles from Fontainebleau, had been occupied by the advanced guard of the enemy. It is certain that there were no French in Nemours. But these two reports seemed to furnish decided indications of the advance north down the Loing, though it must have seemed strange that the German detachment already in Chateau Landon had not sent in any report to the same effect.

Soon came in reports from Beaune as to what was taking place there and in the neighbourhood, but which in no way conflicted with those already received; and these latter, unfortunately, had led to the formation of erroneous impressions at the very commencement of the work of the day. The telegraph station was at the village of Beaune, but the general had at about 8 A.M. left Beaune for Long Cour; so there must occasionally have been a certain amount of delay in rendering reports to Pithiviers. By a wire of 9.15 A.M., v. V. Rhetz reported that a fight had commenced at Maizieres (nearly three miles south of Long Cour), where the enemy, the 18th Corps, had attacked the outposts.* A second wire, which was received at 10 A.M., said: "There is an outpost fight at Juranville [one mile nearer Long Cour], which at this time, 9.15, appears to be dying out. The enemy has shown some hostile infantry battalions, but no artillery. At present our infantry and artillery have easily repulsed them." The Prince now came to the conclusion that the Loing Valley was to be the scene of the hostile operations, and he therefore determined to move his army this day in that direction. To v. V. Rhetz he wrote at 9.30 A.M. a letter, probably despatched about 10 A.M.: "I have received your Excellency's report that the advanced hostile troops have reached Fontenay. The hostile forces advancing by Montargis belong apparently to the 18th Corps" [now actually engaged against the German left] "and whose advance down the Loing, especially on the right bank, must be delayed. Your Excellency will, therefore, send to-day by Chateau Landon a brigade with artillery and cavalry which will take up a position for this purpose, and push forward detachments towards Joigny" [in the direction of the expected arrival of the last, the 40th Brigade, of the corps]. . . . "The IIIrd Army Corps has orders to close to its left, and closely connect with your Excellency at Beaune, so as to take part decisively in any fight that may take place there to-day. . . . According to what happens to-day, of which I must request frequent telegrams, I will settle whether the Xth Army Corps moves into the country between the Loing and the Yonne, and the IIIrd Army Corps from Beaumont to Chateau Landon to occupy the

---

* There is sometimes great difficulty in ascertaining the meaning of the times named in connection with the telegrams quoted or mentioned by Hoenig and v. d. Goltz, for it is not always clear whether these times apply to the writing the telegram or to its receipt in the office or to its despatch thence, through the wire. This telegram is not mentioned by v. d. Goltz; Hoenig called it "Die erste, von 9¼ uhr." An orderly well-mounted could gallop from Long Cour to Beaune in a very few minutes.

position there. The news of the fight developing at Maizieres just received. The 5th Inf. Division IIIrd Army Corps will at once move towards Beaune " [it did not do so]. " The telegram of 9.30, which speaks of the outpost fight at Juranville dying out, just received. I rely the more on the carrying out the march of a brigade of the Xth Army Corps to the Loing to-day." As the IXth Army Corps was retained on the Paris road pending the arrival of the Detachment, the front of the army would have been between thirty and forty miles long.

Telegrams now came in rapid succession. 10.10 A.M. " The enemy has brought into action at St. Loup some guns which are firing slowly. Nothing fresh from the left." It is very strange if this was the first report of affairs at Beaune, inasmuch as hostile artillery had been in action there from eight in the morning. At 11 A.M. came a wire dated 10.47 : " The fight in front is getting weaker, but on the other hand it is extending towards my left flank." The next, 11.8, came very quickly, as it arrived at 11.15. " The enemy is driving in my outposts at Corbeilles and Lorcy [on the extreme left]. I am bringing my corps artillery and the Brigade at disposal to the crossing of the railway and Cæsar's Road [near Long Cour]." Hoenig states that from the 1st Cav. Division on the right came in also reports indicating that the corps must now be becoming engaged in a fight. Soon the telegraph station in Beaune reported it has to cease working, as the enemy is commencing a heavy fire on the town, and then from the Brigade Commander at Beaune came a letter, of which, unfortunately, neither hour of despatch or receipt is now decipherable. " The frontal attack on Beaune from St. Loup, outflanking in strong force our right wing by Batilly, is in progress. Only one brigade here. Cavalry Division warned." From this Division came the report : " The enemy is between Barville and Beaune [in rear, therefore, of the right flank]. The Cav. Division is obliged to fall back to Barville before infantry and artillery." Now at last, at 12.30 or 1 P.M., the Prince mounted his horse and rode to the battlefield, arriving there just at the time when, after some six hours of fighting, a crisis has arrived.

It is, however, impossible to ascertain what other reports may have come in during the morning. Hoenig and v. d. Goltz are not always in accord; the former gives a most important report, not given by the latter; it was sent at 11.45 by v. V. Rhetz to the Prince, and ran as follows: " An infantry action in the neighbourhood of Juranville and Lorcy in which the enemy is showing strong lines of skirmishers but no artillery. I have supported Valentini's Brigade [in action against 18th Corps] by some of Lehmann's Brigade [the reserve Brigade], and I keep in hand the rest of the latter and the Corps Artillery at the Railway Station on Cæsar's Road. No news from my left flank." And he adds the important remark: " But I regard it as not impossible that the enemy is masking by the engagement his march north." Here was an opinion from an experienced soldier on the spot, and it must have contributed greatly to the formation of the erroneous view of the battle taken later on by the Prince. The exact time at which the Prince set out from Pithiviers is doubtful; but it must have been after midday; and the delay in starting could not have been due to ignorance of the fact that something of importance was taking place at the Xth Army Corps. Hoenig criticises severely the conduct of the Prince in remaining so long at Pithiviers. It is possible that owing to the great length of front, Chateaudun to Montargis, from which the enemy might emerge at any point, he considered it advisable to remain to the last moment in a central position at the end of the telegraph wires; but the distance from Pithiviers to Barville, to which place the 1st Cav. Division had retired, is hardly eight miles, so relays of orderlies would have ensured the rapid transmission of messages sent on and their speedy delivery. The Prince may have been physically somewhat lethargic; Hoenig says that when mounted he never moved faster than at a trot.

There had been at the Head-quarters a good deal of letter-writing as usual. At 11 A.M. v. Stiehle wrote to v. Moltke: " The enemy (we believe it to be probably part of the 18th

Corps) sent forward troops by rail to Montargis yesterday [it was on the 26th that this took place]. Last evening his leading troops were at Fontenay [only foraging parties]. This reveals that the probable plan of the enemy is to approach Paris along the Loing, avoiding the open ground of La Beauce, and turning our left flank. Confirming this is the report just received from the Xth Army Corps that it is being attacked at Maizieres. Fortunately, the 5th Inf. Division is already concentrated south-east of Pithiviers and goes as support to Beaune. So soon as the course of the fight permits, a strengthened Brigade of the Xth Army Corps is to go to-day to Chateau Landon, which is already held by a mixed detachment, in order to take up a position on the Loing, and to reconnoitre to the east. His Royal Highness intends, further, to deploy the Xth Army Corps in the district between the Loing and the Yonne, to place the IIIrd Army Corps on the line Beaumont-Chateau Landon, and to concentrate the IXth Army Corps at Pithiviers. Obviously, this state of affairs upsets, for the time, all plans for crossing the Loire below Orleans. The Detachment arrived yesterday (27th) at Bonneval and Chateaudun without fighting, and is resting there. . . . His Royal Highness intends to draw the Detachment to-morrow (29th) towards Janville-Toury, and to hand over to it the protection of the great road to Etampes and those nearest and parallel to it. The Second Army will thus be freed to operate against the Army of the Loire, which is advancing perhaps on both banks of the Loing. . . . I suggest to your Excellency whether, from the troops before Paris a strong occupation of Fontainebleau and Moret could not be carried out. The fight on the left flank of the Xth Army Corps is extending ; we go there ; " but before going time was found to write and send to the Detachment letters similar to that to v. Moltke. These letters were despatched about noon. To v. Stosch a telegram was sent at 11.30 A.M., directing the Detachment to reach on the 29th the Orleans-Paris road at Toury with as strong leading troops of the left wing as possible, and the rest closed up as much as possible. A short march was suggested for the 28th. Written orders showing the pressing urgency would be sent.

It was probably between one and two o'clock that the Prince arrived near Barville at the time when the 20th Corps had reached the limit of their successful advance against the German right; and although the tide of success soon turned, leaving the flank safe, here the Prince remained, and gave orders in connection with the operations on this flank, beyond which any interest he took in the battle did not seem to extend. There is no record of his having communicated directly or indirectly with the General at Long Cour, or having inquired of him what had taken place, or learning his views on the situation; he seems simply to have ignored his existence, yet there is no trace of any ill-feeling on the part of the Prince towards v. V. Rhetz or of any want of confidence in him. And when at nightfall about half-past five the counterstroke had succeeded the Prince prepared to ride back to Pithiviers; but before he mounted his horse, v. Waldersee came to him and made his report on the battle, having been present the whole time and in personal communication with both v. V. Rhetz and v. Alvensleben. The Count remarked to him: "A complete victory has been won, it will be a Rossbach for the French if there is a vigorous pursuit." The reference to the success of Frederick the Great was made designedly. Gen. v. Hartmann had been urged more than once to launch his Cavalry Division in pursuit, but no order to do so had come to him from a senior officer, and on the plea that the ground was too heavy he scornfully ignored the suggestion. V. Waldersee hoped that by this allusion to Rossbach the Prince would be led to give the order. The Prince asked whether the 1st Cav. Division had not moved to the attack; v. Waldersee hardly liked to tell the Prince of the unsuccessful efforts made for this purpose and confined himself to the reply "there may be difficulties in the way." The Prince, however, did not interfere directly in the matter and turning to v. Stosch, said: "According to the report by Count v. Waldersee, the Xth Army Corps cannot be employed in pursuit. One of its brigades must, however, move off to-day to the Loing. But a vigorous pursuit in several directions by the 5th Inf. Division and the 1st Cav. Division promises a great success. Be so good as to convey my wishes to Generals v. Alvensleben and v. V. Rhetz." So any pursuit by the cavalry would not commence until the order had come to v. Hartmann by a roundabout course through some other senior general, and the favourable moment might then have gone by. V. Stiehle rode away to give the orders, and the Prince rode away towards Pithiviers. At the desire of the Prince, v. Waldersee accompanied him on his ride back and the conversation between them continued. The Prince had not seen more of the battlefield than an outlying portion; he had not been near Beaune or any other part of it, where the hecatombs of dead, dying and wounded, told the history of the battle. V. Waldersee, from his personal observation, was convinced that the fight had been far more than a demonstration or a mask for strategical movements, and he endeavoured to induce the Prince to accept as correct his opinion that two hostile army corps had taken part in the battle, and that its issue had been so decisive, that any belief in the advance down the Loing Valley could no longer be entertained. But the Prince firmly held to the opinion that the strength of the enemy had been over-estimated; he still believed that the fight was but the introduction to a powerful offensive movement, and he considered it necessary to put in the Loing Valley stronger forces than had been there up to the present time. The Prince on his way to Pithiviers, where he arrived about seven o'clock, stopped at Boynes to draw up and send a telegram to the king: it ran as follows:

"To H.M. the King, Versailles.

The Xth Army Corps was from nine o'clock driven back from the outpost position; it has successfully held its position at Beaune la Rolande, and was in the afternoon supported in my presence by the 5th Inf. Division and the 1st Cav.

Division. The fight [kampf] was to a certain extent severe [zum Theil sehr ernst]. The enemy was 30,000 strong. Our loss about 1000 men, many hundreds of prisoners. Fight [kampf] ended about 5 P.M."

FRED. CHARLES,
Prince of Prussia.

Nine thousand men not only holding their own successfully all day against the onslaught of fifty thousand, but driving them back off the battlefield with a loss of 8000 to 10,000, only a " Kampf zum Theil sehr ernst!" And this erroneous idea was due to the want of thoroughness in the ascertainment of the facts. It would not have much mattered if the misconception had stood by itself and without any influence on the future, but here it had evil effects on the course of the operations in the days immediately following. And v. Stiehle was, as usual, a mere " ditto " to his chief.

V. Alvensleben when he received the message had not at hand forces for the pursuit; v. Stiehle rode on to give the other order to v. V. Rhetz, but failing to find him sent it to him in writing. The order is reproduced by v. d. Goltz and is worthy of transcription.

" His Royal Highness says that it is of the utmost importance that the detaching an Infantry Brigade with Artillery to Chateau Landon, in order to take up a position in the valley of the Loing, as ordered to-day, shall be carried out tonight with the Brigade most intact. If the attack at Beaune is renewed to-morrow the 5th Infantry Division is there, and at 7 A.M. the 6th Infantry Division and the Corps Artillery of the IIIrd Corps at Boynes ; and also in the forenoon a Brigade of the IXth Army Corps will be available there. We can thus fight with seven Brigades. His Royal Highness expects tonight by the bearer a reply and information about to-day's fight [Gefecht]."

It must have been with no little contempt for the superior staff that v. V. Rhetz read the missive. His reply was to the point: " The sending a Brigade to-night to Chateau Landon is impossible. All three Brigades have been engaged to-day, and all three have put out outposts. All three are short of ammunition and none have finished cooking. As soon as possible to-morrow morning I will move a Brigade on Chateau Landon, but I would remark that it is impossible for only one Brigade to hold the position of Long Cour, and that if I am to take a Brigade away from it, that can only be on the assumption that, meanwhile, it is replaced by a Brigade of the IIIrd Army Corps." So for a few hours the Xth Army Corps was allowed a little peace and rest. It must be mentioned that the intention to cover on the left against German reinforcements Crouzat's advance, fell through owing to the want of unity in the French leading and command.

The Detachment, on the 28th, had been resting on the Loir, and in the evening there came in to Pithiviers from it in reply to the Prince's orders sent in the morning a telegram stating that on the 29th the Detachment, by a march of some twenty-four miles, would arrive with the 4th Cavalry Division at Toury, with the 22nd Infantry Division at Allaines, seven miles west of Toury, the Bavarians at Orgères, eight miles further west, and the 17th Infantry Division in rear of the line, which would face south in prolongation of the line of the Second Army and be in touch with it ; affording thereby that form of co-operation already mentioned as specially agreeable to the Prince. But this telegram was " second thoughts," and represented strict obedience to orders, and not necessarily approval of the strategy ; for only shortly before had come from the Detachment a telegram giving quite another position, and evidently sent before the orders had been received. According to this, the Detachment was to move from the Loir to a position of the shape of an arrowhead, pointing directly south-east towards Orleans ; the point being at Villamblain, on the main road from Chateaudun, and seventeen miles from Orleans. This position represented v. Molke's idea of co-operative strategy, but the idea had, of course, to be abandoned by v. Stosch, who took care, however, to let Versailles know by wire what was being done.

CHAPTER XV

NOVEMBER 29TH

DURING the night 28th-29th reports, seemingly conclusive, that, at all events for the time, the hostile advance down the Loing had been given up, came in from the left. From the Detachment was reported the falling back of very large hostile forces towards Beaugency from the Loir valley. The Prince now awaited, on the 29th, the renewal of the attack. And it is necessary to learn the view taken by v. Moltke of the situation on the 27th, the day previous to the battle, and which is given in a letter of the same date to v. Stiehle, which arrived at Pithiviers apparently in the forenoon of the 29th. The letter commenced with granting the Prince permission to transfer the 6th Cavalry Divison from the Detachment to the Second Army, a most unfortunate and ill-timed concession, as will appear later on. The gravity of the import of the further contents of the letter cannot be overrated: "Our communications are now threatened with serious danger from the South, where General v. Werder cannot protect the whole line Montbéliard-Châtillon. Therefore, the 13th Inf. Division is despatched by rail to Troyes, whence forces will be pushed as far as possible by Joinville. The advance of the enemy by le Mans would be inconvenient, but from the movements of the enemy hitherto this is not probable ; rather, defensive measures at le Mans. . . . If you connect with the Grand Duke it would be desirable for you to attack the enemy. Whether the enemy will attack is a question, but in the defensive he certainly cannot do anything for the relief of Paris. . . . Of decisive weight is your fight in the south against France's only army in the field. If you

are beaten, my plan would be to give up the Investment of
Paris, and to send the Crown Prince of Saxony [Fourth
Army] with Manteuffel to the north, and the Crown Prince
of Prussia [Third Army] with you to the south; and, after
winning some victory, to resume the Investment of Paris, at
the surrender of which we shall recover our siege Artillery."
The situation as it presents itself on the 27th to v. Moltke
is grave indeed; immediately in front he has to hold
back the greatest sortie yet attempted from Paris, aided
by small sorties from other parts of its walls; the communications of all the German forces in France are threatened in their most vulnerable point, and at the point farthest
away from any aid he could send; to his south is a huge
hostile army of relief faced by an inert and inactive 90,000
Germans, apparently awaiting the law from the enemy. The
meaning of the remarkably honest, open, and candid statement in the letter is surely clear enough—so clear, that he
who runs may read; it hardly seems to admit of misunderstanding. What he says to v. Stiehle and to the Prince may
be paraphrased truthfully: " You see the plight in which we
Germans, we invaders are, now that our communications with
the Rhine are no longer safe. Now that the Detachment
is nearer to you, *do something or other, and do it at once*. If
you fail, it won't be your fault, I know, and I won't blame
you. In urging you to attack the enemy, I cannot, of course,
count surely on your success, but *try*, for goodness' sake *try*;
I here tell you what I am ready to do and intend to do if
you fail, and in any case I shall hold your boldness free from
blame." It was almost a counsel of despair, and had the
Grand Duke been in command, with v. Stosch at his elbow,
the offensive, it is well nigh certain, would have been taken
on the Loire immediately after the battle of Beaune la
Rolande; but on the Prince and v. Stiehle v. Moltke's letter
had not the slightest effect.

The situation on the east side of the Paris Road on
the 29th was very peculiar, though presumably not without
precedent in military history. The Germans had again taken

up the outpost line they held before the battle. Close in front at Ladon and Boiscommun respectively were the 18th and 20th Corps, the corps that had fought against them, but which are now impotent for offence and are fearing an attack by the Germans; the Germans still on the defensive as on the previous day, and again awaiting an attack; and with no thought of the possibility of pursuing the enemy they had driven off. Troops on whom the brunt of the battle has fallen are physically unfit to pursue; and here the corps at the outposts, the Xth Army Corps which had done the fighting, was worn out and exhausted, but the IIIrd Army Corps was quite fresh and was close at hand. It could well have undertaken the task, whilst the Xth Army Corps with a little rest and its re-supply of ammunition completed, could have followed in reserve. And had the pursuit been taken up in the early morning, it is possible that very great results might have followed. It would have struck upon the 20th Corps, which was so completely demoralised by its defeat that Crouzat was obliged to report to Tours, that it would be absolutely unfit for any further work until after a rest of several days. It was the Garde Mobile Corps; grandly and heroically it had fought, inspired by patriotic enthusiasm, but without that previous training which is the best preparation to face defeat calmly; so the deepest moral depression had succeeded to the high hopes and anticipations of the previous day. The 18th Corps was composed mainly of *regiments-de-marche*, and seems to have been less affected morally by the defeat. Reinforcements were during the day nearing both flanks of the French line, but a blow driven home on one part might have been decisive. The actual condition of the defeated force was, however, unknown to the Germans, for it had retired again to its previous shelter, shrouded from view physically by the character of the country, and among a population still intent on doing its best to give it notice of the approach of danger and to put pursuers on the wrong track. But there was one source from which might be drawn some fairly sound conclusions as to the power of resistance to pursuit. This was the aspect presented on the morning of the 29th by the battlefield. Suspicions that the overthrow of the French had been great were entertained by some of the German Staff Officers even on the night following the battle ; on the morning of the 29th, the Prince despatched from Pithiviers to the scene of conflict Staff Officers to report to him on the matter ; and in their reports there was no conflict or difference of opinion ; the disaster to the French had been great and overwhelming. But the Prince did not go to judge for himself, and the information being second-hand could not produce in his mind the same impression that would have been derived from personal observation. No doubt it is strange, that inasmuch as he anticipated a renewal of the attack that day, and that in meeting it two of his three corps would have to take part, he should not have, in the early morning, taken that short ride to ascertain how matters stood, and also as chief commander to supervise the arrangements for the expected encounter. But the same considerations as on the previous day may have induced him to remain at Pithiviers ; here he was at the end of the wires connecting him with other parts of the wide area, all of which he had to keep under his observation. Had he himself seen things as they were on the battlefield, he would possibly have found in them a complete justification for immediate compliance with v. Moltke's urgent appeal : " Do go on and hit the Army of the Loire as hard as you can."

About noon this day, the Prince ordered that v. V. Rhetz's troops here should be relieved from any further participation in the operations in the Loing Valley, as Major-General v. Kraatz with the 40th Brigade was near enough to watch now the line of hostile advance from Montargis on Fontainebleau. The corps was to concentrate in the country east of Beaune : then came the IIIrd Army Corps, whilst at Pithiviers, and between it and the Paris road, was to be the IXth Army Corps.

The Detachment after a good march, but occasionally brushing against the left of the hostile army, arrived on the 29th with the head of the 4th Cavalry Division at Toury, and with a small force of infantry at Allaines, five miles short of Toury. The main body of the detachment was facing south-east on a line ten miles long and six or seven miles in rear; the 22nd Inf. Division on the left at Ymonville; the 17th Inf. Division in the centre at Germignonville; the Bavarians on the right at Orgères, with the 6th Cavalry Division ten miles south at Villampuy. Head-quarters were at Viabon in rear of the centre of the line. The Prince intimated to the Grand Duke the approaching exchange of Cavalry Divisions, and he ordered that whilst the Bavarians should hold on to Orgères, the left should extend right across the Paris road as far as Bazoches les Gallerandes five miles to the east of it. The whole front of the Prince's command was forty miles in length and extended thinly across all the lines of approach to Paris.

On the evening of the 29th, the Prince telegraphed to the King: "According to French statements, the enemy yesterday was 70,000 men strong, from the 20th, 18th, 15th and 16th Corps, of which the whole of the 20th Corps was in the fight. [None of the 16th were in the battle, there were only two batteries of the 15th, whilst the 18th Corps was one brigade short.] I sent some battalions of the IIIrd Army Corps in pursuit during the night. To-day little can take place, because the state of affairs on the Loing has not yet been cleared up, and because the results stated above were known only in the course of to-day. To-morrow advanced guards will pursue towards Montargis and Bellegarde."

V. Stiehle, fully aware that v. Moltke and the Prince are not in accord on the strategy for the campaign, naturally wished to learn exactly what were the views held at Versailles; and as a personal interview is worth a sheaf of letters, he wired to v. Stosch arranging a meeting the next day at Bazoches les Gallerandes.

The Prince appears not to have had sufficient self-confidence to act always on his own independent judgment in arriving at a decision. In his message to the King it is evident that he considered pursuit, even if delayed, yet both desirable and practicable; but on finding that his chief Staff Officer disagreed with him, and believing that in any advance he would find himself confronted by a prepared defence, he had sought advice from another quarter without letting v. Stiehle know that he was doing so; and whilst he telegraphed in the evening to the Xth Army Corps to advance in force on the 30th against Montargis, he sent a Staff Officer to consult the general commanding the IIIrd Army Corps, v. Alvensleben, in whose opinion he had great confidence. The officer was to communicate the Prince's view of the situation to v. Alvensleben, and to inform him that he intended to advance the IIIrd Army Corps on Boiscommun, and would afterwards, according to circumstances, continue the offensive on Orleans. V. Alvensleben regarded the proposed operation as an isolated operation of the Army Corps, and dissented therefore from its adoption. He also demurred to proposals to make a reconnaissance in force with each of his divisions. Fortified by v. Alvensleben's opinion the Prince determined to remain on the defensive; but v. d. Goltz states that both corps received, in the evening orders, to reconnoitre in force towards Boiscommun and Montargis.

The position of Montargis and the character of the surrounding country were specially unfavourable for reconnaissance; and the peculiarities were skilfully turned to account for purposes of deception in this " People's War." The town with its large population and many hiding-places, was, at this time, the centre of activity of the Franc-tireurs. A great wood lay in front of Montargis on the right bank of the Loing, as far as Ferrieres (8 miles). The Canal d'Orleans which ran on the west and south-west of the town, the Fessard stream and the Loing acquired great importance because the railway bridges and many others over them were barricaded and occupied by the defenders. From these bridges all the German patrols were met with heavy fire; the German Cavalry had not been trained in swimming, but even if they had been trained, the steep canal banks would probably have formed a powerful obstacle. The patrols were consequently unable to reconnoitre the town itself; this could have been effected by a strong force only. Whether all these facts were known to the Prince is uncertain.

As regards the exchange of the Cavalry Divisions, it is impossible to understand how any leader in war, especially one who was himself a general of Cavalry, could even allow, still less ask for, such an exchange at this time. As both the 2nd and the 6th Divisions were in actual contact with the enemy, the exchange of these Divisions along the front of the armies was impossible. The only solution practicable was that adopted ; the 6th was exchanged for the 4th which was somewhat in rear, at Toury ; and the two effected the exchange by a route-march in rear of the Detachment. During this march both divisions might as well have been non-existent for the battle purposes of the Detachment, and of the Second Army ; but worse than this, the 6th Division that knew the country well was being replaced on the eve of, and during a great battle, by the 4th Division which not only did not know the country, but was tired and well-nigh exhausted.

CHAPTER XVI

NOVEMBER 30TH

EARLY in the morning of the 30th came to the Prince from Versailles two telegrams stating that the expected great sortie had begun towards the south. That the Army of the Loire would now move to the assistance of Paris was therefore in the highest degree probable. The Prince rode now to the battlefield of Beaune and watched the action of the numerous reconnaissances sent to the front by his order. Everywhere they met the enemy, and sometimes in force, so that along the whole line there was fighting. Believing, therefore, a hostile advance not improbable, he held his troops to the position, drawing the IXth Army Corps still nearer.

But his visit to the battlefield was anything but comforting to him, as regards his inaction in the last forty-eight hours. As he was getting into his carriage on his return home, v. Waldersee came to him to report and was invited to accompany him in the carriage. The Prince seemed somewhat dissatisfied, and to think that the day following the battle had not been put to its best use. V. Waldersee turned the conversation on to Beaune. The Prince remarked, "The battlefield reminds me of St. Privat. Yesterday great results might have been obtained, for this corps (the 20th) could not possibly be fit for a fight, and also is not so now. To-day a strong offensive might have reaped its reward, but—" and here the Prince suddenly broke off from this topic. After a little time he resumed : " The favourable moment for the offensive is gone ; the information leads to the conclusion that the French have been reinforced on the line Boiscommun-Bellegarde ; what is going on behind the Forest of Orleans is out of sight. The Franc-tireurs, aided by the country, have done the French good service. Now I am reduced to a waiting attitude. If the French attack us once more, the experience of the 28th to the 30th will stand me in good stead. But a soldier's good fortune seldom comes back to him with the same favour. To-day has already gone by in justifiable doubt; the French were brought forward to the attack at many points; they must have, however, other plans, for it was quite clear that they did not advance beyond the line they had fixed for themselves. *There is for a leader nothing more oppressive than a situation that is not clear, nothing more trying than bands of armed irregular troops, aided by the population and the nature of the country, and relying for support on a strong army in the neighbourhood.*" What a decisive testimony is this to the aid a People may give in war.

What had not been lost by that day of inaction in Pithiviers!

On the 30th, the conference between the two Chief Staff Officers v. Stiehle and v. Stosch took place at Bazoches les Gallerandes. The purpose of v. Stiehle in meeting v. Stosch was twofold: first to learn from v. Stosch the views held by v. Moltke as to the course of the campaign on the Loire, past, present, and future; secondly, to justify the action of the Prince in the past and present, and his proposed action in the future. The campaign on the Loire was only one of four large operations which, together, constituted at this time the campaign of Germany against France; the others being the operations in the north-west, those in the south-east, and the investment of Paris. Each of these four was important, but their relative importance necessarily varied from time to time according to the aspect that the campaign, taken as a whole, presented from time to time, and according to the degree in which danger to the whole campaign was more or less threatening at the scene of each. If danger seemed imminent at one of these points, then in order that this might be warded off, there might be accepted a certain amount of passivity among the German forces elsewhere, so that troops might be diverted to the threatened point. And it was only at Versailles that this relativity of importance could be correctly judged. From v. Stosch, fresh from Versailles, v. Stiehle could learn exactly the importance Versailles attached at this moment to the operations on the Loire, and the result which, from those operations it was considered would contribute most effectively to the success of the whole war. On the other hand, it was the commanders at the four scenes of operations who were, or who ought to be, the best judges of the measures to be adopted for obtaining the results regarded by Versailles as desirable and necessary. Mental vigour depends greatly on physical vigour, and it was no small gain to the counsels at the Loire that there should come a counsellor like v. Stosch, physically fit, and who had not suffered from the fatigues and anxieties of the trying work in the field. Hoenig gives a long account of the conference, but this it seems unnecessary to reproduce here, inasmuch as the subjects discussed were the mode of covering the road from Orleans to Paris, direct or indirect cover, and the time for taking the offensive, now or later on. The views put forward respectively were the same as those with which the reader is already acquainted, and they need not therefore be repeated. The two chiefs parted, not one hair's breadth nearer agreement than when they met.

V. Stiehle, on his return to Pithiviers, gave to the Prince an account of the interview. The Prince considered it desirable, especially as, whilst v. Stiehle had been away, additional information had been gained as to the state of affairs in front of the IIIrd and Xth Army Corps, to send in writing to the Grand Duke his own view of the situation and also his wishes. The Prince informed the Grand Duke that from information gained from prisoners it was clear that " besides the 18th Corps there was another corps in front. Since this did not take part in the battle of the 28th, I believe that for the protection of his right wing, the 15th or the 16th corps has been drawn in this direction." It is difficult to reconcile this statement with that in the Prince's telegram (7.29 P.M. 29th) to the King that " the whole of the 20th corps and also troops from the 18th, 15th, and 16th corps had taken part in the battle." He then

NOVEMBER 30 225

stated his intention of remaining on the defensive in prospect of another attack. One brigade of the IXth Army Corps, the main body of which was at Pithiviers and in the neighbourhood, was at Bazoches les Gallerandes. The Prince ordered, therefore, that on December 1st, the 22nd Inf. Division from the Detachment should relieve this brigade so that it might follow on to Pithiviers, and with its corps act as his own reserve; and he requested that the 22nd Inf. Division should not be employed by the Grand Duke as, if necessary, it would then serve as the last reserve of the Second Army. The Prince gave his opinion as to the hostile forces opposite the Detachment. " It is probable that to-morrow there will be in front of your Royal Highness only the 17th Corps and a part of the 16th Corps; the latter has apparently occupied the north edge of the Forest of Orleans along its whole extent." As a matter of fact, there was on December 1st the whole of the 16th corps, two divisions of the 15th, and two and a half of the 17th corps opposite the Grand Duke, who was now to be deprived of about one-third of his force. The Prince details the mode of withdrawal of the 6th Cav. Division, which, on the following day, is to commence a route-march along the rear of the Detachment, and on December 2nd is to be in position in rear of the centre of the whole line and east of the Paris road; and then comes what may be regarded as a reminder to v. Stosch to " mind his own business." " Until the situation on the enemy's side is clearer, I must reserve to myself the communication to your Royal Highness of my further plans for driving the enemy out of Orleans." How completely the Prince misconceived the situation will soon appear. Specially noteworthy is it that here for the first time in the Loire campaign the mere regaining possession of Orleans appears as the objective of the operations. V. Moltke, up to this time, certainly cannot be credited, or rather discredited, with concurrence in this novel idea.

Very different from the imaginative creations at Pithiviers were the real views and intentions on the French side. The earlier reports of Crouzat on the 28th had caused a great deal

P

of excitement at Tours, and had given rise to great hopes and expectations, so that when the last report was received from him it caused not only deep depression, but senseless wrath and anger. The reply of de Freycinet was full of unjust undeserved personal charges against the General, and was totally unworthy of the Delegation.

On the evening of the 29th, the Delegation demurred to any movement eastward, and directed that the two corps, the 18th and 20th, should be drawn to the west. On November 24th and 26th there had arrived at Tours, from Jules Favre at Paris, despatches in which December 15th was named as the utmost limit for the endurance of the capital. " We cannot hold out beyond that time, even if so long." On November 16th the Government in Paris had estimated that the power of endurance would last to January 8th, 1871. What was the cause of the difference in the limits assigned does not appear. Hoenig thinks that the alteration in the dates may have been a misstatement intentionally made to spur on the Delegation to immediate action. If so, a step more likely to be fatal to success could hardly have been taken. For instead of well-considered and orderly-conducted operations, were necessarily substituted operations adopted in haste and carried out in hurry. And to make matters worse, there came on the 30th, to the Delegation a delayed despatch from Gen. Trochu, which having been sent off from Paris by balloon on the 24th, was first carried to Norway and thence telegraphed to Tours. The despatch announced the intended sortie of the 29th by General Ducrot towards the Loire, probably in the direction of Gien. On the night of the 30th, at 9 o'clock, de Freycinet and the French Generals assembled, therefore, at d'Aurelle's head-quarters to confer on the measures to be taken to meet the new and pressing situation that had so suddenly presented itself. There was no agreement as to any one plan being the best to be adopted, so, finally, de Freycinet produced his own as approved at Tours, and he ordered it to be carried out. Again an attack on Pithiviers, this time converging, and then an advance on Fontainebleau ; the 18th and the 20th corps by the former line, Beaune, the 15th corps on their left against the south and south-west of Pithiviers, whilst to the same objective the 16th corps, supported by the left of the 15th, would move diagonally north-east across the Paris road. The 17th corps, with the help of the 21st from le Mans, would be entrusted with the protection of Orleans. That there were many misunderstandings, arising out of this hastily summoned and probably highly excited meeting, goes without saying.

The discussion occupied so much time that the generals separated in haste, without having had any conference among themselves for mutual understanding, and they hurried away to get out their orders in the early morning at all events. But Chanzy, finding the Detachment in front of his corps, must, necessarily, as a first step in the movement north-east, get the Detachment out of his way, to avoid being attacked on his left during the advance; after submitting his proposal to d'Aurelle, it was eventually agreed that the 16th Corps, covered on the left by Michel's Cavalry Division, should advance north, and dislodge the enemy now there; the 17th Corps to move in support. The advance would be continued next day on Pithiviers. This movement on the 1st must necessarily strike on the Bavarian Corps at Orgères.

CHAPTER XVII

DECEMBER 1ST

On December 1st, at 1.10 A.M., the Prince received from the Xth Army Corps a somewhat belated report of the previous evening, to the effect that according to statements of inhabitants there were 20,000 French in Montargis, and according to those of Prussians left behind sick at Courtenay, to the east of Montargis, large supplies of provisions had lately been passing through the former place to the latter. As a matter of fact, there was no truth in these statements. The Prince, however, ordered reconnaissances towards Montargis and Bellegarde, but as in his order he directed the reconnaissances to be made after the troops had cooked, that towards Montargis could be of little use; but the information generally obtained showed that the French had fallen back, and that no offensive operation against the Second Army was immediately in prospect.

And now the interest shifts to the right wing, the Detachment, for events are so shaping themselves here during the day, that it will be the Grand Duke and v. Stosch, not the Prince and v. Stiehle, who will ward off the second and last effort of the Army of the Loire for the relief of Paris. The Bavarians had thrown forward troops to Terminiers, three miles south of Orgères, and to the villages west of Terminiers. Against this position advanced at about half-past one, one division of the 16th Corps and a Cavalry Division. After much fighting the Bavarians were driven from the position, and they fell back to another at Villepion Chateau. Towards nightfall their defence was broken, and the Corps collected at Orgères and in the neighbourhood. In this brief encounter the Bavarians, who numbered some

7000 men with forty-eight guns, against 13,000 French, with forty-six guns, lost forty-two officers and nearly 900 men. It was, however, nine o'clock at night before a full report on the encounter came to the Head-quarters of the Detachment, which were at Janville, three or four miles west of Toury.

V. d. Tann had at once felt the evil effects of the exchange of the Cavalry Divisions; he needed cavalry on his front, and he applied to the Grand Duke for it, but it could not be given, for the cavalry was not forthcoming. The trusted and trustworthy 6th Division was on its route-march in rear of the Detachment; on the right had arrived the worn-out 4th Division, from which its commander selected the least exhausted Brigade, to move out to the right front. This arrangement was but a poor substitute for the close co-operation that had hitherto been maintained between the Bavarians on the exposed flank and their protectors, the 6th Division. Into the Head-quarters of the Detachment at half-past one had ridden v. Schmidt, the commander of the 6th Division, to report himself to the Grand Duke, who bade him farewell, expressing his deep sense of the value of the services rendered to him by the general and his Division. And then v. Schmidt betook himself to v. Stosch. The interview is so interesting, and was in its consequences so important, that the account of it, as recorded by Hoenig, is here given in full.

With the alert, decided, soldierlike bearing of the cavalry commander, the Chief of the Staff was very sympathetic. But General v. Stosch was surprised, above all, by the detailed knowledge of the country, and the thorough acquaintance with all its peculiarities, that he possessed. V. Stosch remarked that for himself under the circumstances it was very unfortunate that General v. Schmidt should pass over to the Second Army. "And I also lament it," said v. Schmidt excitedly and somewhat bitterly. "I do not grudge to any of my comrades the laurels which undoubtedly are immediately at hand for them, but after I have gone through the Perche country without any satisfaction, I am obliged at this very moment to take a ride in rear of the Army, when I could reap the fruit of all my previous hard work; and very hard work it was. Your Excellency will see that I am speaking only the truth. The enemy is on the point of attacking us. I wish only that you may have an enterprising body of cavalry. In all the world there is no better country for good cavalry than the great district in which we are now. Everything that cavalry could desire, so far as country is concerned, is here; every stone's throw there are villages, farms, small woods and wide although shallow depressions, in which they can conceal themselves in large bodies, and can follow up closely the infantry and dash out and take them by surprise. We are here," he exclaimed, "in the paradise of cavalry; and, moreover, this enemy! His cavalry will never stand against ours, nor have they the spirit of enterprise and the dash to attack our infantry. His artillery is but poorly horsed, and is incapable of moving quickly. His infantry, whether Line, Marche troops, or Gardes Mobiles, cannot stand the ' Prussian Fanfare.' During the last weeks my cavalry have come upon them every day, and have always got the best of it, even if they were well led. This infantry is fodder for good cavalry."

As v. Stosch was still under the influence of his conference with v. Stiehle the day before, he asked General v. Schmidt, without telling him of the interview, whether, in his opinion, " Corps or Divisions had marched eastward for an operation towards Fontainebleau." V. Schmidt gave a most decided negative to the question, and added in his most drastic manner, " The whole lot are still round the salient point, Orleans, but if you do not look out, they will be on the top of you here; all reports from my patrols, and the information from the inhabitants are here in my book with days and dates, and the enemy's regimental numbers. From these, there is not the slightest doubt that strong bodies of all arms have been pushed forward to the road Orleans-Chateaudun; and I know that the 17th Corps is on the march here from the Forest of Marchenoir" [a fact]. In reply to the question how strong the enemy was, v. Schmidt said: " At least 50,000 men; in any case there are at least two Corps. The drawing forward the 17th Corps to the north-east implies an immediate general attack on the Orleans-Chateaudun road." In compliance with General v. Stosch's request, v. Schmidt put together the reports and information received lately; he docketed the important ones with the substance of the contents. To the question whether he believed that the 15th and 16th Corps were on the line Boiscommun-Bellegarde, he gave a negative, and he held to his opinion, even when v. Stosch told him that v. Stiehle believed the contrary.

V. Schmidt's view was prophetic; yet it was of the invaluable services of this leader, thus prepared and able to obtain every possible advantage during the coming battle, that the Prince deprived the Detachment, and incidentally the whole Army. The interview with General v. Schmidt produced a deep and immediate impression on v. Stosch's mind. He could not resist the conviction that the French had shifted their base of operations, and that the second defeat, which v. Stiehle had named as the transition point from the defensive to the offensive, would be inflicted on the Army of the Loire this time, not by the Second Army, but by the Detachment. But v. Stosch was far too enterprising to accept the doctrine that it is only the defensive that should be employed to ward off an approaching attack; like v. Moltke, v. Stosch regarded the attack and the moral effect of the initiative as everything; and here, after his enlightenment by the great Cavalry Leader, he saw that the long-desired chance had now come. But both tact and diplomacy were necessary, and in both arts he was a proficient. He now betook himself to the Duke, and laid before him the situation depicted by v. Schmidt, and accepted by himself as correct. He pointed out to his commander that there could be no doubt that an attack by the French was imminent; but that, at the present moment, the disposition of the Detachment, in conformity with the orders of the Prince, was far too extended to meet an attack successfully. Concentration must be the first step; standing fast with the right wing, drawing forward the left, and then concentrating to the centre. But at the present moment this was permissible only for the Bavarians and the 17th Inf. Division, for he dared not include in the movement the 22nd Inf. Division on the left, which the Prince had expressly said was to be regarded as the last reserve of the Second Army, and which, even now, was not as far to the east as the Prince had ordered. V. Stosch proposed, therefore, to the Grand Duke that, on the very next day, preparations should be made for attack, without giving a thought to the idea of a retreat. "Under existing circumstances, nothing more could be done than to get into line early under such favourable conditions, that there should be no difficulty in closely concentrating if this proved to be necessary later. As matters stood, the roads to Paris would best be protected, if the concentration west of the Orleans-Angerville road was kept in view, and pushed yet more forward. But whatever was determined to be done, the power to dispose of the 22nd Inf. Division must again be obtained. The Detachment could not be tied to a position à cheval the roads Orleans-Angerville [the main road to Paris] and Orleans-Allainville [the Paris road next to it on the west, and diverging from it at Artenay]; the Detachment would accomplish the duty assigned to it if at the right time it brought up all its troops, even to the very last man, and beat the enemy. That would be the best protection of the roads, and probably also, at the same time, the decisive blow for the subsequent capture of Orleans." Provisionally, the question as to the 22nd Inf. Division could be put on one side. "Anyhow, we shall have," added the General, "freedom of choice for the concentration in the favourable position from Loigny to Lumeau. It answers best for the attack and the defence according to the circumstances." The Grand Duke accepted this proposal a little too eagerly to please v. Stosch, and said with a sort of joyous decision: "Let it be so; we will take the offensive to-morrow with our whole force in the direction of Loigny-Lumeau; do what is necessary for this purpose." The Grand Duke's idea was a little premature;

but v. Stosch, having already gained a great deal, did not deem it expedient to suggest a counter-proposal for a closer concentration first as a preliminary to an attack. V. Stosch's plan, now adopted by the Grand Duke, was of vast importance, for it meant in the Loire campaign the change from the defensive to the offensive; and, incidentally, it was a revolution in the control of the German forces on the Loire; it involved the employment of those forces in a direction totally different from that which the Commander-in-Chief considered the best suited for the overthrow of the French. It was more than the substitution of one scheme of operations for another; it was the negation of the scheme of a supreme commander by a sub-commander. And it may be doubted that any General of ordinary social rank, however distinguished as a soldier, and however good might be the Chief Staff Officer at his side, would have dared to propose to the nephew of the King such a radical alteration in the plan of the campaign. But the Grand Duke was a reigning Royalty, his Chief Staff Officer was v. Moltke, present by proxy; and at Versailles was his Staff Patron, the determined v. Blumenthal. Under these circumstances the leader of the Detachment might "do and dare."

The next step that v. Stosch had to take in the matter was one far more difficult to accomplish than that of securing the approval and assent of his own commander. It was nothing less than bringing about agreement in action, between two Royal personages, whose professional views were in discord, and who, personally, were not on good terms with each other; moreover he knew that he himself was regarded at the Prince's Staff as somewhat of an autocratic disposition. He now drew up a letter to v. Stiehle, in which he explained the altered state of affairs on the French side, and requested permission to attack the French, and thus in another form give protection to the Paris road. The letter was sent at 6 P.M. by an orderly officer, and was, it must be borne in mind, written and despatched before all the events of the day at the Bavarian Corps, had come to the knowledge of the

Detachment Head-quarters. The principal points urged in the letter were as follows:

" 1. The enemy is still in strong force at Chevilly; a deserter gives the force as 50,000.

" 2. The enemy is occupying the road Orleans-Chateaudun in greater strength, and has shown everywhere there larger bodies of infantry, and also cavalry and artillery. [This information was based on the reports of Gen. v. Schmidt.]

" 3. The enemy has advanced from Patay and Poupry in the strength of about three battalions against the Bavarian outposts, but he retired immediately when Bavarian battalions deployed against him.

" 4. The enemy has strongly occupied the places in front of the 17th Inf. Division.

" 5. All is quiet in front of the 22nd Inf. Division."

In the letter it was further stated that the Grand Duke was of opinion that obtaining command of the road from Orleans to Chateaudun was necessary for the security of the right wing and for maintaining the communications with Versailles; and he proposed therefore pushing the outposts on the left towards Artenay as far as Dambron-Poupry-Patay, and taking the offensive with the right wing; but as the enemy had shown strong forces there, the employment of the 22nd Inf. Division would be required for a real offensive on December 3rd; on December 2nd the 17th Inf. Division would suffice. In any case, however, serious encounters might take place.

It is very remarkable, according to the account given, that notwithstanding the vital importance of the certain and speedy delivery of the request at Head-quarters, the request was transmitted by one channel only, and that a single mounted orderly officer.

The Prince, when he received the letter at 9 P.M., was not at first disposed to grant the desired permission; but when he learnt from the reports of the IIIrd Army Corps that the French had evacuated Boiscommun, he granted it. V. Stiehle at 9.37 P.M. sent to the Grand Duke a telegram to this effect, but the telegram did not arrive at Janville until midnight, about which hour the orderly officer also returned. Before v. Stosch had sent off the letter to v. Stiehle he had despatched an officer to the Bavarians to ascertain the position of affairs with them ; soon after 9 P.M. this officer brought back to Janville his report ; so alarming was it that at 9.30 P.M. v. Stosch sent to Pithiviers the following telegram, which arrived there shortly after midnight :

"At the advance to-day of the 1st Bavarian Corps against a hostile reconnaisance at Terminiers, resulting in the entry of nearly the whole corps into the affair, the enemy showed large masses, which have been estimated at one cavalry division, two infantry divisions, and much artillery. The enemy pressed forward strongly on the right wing. The fight terminated at about 5.30, and at that time the Bavarians had retired as far as the line from Nonneville in the direction of Courmainville. Specially noticeable is a report of an officer who was sent there from here that the retreat of a portion of the Infantry was not in good order. Information from Artenay states that the 15th Corps is at that place with another corps behind it. It is apparently the 17th Corps that has fought against the Bavarians." At 12.20 on the morning of December 2nd v. Stosch sent a second confirmatory telegram giving some details. V. Stosch's letter had been received at Pithiviers with a certain amount of incredulity, but all doubts as to the impending conflict and its importance vanished when, after midnight, the later reports came in. And now the Grand Duke, at v. Stosch's instigation, took a very bold step ; he felt that necessity knows no law, and therefore, in his latest orders, he drew into his own fighting line the last reserve of the Second Army, the 22nd Inf. Division.

CHAPTER XVIII

DECEMBER 2ND—BATTLE OF LOIGNY-POUPRY

EARLY on the morning of December 2nd commenced the Battle of Loigny-Poupry, essentially a " bataille de rencontre," the Bavarians, whilst moving into position, encountering the French force on its way to the north-east to Toury. It was thus on the German right that the hostile armies first came into contact, and here the Bavarians had, for some time, great difficulty in holding their ground against the impetuous attacks of the 16th Corps. On this right flank also the hostile cavalries were opposed to each other. When the 17th Inf. Division came up on the left of the Bavarians, it was met to the south also by the French 16th Corps; later on the 22nd Inf. Division, when entering the battlefield, had to march away east to stay the advance of two Divisions of the 15th Corps coming up the Paris road. At nightfall Loigny, on the extreme German right, where the 17th Corps has entered into the battle, had been wrested from the French; the Germans held Poupry on the extreme left. The defeat of the French was complete. The isolated character of the French attacks contributed greatly to their failure, this absence of well-timed combination being due to hurry in the preparations for the operation. The Germans owed no small part of their success to the admirable leading of the two Infantry Divisions by Generals v. Tresckow and v. Wittich, who, as they came on the field, displayed excellent judgment in the disposal of their troops to meet the unexpected situations they found confronting them. The Battle of Loigny-Poupry, like that of Beaune la Rolande, is deserving of close and careful study; the former is an example of the higher leading in its best aspect, and of the work of the three arms in combination; the latter is rich in the experiences of the most minute incidents of a battle. At the close of the battle of December 2nd, the Grand Duke and v. Stosch were fully aware of the greatness of the success they had achieved; and they had only one thought for the morrow, the reaping the fruits of that success.

To the leaders of the Detachment there appeared to be three courses of action open to the French; they could retire to the west; they could fall back on Orleans; or, if they received reinforcements, they might offer resistance at Terminiers, only three miles south of Loigny. The last course was regarded as improbable; it was the first course that, from the strategical point of view, and for the prolongation of the war, seemed to be the one which the enemy ought to adopt. The Detachment orders for the next day were framed, therefore, to prevent this escape, and to drive the enemy back on to Orleans. This done, it would be easy for the Detachment to gain the Loire and carry out the strategy of v. Moltke. To the Prince was sent a brief telegram giving the general result of the battle, with the remark : " If the enemy is to be pursued to-morrow, it is absolutely necessary that the Second Army should attack Artenay, and undertake the protection of the Orleans-Paris road."

But the Grand Duke's high hopes were doomed to disappointment, for there came from Pithiviers the Prince's orders, which will be dealt with later on, but which commenced with the sentence, " The Second Army and the Detachment of H.R.H. the Grand Duke of Mecklenburg are to advance to-morrow, December 3rd, to the concentric attack against Orleans," and then, after detailing the movements of the Second Army, the order ran : " The Detachment of H.R.H. the Grand Duke will, according to its own dispositions, advance to-morrow west of the Artenay-Orleans road for a corresponding attack." To learn how it came about that this order was given and rigidly adhered to, we must go to

Pithiviers, and see what had been taking place there during the day.

It was with great anxiety that Prince Frederick Charles had, in the early hours of the morning, awaited at Pithiviers news from the Detachment. Of his Army, the main body of the IXth Army Corps was at Pithiviers, one brigade being at Bazoches les Gallerandes; the other two corps were reconnoitring as on the previous day towards Montargis and Bellegarde. At 10 A.M. came in from the Grand Duke the first report, dated 8.10 A.M., informing the Prince that the whole Detachment was concentrating for the attack on the line Tanon-Baigneux, the 1st Bavarian Corps, and the 4th Cav. Division on the right, the 17th and 22nd Inf. Divisions on the left. Up to ten o'clock the Prince had not received any information as to the state of affairs in front of his own Army; he at once however, resolved to move the IXth Army Corps to the westward to support the Detachment, and he telegraphed to the Duke to that effect, but owing to the distance of the corps from the road, fifteen miles, the earliest time at which the tactical influence of the corps would be felt would be about 4 P.M. At about 10.35 A.M. there came a telegram of a very alarming character from Count v. Waldersee, who, believing that a battle was imminent, had ridden very early to the Paris road. It had been written after 9 A.M. on the Road itself, and it seems to have been handed in at Leon-en-Beauce at 10 A.M., and given out of the telegraph office at Pithiviers at 10.35. It stated that east of the road the enemy had deployed a large force, apparently fifteen battalions, eight squadrons and artillery, and that an advance of all arms on Bazoches was reported. This was the first news of any threatening from the direction of Artenay. The reports now received from the IIIrd and Xth Army Corps did not make the situation more clear, but at 11.30 A.M. the Prince directed General v. Manstein to march his corps towards the Paris road for its protection after the men had dined. He had also ordered the 6th Cav. Division, now on its way from the west, to halt on the Paris road. V. Manstein, before leaving, had an interview with v. Stiehle, who made to him the sneering remark: " The Grand Duke is behaving somewhat in the same way as at a Krieg-Spiel in peace time."

And, now, the Prince, whilst engaged in contemplating the situation and devising plans to meet future developments in this difficult campaign, is suddenly by one fell blow deprived of his position as independent commander in this theatre of war, where the fate of France is to be decided, and he has to do as v. Moltke tells him; for now that the failure of Ducrot's sortie of November 30th—December 2nd has relieved v. Moltke from anxiety at Paris, he is giving his attention again to the Loire. At 1.30 P.M. the Prince received from Versailles the following telegram, dated 12.30 P.M., and despatched at 1.10 P.M. :

" According to report "[Meldung] " received, the main body of the Army of the Loire may be south of Artenay, and the Grand Duke alone may perhaps not be able to prevent their further advance by Toury. His Majesty therefore considers it absolutely necessary that the Second Army now proceeds direct to the attack on Orleans, in order by so doing to bring about the decision. This morning a few of the advanced points of the outpost line before Paris, lost the day before yesterday, have been re-captured from the enemy."

" (Signed) GRAF MOLTKE."

The origin of this peremptory order must now be explained. The course of affairs on the Loire was being regarded at Versailles with the deepest anxiety, and news from the Second Army was awaited with impatience. On the morning of the 2nd none had been received. V. Moltke, therefore sought an audience with the King and laid before him the proposal embodied in the telegram. The King gave his consent, not, however, without considerable hesitation. Quite justifiably the King, owing to the numbering of the four hostile corps said to have been engaged at Beaune, had no reason for believing that there were strong forces opposite the Detachment. Hoenig states also that from private sources had come to the King information which, though not accepted as thoroughly correct, was not without some truth. At the audience the King had alluded to the risk of the Second Army marching westward, if the enemy intended a turning movement between the Loing and the Yonne. V. Moltke had never mentioned to the King v. Stiehle's ideas on this turning movement: he was therefore considerably surprised when at the audience the King brought forward this matter in almost the very same words that v. Stiehle had used in his correspondence with himself; there had been wheels within wheels, revolving unknown to v. Moltke. But he could now, owing to the failure of the great sortie, calm the King's anxiety by pointing out that the Paris Army was no longer in a condition to make any great effort outside the capital. V. Moltke advanced further arguments, and the King yielded, but the King almost directly afterwards heard of the report from the Xth Army Corps that on the night November 30th–December 1st, "according to the assertions of the inhabitants, 20,000 men are in Montargis." Thereupon he doubted the wisdom of the telegram and wrote to v. Moltke: "From the annexed you will see that my opinion that the great Forest of Orleans keeps us in doubt as to what the enemy is doing (is correct) [sic], so that moving into the forest which is some twenty-eight miles long involves at least two days fighting during which time the Second Army can be marched round on the flank and rear if there are 20,000 men in Montargis. I am doubtful whether our order of to-day is still advisable." V. Moltke held to his point and through Col. v. Verdy calmed the apprehensions of the King by pointing out that the report was based only on hearsay, that evidently it referred to the past, and that no corroboration of it had been received. This is certainly an illustration of how belated information may influence judgment on the present.

As regards v. Moltke's telegram of 12.30 P.M., it may be doubted whether in the records of this campaign there exists one more extraordinary in its character. The supreme authorities at Versailles had in the early days of November refused to accept the estimate formed of the local military situation on the Loire by the General in command there, and, in consequence, a heavy penalty was paid at Coulmiers ; now, in the first days of the following month, the same authorities intervene actively in the operations in the same theatre of war, and misjudging completely the military situation, peremptorily order the immediate initiation of an operation totally unsuited to the needs and requirements of the situation. The right wing of the German forces at the very moment that v. Moltke sent the order was engaged in what was almost a hand-to-hand encounter at the spot where the French were making their real attack ; the left wing of the German forces, extended and widely scattered, was engaged in reconnoitring : the centre was so destitute of troops that the direct line of hostile advance on Paris lay almost open to the enemy. To meet these dangers there seems to have been only one course of action possible, namely, to leave in front of the French, east of the Paris road, a small force to demonstrate and hold their own, and then with every available man and gun to hurry to the west, to support the Detachment and to cover the road. But v. Moltke at this critical moment steps in and says, " March ahead all of you at once and attack the city of Orleans." Hitherto, the guiding, paramount principle of v. Moltke's strategy has been the annihilation of the enemy's forces in the field ; now the objective is the capture of an open town. But on the 2nd v. Blumenthal writes : "The Crown Prince told me that the King has now positively ordered the Prince to attack the Army of the Loire. Surely it is impossible for him to ignore such an order, and he must now go forward (*Fabius cunctator*). A Prussian Field Marshal is bound to go forward." This is very different from the order actually sent. The incompatibility of the order with the military situation is so glaring, that any critic, judging even inferentially only, would at once come to the conclusion that v. Moltke, when he obtained the Royal permission to send it, was in ignorance of the actual state of affairs on the Loire, and further, had been misinformed as to them. The latter is clear from the order itself in which v. Moltke gives "south of Artenay" as the position of the main body of the enemy. As we know there was not one main body in the Army of the Loire, but two main bodies, one of which, the 18th and 20th Corps, was well to the east, the other, the 16th and 17th Corps, was to the west, the 15th Corps forming across the Paris road the connecting link between them. It is not clear as to what the words "report received" (eingegangener Meldung) referred. There is no record of it in the archives or journals. Had it been derived from the Intelligence Branch, the word used would have been "Nachrichten" not "Meldung." Hoenig is, however, inclined to believe that this must have been its source; and so thick is the Fog of War that v. Moltke seems to anticipate the greatest danger to lie on the Paris road. But still more extraordinary and inexplicable is the fact that when v. Moltke at 1.10 P.M. issued the order he was not aware of the battle then raging at Poupry; nor, although from midnight December 1–2, there was no longer any doubt at Pithiviers as to the critical state of affairs on the west of the road, does there appear to have been any intimation to this effect to Versailles, although v. Stiehle himself had on the evening of the 1st told v. Waldersee he believed that there would be a fight at the Detachment next day. And all this is still more strange because the battlefield was little more than fifty miles from Versailles. Toury, the German telegraph station on the Paris road, was only six or seven miles distant from the left of the battlefield. The battle commenced at about 8 A.M. and lasted until dark. Yet nobody seems to have sent to Versailles during the day any news whatever about what was taking place, but between 5 and 6 P.M. v. Waldersee wired to the King a short but very clear summary of the successful encounter.* The inappropriateness of v. Moltke's order was

* The following extract from a letter, which I had both the pleasure and honour of receiving, from Field Marshal Graf v. Waldersee nearly two years ago, is conclusive : " On the evening of Beaune la Rolande, as well as that of Loigny, I telegraphed to the King William that a *complete* victory had been

DECEMBER 2   243

clearly due to the absence of knowledge of the military situation. And now we pass to the consideration of the action taken by the Prince on the receipt of this inappropriate order. And here we meet the question of literal obedience *versus* intelligent disobedience, the latter, be it remarked, a form of leading in high favour in the German Army.

It certainly seems, that peremptory as was the order, there was open to the Prince an alternative course to that of unhesitating and immediate compliance with it. The telegraph wire connecting Pithiviers and Versailles could work quickly enough when necessary, as shown by the fact that twenty minutes had sufficed for the delivery of the order after its issue. Without, therefore, any appreciable delay in the execution of the order, the Prince could have assured himself that the King and v. Moltke were fully aware of the situation on the Loire when the order was issued. A wire, "Detachment concentrated this morning to attack on line Tanon-Baigneaux. Waldersee reports hostile advance in strong force along Orleans-Paris Road. Does your order hold good?" would have removed at Versailles all possibility of a misunderstanding of the situation; and then if notwithstanding, the order was confirmed, all responsibility for the consequences rested on the right shoulders. But the Prince was silent; it is said that if speech is silver, silence is gold, but here the gold was coinage of the counterfeit class; for whilst it bore the stamp, " unhesitating obedience to orders," it led eventually to results that were simply deplorable.

But even if the Prince determined, as he did, to accept the order in silence, and at once to comply with it, the mode in which he would comply depended obviously on his interpretation of it. " Die II. Armee nunmehr direct zum Angriff auf Orleans schreitet, um die Entscheidung herbeizuführen." Taken literally, it reads, " attack the city of Orleans by the shortest road "; and the corollary reads, " on the capture of

won. The order to Prince Frederick Charles of the 2nd December to commence the attack on Orleans was given by General v. Moltke before he received tidings that a battle had begun on the west of the great Chaussée."

the City of Orleans the decision of the conflict with the Army of the Loire depends." But of course the order construed liberally and not literally runs, "At once give up your defensive attitude and energetically assume the offensive." The substitution of a city for the hostile forces in the field as already noticed is very remarkable. Hoenig says that at this time there was a general feeling, shared also by the King, the Prince, and the Grand Duke, that with the recapture of Orleans the war would come to an end. On what grounds this assumption was based we do not know. Sometimes there attaches to the possession of an open town or city either on or away from a river, some strategical advantage, so marked that the future course of the war will be greatly influenced by its retention or its capture. But here in the case of Orleans, the importance attached by both sides to its possession seems to have been to a considerable extent fictitious. In November it was natural that the first objective of the then newly-formed Army of the Loire should be the ejection of v. d. Tann's force from Orleans and its repossession by its rightful owners. The recapture exercised a great beneficial moral effect on the country, and it covered the future concentration here, but the value of Orleans to the French strategically may be regarded as doubtful. De Freycinet regarded Orleans as merely a *point d'appui;* General Borel, the Chief Staff Officer of the Army of the Loire, had never assented to the alleged advantages of the position; as a Bridge Head for a force advancing from the south, it was, in its prominently salient position, exposed to isolation by attacks coming from both above and below the city; moreover, in the French counsels there was great diversity of opinion as to which among the several theatres of war available for the Army of National Defence would be most favourable for its operations. Save in its proximity to Bourges, the chief arsenal, Orleans had little to recommend it in connection with offensive operations on a large scale. The Germans had originally taken it in order to keep the country between it and Paris clear of the annoyances inflicted on them by the half-trained troops and the bands of irregulars, and also on the erroneous supposition that it would serve as a sort of half-way house to Bourges and Tours. And, moreover, so long as Orleans and the surrounding country on the right bank were in the possession of the French the occupation was a standing menace to the Germans. For, as has been apparent from this narrative, the Orleans position was a screen impenetrable to hostile observation, and therefore they could not tell whether it was being used as a real cover for the concentration of some hundreds of thousands of the enemy, ready to issue forth suddenly at the first favourable opportunity for action, or whether there were there but a few thousands, sufficient however to simulate the presence of ten times their number. As a strategic point for a German offensive it was of no value.

It may have been that the Prince, irritated by the severe censure implied in the order and by the form in which the order was drawn up, determined to give vent to his resentment by interpreting it according to its exact wording, and with complete disregard of the consequences. " He may have said to himself, ' Those people at Versailles at the centre of authority seem always to think they know so much better what ought to be done far away from them than I do, who am on the spot, that now I will give them their heads and do just as they tell me, only they must not blame me later on if we find ourselves in difficulties and obtain but a poor return for a huge casualty list, and are obliged to begin the business all over again.'" On this matter we may well withhold our judgment.

The ground-work of the plan of operations selected by the Prince for the literal execution of the order was to leave the 1st Cav. Division and an Infantry Brigade to watch his own left flank and rear towards Montargis; to send the IIIrd Army Corps from the north-east to the south-west through the Forest of Orleans; and with the IXth Army Corps to push back the enemy along the main road to Orleans, the Detachment cooperating with this corps by attacking from the west the enemy's positions on the road and in its vicinity; the Xth Army Corps to form a reserve at the centre to the whole force. When v. Moltke's order was received, the dispositions on the left wing were not favourable for its speedy execution, both the IIIrd and Xth Army Corps being engaged in reconnoitring to the south and south-east. Telegrams were at once sent to them giving general directions, and at 2.30 P.M. written detailed instructions followed. The IIIrd Army Corps was recalled to Pithiviers, the Xth Army Corps to Beaune and Boynes. But so scattered and so distant were the corps from the points named as rendezvous that it was only by hard marching, prolonged into the night, that these were reached. The marches were flank marches, and specially difficult and dangerous owing to the proximity of the hostile outposts, but this movement, of which the knowledge would have been invaluable to the defenders of the forest, was apparently almost unnoticed by them.

The orders for the actual advance on the 3rd were not sent out until 10 P.M. Omitting some clauses not essential to the consideration of the subject, they run as follows, and, it may be added, they are remarkable for their terseness and incompleteness.

"The Second Army and the Detachment of H.R.H. the Grand Duke of Mecklenburg are to [soll] advance to-morrow December 3rd to the concentric attack against Orleans."

(The word "soll" clearly indicates that the Prince in issuing the order is carrying out one he has himself received.)

"The IXth Army Corps will move to-morrow on Artenay, which place it will attack at 9.30.

"A flank detachment from the 25th (Grand Ducal Hessian) Division will march along the Roman road Bazoches-S. Lyé. This detachment will march into the forest as the fight on the main road makes progress, endeavouring as far as possible to maintain touch with the right.

"The IIIrd Army Corps will march in several columns on a wide front towards Chilleurs aux Bois, proceeding to the decisive attack on Chilleurs at 10.30, capture this place and the edge of the forest, employing its artillery to the utmost, and will push forward a strong advanced guard to Loury. The main body of the corps must reach Loury to-morrow. Within the forest, pioneer detachments are to lead, in order to remove obstacles.

" Headquarters, Loury.

" The Xth Army Corps will march to-morrow out of its cantonments, so that in the course of the afternoon it will arrive at Villereau with its right wing, and Chilleurs aux Bois with its left wing [on a front of six miles, the left six miles from Loury]. It will occupy close cantonments on this line. Head-quarters, Chilleurs aux Bois.

" Hartmann's Cav. Division with the infantry brigade attached will take up a position according to the judgment of the commander, so that it can watch the district between the Essonne and the Loing, and the roads running along the latter river.

" All important incidents, especially any possible advance of the enemy, are to be reported direct to General Count Moltke at Versailles by telegraph, and also by means of orderly officers.

" The Detachment of H.R.H. the Grand Duke will, according to its own dispositions, advance to-morrow west of the Artenay-Orleans road for a corresponding attack.

" The attack on the hostile position, Gidy-Cercottes, will if it is occupied be aided by an infantry outflanking attack of the IXth Army Corps on Cercottes in the forest.

" My Head-quarters go to-morrow after the fight to Chilleurs aux Bois."

It will be remarked that no directions are given for keeping up the connection between the IIIrd Army Corps and the rest of the army, nor is there vouchsafed any information as to the enemy.

In this plan and scheme there is no strategy, notwithstanding the fact that on this long front of forty miles there is plenty of scope for its employment. It is all tactics, tactics of a kind almost barbaric : those of weight and brute force. The influence of ground on tactics, and the selection of the ground most suitable for a force weak in infantry but strong in the other arms are alike ignored. The IIIrd Army Corps with its numerous artillery is to be plunged, isolated, into the densest of woodland, a theatre of war most favourable for its half-trained defenders; what becomes of the enemy is a matter of indifference, so long as the pressure on the main road suffices to force him back; and it is precisely on this line of advance that will be found, in all probability, numerous localities well prepared for defence.

Since it is difficult to suppose that any commander would have issued for December 3rd orders, irrespective of what had taken place at the Detachment on the 2nd, it is desirable to endeavour to ascertain from the documents before us what information had come to the Prince from the Detachment, and at what times it had been received by him.

At 3 P.M. he received from the Grand Duke a telegram informing him that at 1 P.M. the 17th and 22nd Inf. Divisions were advancing on Terminiers, and that the much-shaken Bavarian corps and the 4th Cav. Division were holding the right wing. The enemy appeared to be falling back in the direction of Bonneval.

At 5 P.M. came another telegram from Janville, 3.51 P.M.

"At 2.30 P.M. 17th Division captured Loigny, and is successfully advancing, followed by the 1st Bav. corps, with the 4th Cav. Division on the flank, direction Nonneville-Orgères; the 16th French corps in front of it.

"Twenty-second Division advancing successfully on Artenay. Apparently the 15th French corps in front of it."

At 9.30 P.M. came a message, 6 P.M. Janville, from v. Waldersee, briefly describing the successes of the battle, and concluding with the words, "I regard the battle as a brilliant victory."

Hoenig states that it was whilst the Prince was issuing his orders for the 3rd that he received from v. Stosch a telegram from the battlefield.

"At 4.30 P.M. enemy driven back on Terminiers and also

DECEMBER 2   249

on Artenay. Many prisoners taken, eleven guns captured. If the enemy is to be pursued to-morrow, it is absolutely necessary that the Second Army should attack Artenay and cover the Orleans-Paris Road." This telegram was followed by a letter which described the events of the day and was received before midnight. Yet on the orders issued, with these telegrams before him, the Prince absolutely ignores the fact that only a few miles away a decisive victory has been won on the right wing of what was actually his own command. Whilst the orders were yet on their way to the Detachment, v. Stosch at 11.16 P.M. sent to the Prince a further telegram which arrived at Pithiviers at one in the morning. It commenced with the words, " In order to secure the successful results of to-day, the pursuit will be taken up to-morrow," then followed the arrangements made in consequence. Later on he telegraphed : " A comparison of the information obtained with regard to the hostile troops which were in the engagement yesterday shows the 16th and 17th Corps against the 17th Division. It is, therefore, very probable that the Detachment will have to fight again to-day." Hoenig says that in earlier reports the 15th Corps had already been mentioned, but that the Prince did not believe that these three corps would be encountered in the new direction of the operations. Until four in the morning the Grand Duke and v. Stosch waited in the hope that the Prince would, on the later reports sent to him, modify the original orders, and then, but not till then, did the Grand Duke issue fresh orders in conformity with the views of the Prince. Hence so far as the planning the future campaign on the Loire was concerned, the Battle of Loigny-Poupry might as well not have been fought.

At 11 P.M. v. Stiehle sent to v. Moltke a letter with the orders issued by the Prince and a brief account of the events of December 1st and 2nd, and in the last paragraph we read : " The offensive movement of the Detachment of H.R.H. the Grand Duke had been so arranged with General v. Stosch that an endeavour should be made to secure a crossing over the Loire below Orleans, but as to-day's telegram seems to make great haste necessary, the endeavour will be made to reach the objective Orleans by the direct road." There is nothing in v. Moltke's published correspondence nor in Hoenig's work to show what effect was produced on the mind of the Chief of the Staff of the German forces by the perusal of this letter. If v. Moltke had abandoned his strategy of the first war in favour of a second form of strategy; if for the annihilation of the hostile forces in the field he had substituted the capture of an open town, it must have rejoiced his heart to find his order interpreted to the very letter; if not, and if he still held to the old faith, then the letter must have foreshadowed to him the beginning of the great blunder of the whole struggle, the initiation of a course of action that might prolong the war, involve the Germans in fresh campaigns, and cost them dearly in blood and life. Some day the truth may be revealed.

CHAPTER XIX

DECEMBER 3RD—FIRST DAY, SECOND BATTLE OF ORLEANS

IT sometimes happens when the line of action taken in war by a leader appears to have been dangerous and even foolhardy, and yet has resulted in a brilliant success, that there is attributed to him a species of marvellous insight into the state of affairs on the side of the enemy and his moral condition. But though the Prince achieved his aims on December 3rd and 4th, the success of the dangerous and hazardous operation adopted was in no way due to his possessing any insight of this kind. Rarely has any leader entered so completely blindfolded into a battle as did Prince Frederick Charles into the second battle of Orleans. Of even the general disposition of the enemy he knew very little; of the position of even the larger hostile units, such as the Army Corps, he was equally in ignorance, and he refused to accept as correct the approximately correct information furnished to him by the Detachment. He was aware that, for at least a fortnight, a vast amount of labour had been expended in putting into a state of defence the position he was about to attack, and that in it were heavy guns; but of the system of works, he could see only the fringe, and he was not certain even whether on the river itself there was or was not a Bridge Head. As regards the *moral* of the enemy he was equally in the dark, except as regards the 15th Corps, the best in the French Army, the corps that had fought victoriously at Coulmiers and was in no way shaken; the battle of December 2nd must have seriously injured the *moral* of the 16th and 17th Corps, but this had no influence on his judgment, because he refused to believe that that encounter had been of the serious character attributed to it by both v. Stosch and v. Waldersee. That the 18th and 20th Corps, his opponents at Beaune la Rolande, had been very severely shaken, he did not even admit until his delayed visit to the battlefield on the 30th, and then he believed that the opportunity for taking advantage of the demoralisation of the corps had gone by. With respect to the leaders and the leading of the French, the enemy was to him 200,000 men under one supreme commander only, General d'Aurelle, who had already, as a tactician, made his mark at Coulmiers. No doubt an early gallop to the battle field of Loigny-Poupry, and a personal conference with the Grand Duke and v. Stosch, might have enabled him to get nearer the truth, but the Prince of December 3rd does not seem to have been the same man as the Prince of August 16th, who had hurried in two hours from Pont-a-Mousson to Vionville; and, possibly, the prospect of an interview with a royal Prince he personally disliked, and with a Chief Staff Officer who held views opposite to his own, was not specially attractive.

On the morning of December 3rd began the two days battle. No doubt, if war be a science and an art, it ought to be carried on in conformity with the principles derived from the experiences of the past; and, as a rule, war thus conducted is far more likely to be successful than is war carried on in disregard of those principles; but the so-called " game " of war, like all other games, is one of probabilities, and a disregard of probabilities may sometimes result in pulling off a great *coup*; and so it was here in the attack on Orleans, and in no part of the widely extended battlefield more markedly so than on the east of the Paris road, in the great Forest of Orleans, when, during the thirty-six hours from 9 A.M. on December 3rd the IIIrd Army Corps was, according to probabilities, marching to certain destruction; when the dangers surrounding it were apparently overwhelming: and yet the corps not only issued from the perils unscathed, but succeeded in depriving the defenders of the city of Orleans of the aid of some 40,000 to 50,000 men, simply by frightening them away. It is on this side of the road during the two days that we gain experience of how deeply indebted to sheer good fortune may sometimes be even the ablest generals. The day's work of the IIIrd Army Corps will be dealt with first, and as a preliminary step, the position of the French must be given. At and north of Artenay were the second and third Divisions of the 15th Corps, and when during the 3rd they fell back towards Orleans, their line of retreat lay on and near to the Paris road. The village of Chevilly is on this road at the northwest angle of the forest. No troops had been specially told off to protect the five miles of front between this road and the Roman road; but the protection of some portion of it would naturally fall to the retiring troops. The Roman road was guarded outside the forest, but near to the edge by the fortified localities of Villereau, St. Germain-le-Grand, and Neuville aux Bois. At Neuville were some 8400 rifles and twelve guns; at Villereau 1850 rifles and eight guns; these troops were the left of the first Division of the 15th Corps, and were under General Minot. Chilleurs aux Bois, the next point of entry, and assigned for attack to the IIIrd Army Corps, lies a good mile outside the forest; the village of Santeau is the same distance further towards Pithiviers. At this entrance was des Pallières with 8500 rifles and thirty-eight guns. At Courcy aux Loges, on the next road from Pithiviers, was the right of the Division, 2070 rifles and six guns. The front of this Division of some 20,000 men was eleven to twelve miles. At Chambon, three and a half miles east, and also on a road, was the left flank of the 20th Corps, which, with the 18th on its right, faced north-east towards Beaune and Montargis.

As the Prince, when despatching the IIIrd Army Corps on its mission, believed that the French were in very strong force on its left, with troops also in strength at Chilleurs, the course he adopted was certainly a departure from his usual caution. In fact, his whole leading during the two days was that of a man who, forced by superior authority to adopt a line of action he regarded as both dangerous and hazardous, went recklessly ahead, regardless of possible consequences. The task set to the Corps, namely, after a severe night march to march ten miles to the edge of a forest, drive back the enemy from this edge which had been prepared for defence, and on narrow and obstructed roads to force him back five miles on his natural line of retreat, was a tolerably large bit of work for a short November day; yet grand old v. Alvensleben managed to accomplish the wishes of the Prince, the ten years' commander of the Corps in old days. Nothing, during the whole campaign, was beyond the Brandenburgers. V. Alvensleben was fully aware of the difficulties confronting him, but it was only to his Chief Staff Officer, Colonel v. V. Rhetz, that he spoke of them. Outwardly, to others, he appeared quite unmoved. In the march of the previous night he had brushed against the hostile outposts, and, for aught he knew, the enemy might, in consequence, be specially on the alert; that if he arrived at Loury in rear of the enemy, his presence there on the night of the 3rd would be known to them, he could not doubt; and in front of him at Loury would be the Loire and the fortified Orleans. In the Army Orders there was no mention of the provision of any connecting link between him and the IXth Army Corps on his right, so in the intervening forest the enemy might, unknown to him, be. And what an encumbrance were his own eighty-four guns. To take all these with him along the forest roads, obstructed as they were sure to be, would be great labour; whilst, also, the teams could easily be crippled by a few shooters concealed in the underwood. To leave the guns in rear needed a strong escort, and a consequent diminution of the comparatively few infantry (14,750) of his force. He remarked, somewhat in the spirit of raillery, "We are ordered to beat the enemy, so we will beat him; the position of the General is not usually with the outposts, at least not in wooded country of this kind, but since we cannot command unless we are at the out-posts, we will go there." He also said "the General in command should not be under the fire of the enemy, and I shall only go there if necessary, but if I find myself there by chance it will not be proper for me to ride away." V. Alvensleben estimated the strength of the enemy at one Division on the Loury road and one and a-half to two corps to the east of it—a very close estimate. "I went," he afterwards said, "I was fully aware, into a den, of which the door closed of itself after my last man had passed Chilleurs. With every step forward diminished any chance of support, and also the possibility of withdrawing or of sending any news about myself, or of receiving news; and if I did fortunately succeed in arriving at the southern edge the situation of my corps before the city could become very unpleasant. No use was there in previous calculations and speculations. I knew nothing as to the state of affairs south of the forest: of only one thing was I sure, the impossibility of employing all my guns. And was it quite out of the question that the Prince's attack might be repulsed, that I should be for one or two days in front of the Bridge Head, and with the enemy on my line of retreat? In this case we should certainly hold out, but my corps could hardly escape a catastrophe."

It was at Santeau that des Pallières determined to first oppose the German advance. An artillery duel of great vivacity commenced at 10.30 A.M. and the issue was greatly to the advantage of the Germans. So severely did the French artillery suffer that about midday des Pallières ordered it back to Orleans; the infantry were to cover the retreat and fall back to the edge of the forest, holding the edge on both sides of the road; but the Germans did not allow the retirement to be made undisturbed, and the retreat of the rear-guard became a flight. Chilleurs soon fell into the hands of the pursuers, who also captured the edge of the forest.

Three miles within the forest at this point there is met a perfectly straight cross road, the Allée de Nibelle, running from east to west, and striking the Paris-Orleans road at rather more than a mile on the Orleans side of Chevilly; it cuts the Loury road two miles north of the village. Des Pallières now led his troops back to the Allée, sent his heavy batteries to Orleans by Loury, and turned westward along the Allée with the rest of his column. The road to Loury was thus left completely open to the IIIrd Army Corps.

An explanation of this conduct of des Pallières is necessary. General d'Aurelle, on becoming acquainted with the result of the battle of Loigny-Poupry, determined to give up the offensive and to commence a retreat on Orleans, and, in consequence, issued, among other orders, one 4.50 A.M., 3rd, to des Pallières, which he received at 5.20 A.M. on the 3rd, ordering him to retire west on S. Lyé and Chevilly. Although there was a field telegraph station at Neuville in connection with d'Aurelle, the latter does not appear to have been informed by des Pallières of the attack of the IIIrd Army Corps. It seems somewhat remarkable that des Pallières should have interpreted the order purely according to the letter. But although he removed, thus voluntarily, all bars and locks on the gate opening into the den at Loury, the advance into it and passing the night there was in the highest degree dangerous. With unity of control on the French side, the giving up the door would have been the luring the corps into a trap, and its sure capture.

It must have been half-past three on this short November day that the last of the defenders of the wood edge disappeared. V. Alvensleben had given his troops a short rest whilst he drew up orders for the further advance. In this advance guns would be of little use, so the General left outside the wood the six batteries of the Corps artillery, and the four batteries of the 5th Division, under an escort of five battalions, taking with him only the twenty-four guns of the 6th Infantry Division. From the entrance into the wood a glade, diverging slightly from the road, led direct south, striking at the level of Loury, and at one and three-quarter miles east of the village, on a cross road to Sully la Chapelle, which is on the road from Courcy; at the crossing is a large clearing. The 6th Infantry Division advanced down the main road, the 5th down to the clearing. The march began soon after three o'clock. V. Alvensleben was in a state of great anxiety, but he completely concealed it from

DECEMBER 3 257

the officers round him, few of whom understood the perilous position in which the corps was. During the march the sound of rifle-fire from the dispersed fugitives was heard around. Very soon darkness came on in the dense wood, but the men, elated by the success of the morning, marched on in high spirits. The pioneers and leading troops had to clear away the paving-stones, purposely torn up and strewn about the road; they had to make cuttings passable and to clear away barricades in the glade. The work in the dark was difficult; nevertheless, the troops came stumbling onwards by degrees. Two hours were needed for the first three miles; and now, as the advance continued, heavy rifle-fire suddenly resounded to the right rear in the direction of Neuville aux Bois. V. Alvensleben considered it inadvisable to halt until the meaning of the firing could be ascertained, though it was too heavy to be merely an outpost affair, so he contented himself with sending cavalry for information, and at the same time covering by infantry his flank and rear. The rifle-fire increased in intensity, and guns were also heard. In total darkness the village of Loury was reached; not a light was to be seen; the only thing to be done was to place outposts on the approaches from the west, south, and east. Meantime, at 6.15 P.M. the firing to the north-west had died out, but the approach of hostile parties from the east had been reported. After the outposts had taken up their ground a fight suddenly broke out between those towards Neuville and hostile troops who, at eight o'clock, coming from that direction, collided with them; but the French, after creating at first a certain amount of confusion, were driven off.

The rest of the night passed quietly, and when day broke there was not any enemy in view, but there were found close at hand five guns that had been abandoned by the hostile troops. And now to show how it was that the perils to which the IIIrd Army Corps had been exposed during these twelve hours had remained only perils. The march ordered by the Prince had been found practicable so far, but this did not show any foresight on the part of the Prince. V. Alvensleben had done his best to prepare to ward off the dangers by which he was encompassed, and that was the utmost that the General on the spot could do to contribute towards success. The credit for the success must be given to the French commanders only. It has been mentioned that the left flank of des Pallière's division was, in the morning, at Neuville aux Bois under Minot. It was against this detachment that the left flanking force of the IXth Army Corps and later the Xth Army Corps, had struck in their advance south ; Minot had received orders from des Pallières to hold on to the last extremity to cover the westward flank march of the division, and then to fall back south-west on S. Lyé. When des Pallières arrived in rear of Neuville aux Bois, at four o'clock, a peasant came to him from Neuville and undertook to take any orders to General Minot. Des Pallières, knowing how bad was the road from Neuville to S. Lyé, and fearful that Minot during the march might be attacked in flank, told the peasant to tell the General that he might retreat south-east through Rebréchien, by the road which runs into the Loury-Orleans road, two and a half miles on the Orleans side of Loury, and he expressed to him the hope that the enemy, who had been fighting during part of the day, would not have passed Loury. It is doubtful whether the message was received. Minot had, however, already selected the Rebréchien line of retreat. Of the fight at Chilleurs he had received no information, and he was not aware that the Germans had penetrated into the wood. Not far from Neuville the road he followed bifurcates, the left, the better road, going to Loury, the right, a forest track, to Rebréchien. It was quite dark, and there was a heavy snowstorm, and at the bifurcation the wrong branch, that to Loury, was followed. At the head of the column were two batteries. It was this column that, marching without any precautions for security, struck on the outposts of the IIIrd Army Corps at eight o'clock, as already described. At first there was alarm and confusion on both sides, but with the well-disciplined troops this was only temporary ; with the less well-disciplined troops it developed into panic. In spite of the heroic and desperate efforts of the French gunners, it was impossible to save more than seven of the twelve guns. The column itself broke, and the men fled through the wood to Orleans.

The small detachment on the right flank at Courcy seems to have been forgotten by des Pallières. The colonel sent for orders, but finding Chilleurs in the possession of the Germans, he retreated to Orleans, by the outer of the four roads. It was this detachment that had been reported to Alvensleben as coming from the east. And there had been also peril impending from the north-east from the 20th and 18th corps. Since November 30th these two corps had been receiving their orders, not from d'Aurelle, but from Tours; but in order to carry out the schemes which now emanated from the Delegation, there was sent, on the 2nd, by Gambetta to d'Aurelle the following order of 4 P.M., which, however, d'Aurelle did not receive until the night of the 3rd: "From to-day, December 2nd, it is necessary that for the operations now undertaken, you issue your strategical orders to the 15th, 16th, 17th, 18th, and 20th corps. I have, until yesterday, December 1st, myself directed the 18th and 20th corps, and for a time the 17th; I now hand over to you this duty. From earlier reports, I do not believe that serious opposition will be encountered by you either at Pithiviers or at the other points. In my opinion, the enemy is only attempting to mask his movement to the north-east to meet Ducrot. The column with which you had to deal yesterday, and perhaps have to deal with to-day, is doubtless only an isolated detachment which is endeavouring to detain us. But the main body must be, I repeat, on the way to Corbeil [fifteen miles from Paris, on the Seine]. At this moment we have reoccupied Chateaudun."

Very intricate is the controversy that has arisen on the question of responsibility for the leading of the two eastern corps at this critical period. De Freycinet maintains that this telegram is not to be taken " à la lettre des mots employés par lui," and that d'Aurelle was already in command of them ; d'Aurelle declines to accept the responsibility earlier than the receipt of this telegram. Anyhow, it was not until 7 P.M. on the 3rd that Bourbaki, who had superseded the very recently appointed

Billot in command of the two corps, received from d'Aurelle orders to concentrate to his left, and to support des Pallières, who at this time had, as we know, totally disappeared from the scene; so during the two critical days of the 2nd and 3rd, the two corps remained quiescent, quite ignorant of what was taking place on their own side, or on that of the enemy. It must be mentioned here that at night the Xth Army Corps had arrived with its left at Chilleurs, and had failed to wrest with its right Neuville from Minot's troops.

On the main road, in the centre, the IXth Army Corps had since morning progressed some five miles, after a series of combats for the possession of villages, commencing at Assas, north of Artenay, and capturing La Croix Briquet about four in the afternoon, when it began to darken. But at a quarter before three the Prince had issued a remarkable order: "I shall consider to-day's work finished when, after a thorough preparation by artillery, the village of Chevilly and the angle of the forest east of it are in possession of the IXth Army Corps, and are, under all circumstances, held by them. The 17th and 22nd Inf. Divisions will similarly, after a bombardment, capture the Chevilly château and the angle of the forest south of the village, and hold firmly on to them. If the day is not long enough the attacks must be continued after dark." A night attack through a forest, on strongly fortified localities, yet two miles distant!

It has already been mentioned that in front of the main position prepared round Orleans, there was also a prepared advanced position. It was at the localities in the latter that the IXth Army Corps had hitherto been engaged. Chevilly was one of the most important localities in the main position. D'Aurelle did not intend that his retirement should go further than this position, and he expected that at Chevilly, des Pallières would arrive during the day with his Division.

And now we shall again come on the old factor in war, sometimes friend, sometimes foe, "personlichkeit." During the day the Detachment had been pushing its way on, by constant fighting against the French Army on the west of the Paris road somewhat into the front of that army, and also at the same time guarding its own right from any attack on that flank, and, with its left, outflanking the French positions on the Paris-Orleans road, which were being attacked in front by the IXth Army Corps. General Chanzy, the French leader, opposite the Detachment, was a bold, enterprising and competent commander, and both to cover the retreat of the 16th and 17th Corps ordered by d'Aurelle, and also as a diversion to relieve the pressure on the 15th Corps, he kept v. d. Tann on the right fully occupied.

The Prince had not intimated to the Grand Duke where he was to be found during the 3rd; he apparently did not know until one o'clock in the afternoon what alterations the Grand Duke had made in the original orders to comply with those issued by himself, and so little interest did he take in the proceedings of the Detachment on either this or the preceding day, that though at one o'clock the two commanders were very little more than a mile apart no interview took place between them during the day. About this time the Prince sent to v. Stosch an order intimating to him the way in which the two Infantry Divisions should be employed; and in his mind there was still the "idée fixée" that the Detachment had made much ado about very little. That on the 2nd it was the main body of the French left wing that the Grand Duke had encountered he still disbelieved. "Believe me," he said, "the Grand Duke has nothing of any importance in front of him." The preparations for the attack on Chevilly had been almost completely carried out when, suddenly, there came a counter order. About five o'clock, when it was getting dark, v. Stosch, who, with the approval of the Grand Duke had gone to seek a personal interview with the Prince, came to him at the little village of Creuzy, some three miles from Chevilly, to put before him the state of affairs at the Detachment, and also because he thought that the night attack on a position that was fortified, but of which little was known, was a great risk. V. Stosch informed the Prince that a hostile force of one Division was threatening the right flank of the Detachment, and that the Bavarians had now their 1st Division in action against it, and the fight was not yet ended ; and he mentioned that on the previous day there had been in front of the Grand Duke the 16th and 17th Corps, and strong forces of the 15th Corps ; he also added that the whole Bavarian Corps was hardly as strong as a weak Division, and that the 17th Inf. Division must be left out of consideration ; the 3rd Division of the 15th Corps was opposite to it. The Prince listened with marked attention and then said : " Many prisoners of many regiments of the 3rd Div. of the 15th Corps have been captured in Artenay " [they were stragglers from the Division on December 2nd] ; " the Grand Duke has made a mistake, this Division cannot be opposite to him ; he has nothing much opposed to him, and he has been deceived by a demonstration, and has again allowed himself to be drawn away from the real point for attack." This reference was to the conduct of the Detachment on the 2nd, the day of Loigny-Poupry. As time was of importance, v. Stosch did not carry on the discussion, but said that it was impossible to tell whether it would be possible to continue on the morrow the convergent attack on Orleans ; that must depend on the news from v. d. Tann about the strong hostile forces showing themselves at l'Encorme * on the right rear ; the Detachment might be compelled to move with the main body westward. To the Prince the words " strong hostile forces " seemed unworthy of credit. " They are only franc-tireurs and Gardes Mobiles," he said, and with marked emphasis he added, " Orleans is the parole ; the Detachment will advance against it to-morrow with all its forces." To this v. Stosch made no reply. The force at l'Encorme was not " franc-tireurs " : it was Barry's Division of the 16th Corps which comprised more Marche troops than Gardes Mobiles, and was making a diversion against the flank of the Detachment, whilst the 3rd Division of the 15th Corps was resisting its advance. But, apparently, in the Prince's mind, the Detachment was always in the wrong.

* A hamlet one mile south-west of Sougy.

DECEMBER 3

V. Stosch felt it, however, to be his duty to suggest to the Prince the danger of the night attack. The Prince, without in any way replying, turned to v. Stiehle and counter-ordered the attack. Then in a quieter manner he said to v. Stosch: " Night attacks are always bad, they should only be undertaken when success is certain ; I dare not run any risk. Under the present circumstances I am not certain of success. I had relied on the flanking movement of the whole of the Detachment. The Grand Duke will remain for the night in his present position." V. Stosch was already riding away when the Prince repeated the words, " But to-morrow we must be in Orleans "; v. Stosch replied, " It will not be our fault if we are not." Such is the account given of the interview by Hoenig, and subsequently endorsed by v. Stosch himself. And yet v. d. Goltz, the writer of the semi-official history of the Second Army, has another and a very different tale to tell. He says : " After it had already begun to get dark, General v. Stosch, the Chief of the Staff of the Detachment, came to the Commander-in-Chief and represented to him that the Grand Duke's troops, exhausted by the severe fight of the previous day, and tired out by to-day's marching with fighting, were hardly able to take part in a determined attack on the Chevilly position. The Field-Marshal felt himself compelled to postpone to the next day the capture of Chevilly and the edge of the forest."

To the truth of this account v. Stosch has given a direct denial and he furnished Hoenig with a statement of the conversation. V. d. Goltz must have obtained his version second-hand, as only three persons were present at the interview, the Prince and the two Chief Staff Officers. What inferences are to be drawn from this extraordinary discrepancy must be left to the reader.

And now the fighting came to an end for the day, and at Chevilly occurred an incident illustrative of the saying " seeing is believing." The orders to the Detachment were that it was to remain on its present ground; v. Wittich did not see the force of the order : " there was nothing for my men," he writes, " but the bare plain covered with wet snow, a bivouac without straw, wood, water or food. My troops had been fighting during the whole of December 2nd ; the leading troops had arrived at 10 o'clock that night, the last at one in the morning, in the icy bivouac at Anneau, where they had little to eat; they had fallen in before daybreak, and had been in fighting formation all day, without taking into account the duty that must now fall to the advanced guard ; so I had determined to go back to Poupry [five miles] for the night and come back next morning. I waited, however, for the receipt of information from my cavalry regiment, which I had ordered to reconnoitre towards Chevilly and the Chateau after the artillery fire had ceased. Reports came in from it that the enemy had evacuated both the village and the château." The result was that both the Infantry Divisions passed the night under shelter there.

D'Aurelle had come to Chevilly at 2 P.M. and awaited there the arrival of des Pallières. But no news of him came, and d'Aurelle saw the chance of being able to hold on at Chevilly gradually diminish. Towards 4.30 P.M. he accepted the needs of the situation and gave orders that Chevilly should be held till darkness set in and then the troops should fall back to the next prepared locality, Cercottes, three miles nearer Orleans. The last French infantry left the village just at the moment that the German infantry, about to advance to storm it, were held back owing to the counter-order.

CHAPTER XX

DECEMBER 4TH—SECOND DAY, SECOND BATTLE OF
ORLEANS—CAPTURE OF THE CITY

THE Prince's orders for December 4th were sent out from Artenay at 9 P.M. and ran as follows: "The attack will be continued to-morrow, December 4th. The IXth Army Corps will advance at 8 ~~P.M.~~ A.M. by the village of Chevilly, occupied by our troops to-day, and will extend with infantry into the wood eastward in order to co-operate later on in an enveloping movement on Cercottes.

"The left flank detachment of the IXth Corps will continue at 7 A.M. its advance by S. Lyé on the Roman Road as ordered.

"The IIIrd Army Corps will advance along the Chilleurs-Loury road towards Orleans, covering itself on its left flank against any forces coming perhaps from Bellegarde, and has, as objective, to bring artillery into action as much as possible against the town of Orleans. The Corps will move off at 7 A.M.

"The Xth Army Corps will march in several columns towards Chevilly, where the head is to arrive at 1 P.M. and will take up, as reserve, a position north of the place. The artillery columns will accompany the corps in order to be able to assist in the supply of the other corps if required.

"The 6th Cav. Division will be south of Artenay at 8 A.M., and follow behind the right wing of the IXth Army Corps.

"The Detachment of H.R.H. the Grand Duke proceeds at 8 A.M. to-morrow in the first instance to the enveloping attack on Gidy in co-operation with the attack by the IXth Army Corps.

"Reports to be sent to me on the right flank of the IXth Army Corps."

This order is a remarkable illustration of how even experienced soldiers are liable to fail in drawing up orders. The Prince had set his heart on the capture of Orleans *on the 4th*. " To-morrow we must be in Orleans," he had with marked emphasis told v. Stosch in the early evening. As Hoenig remarks, it was the capture of Orleans on this day that was the purpose of all the movements ordered, and yet in the order there is not even an indication of this purpose. It is quite possible that v. Manstein, being near the Prince, may have received from him a verbal intimation similar to that given through v. Stosch to the Grand Duke, but v. Alvensleben was left completely in the dark on the matter; and he cannot learn from the order more than the fact that the other Corps are to advance against a series of positions, and also that for some purpose not communicated to him he is to endeavour to shell Orleans.

When this order was issued, the Prince knew nothing whatever as to the progress actually made by the IIIrd Army Corps. At 7 P.M. had come in to Artenay a message sent at 1 P.M. by v. Alvensleben. " The enemy has had in action the 15th Corps 1st Division in front of Santeau in a strongly fortified position, and has shown three batteries and two mitrailleuse batteries. He has been driven back from Santeau, and he retired to the position of Chilleurs, and has also abandoned this. The wood is being attacked. One gun taken, 200 prisoners. Our loss small up to the present." The delay in the delivery of the message was due to v. Alvensleben not being aware that the Prince, instead of making Chilleurs aux Bois his headquarters, as notified in the final paragraph of the Army Orders of the previous evening, had shifted them to Artenay. The orderly officer who brought the message had had much difficulty in finding the Prince. As regards the left flank detachment of the IXth Army Corps, the Prince knew that it had encountered serious opposition. From the Xth Army Corps no news had arrived.

Again, as on the 3rd, we will begin with the left wing of the attackers.

DECEMBER 4 267

Owing to the bad weather and a heavy snowstorm, the officer carrying the message to the IIIrd Army Corps lost his way, so it did not come to hand in time for the corps to move off at 7 A.M., the hour named; but the General had everything in readiness for the march. The 6th Division was to follow the main road to Orleans, protecting its right by a flanking detachment; the 5th Division protecting itself on the left by a flanking detachment, and by officers' patrols, was to take a side road a little to the east to Chécy on the Loire. On arriving at the south edge of the wood the Divisions would halt and await further orders. The sixty guns left at Chilleurs were to follow on the main road. They had, however, to be brought up before the march commenced, and since, in the forest, were numerous dispersed French soldiers, the protection of this long line of guns from a sudden dash on them at some point or other was no easy task. A peculiarity in the Army order was, as just mentioned, that in it the IIIrd Army Corps alone was directed to attack Orleans on this day. But to v. Alvensleben there was something ridiculous about the order; in one respect the carrying it out was impracticable, as a glance at the map showed. "Armchair (salon) strategy," he remarked: this order to bring artillery into action against Orleans further decreased the little value he attached to the strategy of the Second Army. The danger from Bourbaki on his left rear he thoroughly understood, and the left flank detachment was, therefore, intended to act, if necessary, as a rearguard; it would be supported by the 5th Division. The divisions arrived about noon at and near Boigny, five to six miles from Loury, and halted. The 6th Division was directed to continue its march on Orleans, the 5th to march by Bourgneuf to the river road, a little west of Chécy, and thence to proceed to Orleans. The 6th Division, soon after moving off, was met with infantry fire. The hostile troops were from the 1st Division of the 15th Corps that had fallen back on the previous day. They were good troops, and occupied the village of Vaumainbert $2\frac{1}{2}$ miles from Orleans; and here, at 2 P.M., they offered a determined resistance. Not until nearly four o'clock, after a tough fight, did the Germans capture the village ; and then, v. Alvensleben, learning that in front of him was a real Bridge Head, determined to defer the attack to the next day. He was urgently pressed on all sides to continue the attack so that the IIIrd Corps might be the first in Orleans, but he wisely refused to allow such a foolhardy attempt in the dark. In order, if possible, to let the centre column know of his arrival before the city, he ordered his artillery commander to bring a battery into action somewhere or other, and to throw some shells into Orleans. The sound of the guns would thus signal to the troops on the main road his arrival. So close was the country, that only with difficulty was found a place for a whole battery to come into action. At last, a grass plot in front of a villa was discovered ; a heavy battery was unlimbered and twelve shells were fired, and then the battery limbered up just in time, for hardly had it gone, than eleven heavy shells, fired from Orleans, fell on the lawn.

From the left had come in to v. Alvensleben very alarming reports. The left flank detachment, consisting of two battalions and one squadron under the command of Lieut.-Colonel v. l'Estocq, had, at 2 P.M., arrived at Chécy, and was about to go into cantonments, the main body of the Division having arrived at Bourgneuf about a mile to the north, when a report came in to Colonel v. l'Estocq of the approach of an enemy from Pont aux Moines, at a canal-crossing two miles to the east. Soon the hostile infantry skirmishers, followed by several columns, made their appearance.

The enemy was the 20th Corps led by General Crouzat. A position somewhat in advance of the village was at first taken up by two companies of the detachment, but gradually the French came forward to the attack in increasing force so that the Germans had to confine themselves to the defence of Chécy itself. At about three o'clock a battalion and a battery arrived from the 5th Division, and the battery came into action. The French now began to break off the fight and to fall back towards Pont aux Moines ; the Germans reinforced by another regiment followed. The French barricaded the further portion of the village as well as the bridge by which they had recrossed the canal, and then gradually disappeared eastward. The good star of the Germans had been in the ascendant, for it was a whole corps that was advancing toward this small detachment, and it was a whole corps that retired when this handful of men opposed its advance. In compliance with an order of the previous evening from de Freycinet, Bourbaki, with the 20th Corps under Crouzat and the 18th Corps, was marching to Orleans from the position of the previous day, and had been moving along roads almost parallel to the march of the IIIrd Army Corps. The march had commenced at four in the morning. After the troops had begun to move off, Bourbaki received from d'Aurelle the following despatch: "We have been fighting for three days in succession against large forces. Our losses in the 15th, 16th, and 17th Corps are very large. We have gone back to our line in front of Orleans. The enemy has captured one of the most important points. I am am afraid now that it will be impossible for the Army of the Loire to hold on to the right bank of the Loire. There is no bridge between Orleans and Gien [a mistaken statement, there was one at Sully]. The 18th and 20th Corps under your command must, if they have to cross the Loire, do so at the last-named place. Give your orders, therefore, for the eventuality that the retreat by Gien may be necessary." During the last twenty-four hours orders and counter-orders had been showered on Bourbaki from de Freycinet and d'Aurelle. Crouzat had during the day been fully aware of the march of the IIIrd Army Corps, which he had watched carefully. At eleven o'clock an orderly officer came to him and said, " We are in the midst of the Prussian Army," and gave to him a report received from the Maire of a village that the whole Prussian Army was around Orleans: at 2 P.M. Crouzat arrived at Fay aux Loges, four or five miles short of Pont aux Moines, and whence a road leads direct to Jargeau on the Loire. After a conference with his Generals, he determined to march by the right bank to Orleans, sending his trains and artillery by the left bank after crossing at Jargeau. The leading brigade, soon after passing Pont aux Moines, found themselves attacked by the two German companies. Crouzat had sent an officer to report on the bridge at Jargeau. This bridge had been destroyed, but the inhabitants had restored it and made it practicable. Crouzat now believed the Germans were behind him, and as the Loire was in front of him, his mind was much relieved by the report. He now caused the corps to retire to opposite Jargeau, and by the following morning it had crossed to the left bank. The 18th Corps had followed a road further east, and also turned south, reaching the Loire higher up and crossing on the night 5th–6th. So the IIIrd Army Corps escaped in a marvellous way being captured in the very den of the lion.

In the centre on the Paris road, the tactics adopted were those of sheer weight in a concentrated form, and in complete disregard of both the strategical and tactical situation on either the extreme right or the extreme left. Chevilly, which had been abandoned on the previous evening by the French, and occupied by the 22nd Inf. Division, was the starting-point for the attack by the IXth Army Corps down the main road.

The road and the railroad run parallel to each other at a distance of two to three hundred yards apart. On leaving Chevilly they enter a wood defile, two miles long, caused by the projecting of an angle of the forest to the west, the woods on either side being very close and with dense undergrowth. At half a mile beyond the end of the defile is the strongly fortified village of Cercottes, connected by entrenchments with Gidy, a village, two miles west, and also fortified, whilst in front of this line were outlying posts bearing on the exits from the wood. These entrenchments were the right of the main fortified position of the entrenched camp west of the Paris road, and were occupied by the French. Along the main road went into the defile the 36th Inf. Brigade, a regiment of Cavalry and the Division Artillery; along the railroad, advancing *pari passu*, the other column, the 35th Inf. Brigade and a battalion. The corps artillery followed along the main road. Fighting went on all day, and at seven o'clock, after dark, the French had been driven back, or had fallen back, so far that the railway station, les Aubrais, close to the walls of the city, was in the hands of the Germans. The Prince had, even late into the afternoon, held to the belief that on this day he would enter the city; but at 7.15 P.M. v. Manstein, very heavy-hearted, reported that in face of the determined opposition and the great difficulties of the locality, he must abandon for the night any further attempt to advance, so here the IXth Army Corps came to a standstill, close to the city, for the night, as the IIIrd Army Corps had already done.

And now to the right flank. At last, the Prince has had a personal interview with the Grand Duke, for at 9 A.M. to the surprise of the latter, the Prince came to him at Chevilly château where he was. The interview is described by an eye-witness as short, stiff and frigid. The Prince listened coldly to the Grand Duke, and gave him his instructions in the most distant manner. The Grand Duke expressed his belief that the enemy was retreating over the Loire. The Prince held a contrary opinion, that the retreat was on Orleans. Both seem to have regarded the surrounding the Army of the Loire as the end to be attained, but, unfortunately, the orders of the Prince, which involved the whole Detachment in the struggle on the Paris-Orleans road, rendered the envelopment of the French left wing very improbable. Before the brief interview came to a close, the Prince repeated to the Grand Duke the words of the previous evening that Orleans must, under all circumstances, be occupied this day. This injunction must be borne in mind in view of after events.

It would seem to have been the Prince's plain duty to have learnt fully from the Grand Duke the work of this and the preceding day on the west of the road; to have ascertained his view of the situation, and the grounds on which it was based. But the Prince's "personlichkeit" exercised baneful influence here, and the two leaders, on whose thorough and cordial co-operation so much in the future depended, had parted after a few words.

Chanzy will soon be withdrawing, not on Orleans, but down the right bank of the Loire clear of the net the Grand Duke would throw round him, but of which the Prince does not seem to understand the manipulation; and the Grand Duke has to confine himself to making his way westward of the road and down to the Loire, aiding the advance of the IXth Army Corps. All the numerous localities here in front of the Detachment had been prepared for defence so that the French when falling back could find at every step shelter whence to delay their pursuers. But the retreating force, containing as it did very many poorly trained and indifferent troops, was already nearly worn out by hard marching, fighting, defeat, want of food and rest, exposure to bitter winter weather, and by being sent about hither and thither by orders and counter-orders. These are conditions most favourable to panic, or rather, under them panic was sure to come sooner or later, and so it came to pass here. At this time the general direction of the retreat was on Orleans. V. Stolberg with the 2nd Cav. Division had been in close observation of this ground for more than a fortnight and must therefore have formed a fairly correct opinion of its character. The Grand Duke, soon after midday, was with his left flank nearing Ormes, which village is at the junction of the two roads leading to Orleans, from Chateaudun north-west, and Coulmiers west, and is five miles from the city. There was now in front some open ground suitable for cavalry action. The 2nd Cavalry Division was brought forward; the 4th Hussars as advanced guard, the 3rd Brigade on the right, the 4th on the left, and the two Horse Artillery batteries in the centre. Very soon the advanced squadron saw ahead troops standing dismounted behind some entrenchments. The squadron at once charged, and found the enemy to be a battery of Horse Artillery, with its guns laid fortunately in another direction. There was not time to swing the guns round, and the whole battery,

2 guns and 4 waggons, with 4 officers, 75 men, and 79 horses fell into the hands of this handful of Cavalry, only 65 sabres. Now, south of Ormes, was seen by the 5th Hussars of the 4th Brigade, another battery limbering up. Three squadrons of the regiment at once made for the battery, but on the Chateaudun road they came upon three hostile squadrons, which they completely routed, taking many prisoners and pursuing the remainder towards the Loire.

The wide-reaching effect and decisive consequences of this charge, this overthrow of merely three squadrons, would be, incredible did not the French and the German historians alike concur in their narratives. The scene of the charge was between Orleans and the troops falling back from the north-west on to Orleans and to the prepared entrenchments outside it.

The remnants of two French Divisions retreating were already at the road junction, but panic had set in and it spread at once in all directions. The French now strove to stem v. Stolberg's advance by bringing artillery into action, but these were soon driven off by the German Horse Artillery, which was well to the front. The French in their wild flight completely broke up two of the Gardes Mobiles Regiments, a Marche Regiment, and a battery. Owing to the converging character of the retreat of the French Corps, strong bodies of no less than four Divisions were involved in the disaster. Lehautcourt says: " The retreat which commenced in great disaster is continued in the midst of ever-increasing confusion. Demoralisation quickly assumes terrible proportions. There is no longer any command, any direction; isolated parties of infantry and entire bodies of troops are mixed up with trains and batteries. Some make for Orleans, most gain Meung, Beaugency, Mer, or even Blois." Under these circumstances the occupation of the prepared position was no longer possible, and for all purposes of holding off the Germans, or even of delaying their progress, it might have been non-existent. It was between one and half-past one

s

when the charge was made, and the panic continuing to the evening and into the night set in.

The Grand Duke, finding now that the defences of Ormes were unoccupied, directed the Bavarians to march on south towards the Loire to Ingré, and assigned to the 17th Inf. Division the road from Ormes to Orleans. V. Stolberg's Cav. Division had collected at Ormes, and at about 2 P.M. a Bavarian General Staff Officer, with two squadrons and two guns arrived there on their way south to the Loire to harass the French in their passage over the river. In compliance with his request for support, v. Stolberg at 2.15 moved off with his whole Division towards the river, and turning to advantage the knowledge he had acquired of this ground during v. d. Tann's occupation of Orleans, he struck an hour later on the Orleans-Blois road close to the river, and at about two miles from the city. Protected by some dismounted cavalry pushed forward, he at once opened fire on the westernmost boat bridge, one of the four bridges over the river, and also on hostile columns moving from Orleans down the opposite bank; the bridge was at once cast free by the French and drifted under shelter.

Along the Ormes-Orleans road had proceeded the 17th Inf. Division, with an advanced guard of two and three-quarter battalions and two batteries under Colonel v. Manteuffel. At 4.15 P.M. v. Manteuffel arrived at le Grand Orme, 2 miles from Orleans, without having met any serious opposition. It began to get dark, and in this close country view over the ground was no longer possible. At 5.30 P.M. the Grand Duke, whose knowledge of the actual state of affairs with the Detachment at this time seems to have been limited to those of the 17th Division, ordered a halt for the night, as his view of the situation was similar to those held by the commanders of the IIIrd and IXth Army Corps as to the madness of a night attack on the City. For cantonments the road was assigned to the 17th Division, of which the head was to be at Orleans. So, whilst the main body of the Division remained at the railway embankment, one mile from the city, v. Manteuffel

DECEMBER 4

resumed his onward march, and at six o'clock the point of the advanced guard found itself at the entrance gate to Orleans. It was a closed gate of trellis work. As soon as v. Manteuffel had received the report from Lieut. v. Lücken, who now with sixteen men was standing outside the gate, he proceeded thither; he saw a guard behind the gate. There was a lantern alight at the gate. The street beyond was badly lighted, but French soldiers were visible in the street and houses. V. Manteuffel ordered the guard to open the gate, but they declined as they had no orders to do so. V. Manteuffel directed therefore the Commander to be sent for, and at the same time reported to v. Tresckow in rear. But now he had to go away, having been sent for by the Grand Duke, who was at a house between the advanced guard and the railway.

It is necessary, however, in order to understand the transactions at this gate and the subsequent course of events, to learn the action of the leaders of the French Army during the day, because that action affected the whole course of the operations. During the night, December 3rd-4th, to General d'Aurelle there had come in such overwhelming evidence of the demoralisation and distressful condition of his army, that sadly he came to the conclusion that it was impossible to hold on to the right bank of the Loire; and at four o'clock in the morning he telegraphed to Tours to that effect. In the message he said ; " I must therefore tell you that I regard the defence of Orleans as impossible. Painful as it is to me to say this, it is my duty to tell you so, because thereby a great catastrophe may be averted. If we had time to restore order, so as to enable us to take the field anew, resistance might be again resorted to, but the enemy will attack us again tomorrow,* and with grief, but deep conviction, I repeat to you that our troops, exhausted and demoralised by the last two days, will not make a stand. There is only one course open to us, and that is retreat. I have arranged it as follows:

* The telegram appears, therefore, to have been written before midnight, but held back in the hope of news from des l'allières.

the 16th and 17th Corps to fall back on Beaugency and Blois, the 18th and 20th on Gien, the 15th will cross at Orleans and march into the Sologne. Thus there will not be any blocking of roads, and the subsistence of the Army is easily provided for." At the same time the General intimated his decision to the Intendant-General in Orleans. Hardly had the telegram been despatched to Tours, when from de Freycinet came a telegram, 10.50 P.M., December 3rd, criticising the disposition of the troops, and directing a concentration of the whole Army at Orleans. At 5 A.M. on the 4th, de Freycinet sent an objectionably worded telegram, refusing to endorse d'Aurelle's views of the necessity of a retreat, and reiterating the orders for a general concentration. At 8 A.M. on the 4th d'Aurelle replied: "I am here on the spot, and am better able to judge the situation than are you. With not less sorrow than you have I resolved on this extreme measure. The enemy has surmounted all obstacles up to Cercottes, he has mastered all the issues from the forest: the position of Orleans is, therefore, no longer what it was. It is now surrounded, and has lost the support of the forest, it can no longer be defended with troops exhausted by three days fighting and hardships, and who, owing to their great losses, are demoralised. Besides, the strength of the enemy exceeds all my anticipations, also the figures you gave me. Time presses, and will not enable me to carry out the concentration you speak of. Good resistance cannot be organised. In spite of all efforts which could be made, Orleans will, it is fated, be in the enemy's hands this evening or to-morrow. That will be a great misfortune; but the only means to avoid a greater catastrophe is to have the courage to make a sacrifice whilst there is time. The Army of the Loire can be of great service to the National Defence, but on the condition that it can collect at those points where it can have time to get into order again. The attempt to concentrate at Orleans is to invite useless destruction. I believe, therefore, that the orders issued must be adhered to. As to the orders you have given to Bourbaki [to concentrate towards Orleans] it is not for me to alter them. I leave it to you to hold to them or to recall them. I must, however, draw your attention to the fact that this movement towards Orleans, in front of the enemy, who is master of the forest, may turn out still more dangerous, because Bourbaki can cross only at Orleans and Gien [not correct]. The restoration of the bridge at Chateauneuf is not yet completed." D'Aurelle, for the present, maintained his determination. This accounts for much of the falling back of the French before the Germans during this day. At 11.15 A.M. the Delegation sent to d'Aurelle its sanction for the evacuation of Orleans.

But now d'Aurelle, coming to Orleans before he received at Saran this sanction, learnt that des Pallières had arrived, and having great confidence in this general, and knowing that his Division was the best in the army, suddenly changed his plans. He was aware of Minot's disaster, and of the real condition of the Division, but he seems to have lost his judgment; he telegraphed at 11.55 A.M. to Tours, "I am altering my plans, directing the 16th and 17th corps to Orleans, calling here the 18th and 20th, I am organising the defence, I am at Orleans." Counter-orders were at once issued. The confusion arising from this change of plans was one of the most powerful aids to the success of the Germans.

Naturally the Delegation at Tours was delighted at the change of intentions, and wired at once to d'Aurelle the expression of its great satisfaction. But events proved too strong for d'Aurelle, and he gradually came to the conclusion that he must revert to the original idea of abandoning Orleans and the right bank of the Loire; at 4 P.M. his mind was made up, and orders were issued accordingly. To des Pallières was left the covering the retreat. The operation required both time and organisation, for there were some 3000 waggons in the city which, moreover, had been a principal store depôt for the army of the Loire. During the night all was to be sent away.

It was at half-past five in the afternoon that the Prince began to be anxious as to the possibility of Orleans not being captured on this day. Of the IIIrd Army Corps he had heard nothing. To v. Manstein he sent an officer to ascertain whether the General thought he could enter the city on that day. By 6 P.M. the officer returned with the answer that it was doubtful. So at 6.45 the Prince issued orders for the cessation of the fight and its renewal next morning. Subsequently there arrived a report, 7.15, from v. Manstein, and later on, at 9 P.M., one from v. Alvensleben, 4.30, both to the same effect that their attacks on the city had been broken off. To Versailles the Prince reported that the Army would stand ready to take Orleans next day. But storming the city was precisely what the Royal Head-quarters were anxious should be avoided.

At 7 P.M. there were in Orleans some thousands of troops; the number is almost impossible to ascertain: it was at that hour that a Zouave came to des Pallières and informed him that he had been sent by a Prussian officer [v. Manteuffel] who wished to speak with the commandant. The Zouave added that the enemy was in possession of the St. Jean suburb, and that there were but few of the 3rd Division of the 15th corps in front of him. There had been some 1500 men here, but under cover of the darkness they had stolen away. A Staff Officer, Captain Pendezec, was sent to learn what the German General wanted. A battalion was also despatched in this direction to keep the enemy back. Some 300 yards outside the gate was a Prussian officer, who conducted Pendezec to General v. Tresckow in a house close by. Pendezec estimated the Germans he saw at four to five battalions [there were only two]. After Pendezec had given his name v. Tresckow spoke to the following effect : " I have occupied the St. Jean suburb, as you yourself see; in the north, on the road from Artenay Prince Frederick Charles has advanced as far as the gate on the railroad in the Bannier suburb. If you wish, I will have you taken there to convince yourself. I intend to occupy Orleans to-day, but would like to avoid a street fight, which will injure much both the city and the inhabitants; so for that reason I have halted here. Be so good as to convey to your Commanding Officer my summons that he evacuates the city by half-past eleven. I shall then occupy the city as far as the Artenay road. If the commandant refuses, my batteries, which are now in position, will immediately open fire."

This was a game of bluff indeed. And to avoid mistake, the General took out his watch, and requested the officer to compare the time with his own watch.

Des Pallières, on the return of the envoy, seems to have at once believed all that v. Tresckow had said, and to have regarded the terms offered as an unexpected piece of good fortune, for, after a little thought, he told Pendezec to go back to him and tell him that at the hour named the portion of the city specified would be given up to him. And the French were quite content with the agreement, for they knew what v. Tresckow did not know, that there were hardly any troops in front of him, and that by following the river bank he could probably without firing a shot gain access to the centre of the city, and possession of the main bridge over the Loire, along which were now hurrying the waggons and the troops from other quarters.

But now came in from d'Aurelle, to whom des Pallières had reported what he had done, an order which, whilst approving of the capitulation, directed that the entry of the Germans should not take place until ten o'clock the following morning. So on the almost hopeless mission to gain an extension of time, General d'Aries was despatched to confer with v. Tresckow, whom d'Aries met now on foot in the street. V. Tresckow repeated his threat of bombardment, but eventually agreed to give an extra hour, but curiously enough, owing to his own watch having stopped he really gave an hour and a half. The Grand Duke approved of v. Tresckow's action in the matter. Meantime had come in the Prince's orders to defer the attack until the next day; but the Grand Duke determined to defer sending an answer until the negotiations were finished. And at 10.30 he despatched a report that the city would be given up to him at 11.30. And at 1 A.M. the Duke at the head of the 17th Infantry Division and a Bavarian Brigade marched with bands playing into the surrendered city. Great amount of controversy has arisen as to the conduct of the Grand Duke, on his having taken so serious a step on his own responsibility without submitting the question for the decision of the Prince his commander. It is unnecessary to discuss the matter here. The Grand Duke had carried out the Prince's injunctions almost to the letter, but when at three in the morning the report arrived at the Army Head-quarters, there was a scene, over which Hoenig draws but the thinnest of veils. V. Waldersee said: " It was a thunderbolt. The Prince was beside himself. He had intended to make a formal entry into Orleans ; his joy had vanished, and all owing to the Grand Duke, of whom he had an enduring dislike."

It was from the Grand Duke that the King first heard the news. And the reply to the Grand Duke could have been hardly pleasing to the Prince. " It is with the greatest pleasure that I tell you how I appreciate your threefold victory. I send you my thanks and bestow on you my order ' pour le mérite ' with oak leaves. To Generals v. Wittich and v. Tresckow the same decoration without oak leaves. What important consequences these victories, and the reoccupation of Orleans."

To Queen Augusta at Berlin the King telegraphed: " Orleans has been occupied to-night without storming. God be thanked."

On the German side there was no real thought of pursuit, the objective had been the capture of the city, not the destruction of the hostile army in the field ; so the enemy was a secondary consideration. At 6.30 in the morning of the 5th the Prince had ordered the Detachment to march down the right bank of the Loire and to occupy Beaugency, but on the Grand Duke representing to him the tired condition of the troops, the Prince allowed the advance to be postponed until the following day ; a general rest-day was therefore given, although in the IIIrd, Xth, and even the IXth Army Corps were plenty of troops fresh enough to follow up the enemy. V. Waldersee was under the impression that both the Prince and the Grand Duke believed that with the capture of

Orleans the campaign was at an end. V. Moltke on the other hand, considered a rapid pursuit of great importance, but when his orders were received the favourable opportunity had gone by. The mistake had been made and was beyond recall. The Army of the Loire had been most severely shaken and a large portion of it utterly demoralised; but the Army still existed; it was now in two bodies. The 16th and 17th Corps, that the Prince had been mainly instrumental in allowing to escape, fell back down the right bank only a few miles, to Meung and Beaugency, where joined by the 21st Corps, their leader Chanzy opposed with them the advance of the Detachment. On the 7th at Meung, and on the 8th, 9th, and 10th, at Beaugency, Chanzy, before retiring further, held his enemy at bay; then he went west, and on the 16th commenced his retreat to le Mans, having in these operations inflicted on the Germans a loss of nearly 200 officers and 4000 men. Later on this portion of the Army of the Loire compelled the Germans to undertake the campaign of le Mans. The other body, the 15th, 18th, and 20th Corps under Bourbaki, went eastward, where with the 24th Corps they carried on the campaign on the Lisaine.

CHAPTER XXI

CONCLUSION

THE power shown by the hardened soldiers of Germany to hold their own successfully in the field against numerically superior forces, the failure of the leading of the French improvised army when those soldiers had simply marched straight against it, the demoralisation produced by the profitless endurance of suffering and misery, and the exaggerated importance attached to the possession of Orleans, all combined to completely take the heart out of the future National Defence so far as the participation of the People in it was concerned. Henceforth it is almost solely a matter of relative manœuvring power in the opposing forces in the field. But the more, and the more closely and in detail the history of the French National Defence from October 11th to December 4th–5th is studied, the more convincing become the ill-fated but grand efforts of Gambetta and de Freycinet as proofs of the soundness of the principle, that in every defensive land-war against invasion, the whole People should take their part.

The foundation-stone on which every such National Defence rests, the pivot on which such defence turns, is the highly-trained, thoroughly equipped, thoroughly disciplined, and well-staffed Field Army; supplemental to this are the formation of the dense Fog of War, the local hand-to-hand defence of every yard of ground, and the determined holding out in every village, town, or city which is an objective of the invader. It is with the manhood, aye, and with the womanhood of each particular territory that it rests to determine whether this supplementary, but vitally-important, aid to the work of the Field Army shall be given or not given.

CONCLUSION

And when we call to mind the fact that after having organised our Field and Fortress Armies, there will still be available a vast number of men, either volunteers, ex-volunteers, or members of rifle-clubs, besides a multitude who know how to pull a trigger, and all of whom are desirous, yes, and absolutely determined to do their best to defend their country and their homes, we must feel it would be little short of suicidal not to utilise their services. The national wealth of fighting men in this country is enormous; all that is necessary to enable the country to profit by the possession of this wealth is simply carefully-considered and thoroughly-completed territorial organisation. Prince Frederick Charles, as we know, regarded suitability of country as a necessary condition for the successful employment of irregular troops in connection with a Field Army. It will not be *viâ* Salisbury Plain, but through the close country that extends down to the sea coast, southwest, south, south-east, east, and north-east from London, the main objective of the invader, that the hostile army will advance; and here, especially, and to a great extent in many other parts of our Island, this necessary condition is forthcoming. Smokeless powder and the repeating rifle have increased greatly the power of defence of this kind, for, paradoxical as it may sound, the absence of smoke thickens the Fog of War both on and away from the battlefield. And, moreover, as the cyclist manœuvres carried out under the supervision of Major-General Sir Frederick Maurice in Sussex in 1901 clearly showed, the numerous good roads and lanes in England lend themselves to the very rapid concentration of riflemen from distant parts either to reinforce local defence or to thicken the Fog of War. But organisation, sound, fully-completed, and practically-tested, is the indispensable, the necessary basis for participation of the People in the War. Most of the country which was the scene of the "People's War" in France I have visited, more than once; the country which would be the scene of the principal "People's War" against invasion in England I also fairly know. What Frenchmen and Frenchwomen did for their own country in the dark days of October and November 1870, Englishmen and Englishwomen will, with no less courage and patriotic self-devotion, assuredly do in any dark days that may lie before us, though at present hidden in the dim future. Let us be wise in time during the day whilst we can work, and not delay until the night cometh when work can be done only with trouble and confusion.

On February 29th, 1804, Mr. Pitt, in the House of Commons during the debate on the Defence of the Nation, spoke the wise words that follow:

"A great mass of our population may be made fit to serve many useful purposes in the hour of danger, and I should be therefore glad that previous measures, calculated to call it into action with effect, were concerted and carried into execution . . . ; but I wish to give to the Lord Lieutenant of each county, and to a General Officer, the power of calling forth, and arming at a moment's notice, the whole of the active population. This measure should, however, be arranged beforehand; leaders should be appointed, companies formed, AND NO MAN SHOULD BE ALLOWED TO RUN ABOUT IN CONFUSION, CRYING OUT, 'OH, THAT I COULD BE ANY WAY USEFUL TO MY COUNTRY!'"

Let us of this generation, a century later, apply to practice the words of wisdom of this great statesman.

www.ingramcontent.com/pod-product-compliance
Lightning Source LLC
Chambersburg PA
CBHW071000160426
43193CB00012B/1851